Government Reference Books

GOVERNMENT REFERENCE BOOKS 70/71

A Biennial Guide to
U.S. Government Publications

COMPILED BY

SALLY WYNKOOP

SECOND BIENNIAL EDITION 1972

LIBRARIES UNLIMITED, INC.

Copyright © 1972 Sally Wynkoop
All Rights Reserved
Printed in the United States of America

Library of Congress Card Number 76-146307
International Standard Book Number 0-87287-062-6

LIBRARIES UNLIMITED, INC.
P.O. Box 263
Littleton, Colorado 80120

Z
1223
Z7
G68
1972

INTRODUCTION

The second edition of *Government Reference Books* is a comprehensive record of reference books published by the U.S. Government Printing Office and the many government agencies. Over 1,000 entries, with annotations, are listed under appropriate subjects.

The reader should know that this edition contains 451 more entries than the first edition (published in 1970), which covered 1968-69 imprints. This increase in the number of reference books covered is due to more comprehensive coverage of important reference materials published during 1970 and 1971 by GPO and various government agencies. In addition, for the convenience of the reader, a list of 100 periodicals of reference value is included. Information pertaining to serial publications has been updated, including notes on any changes in scope or coverage.

The need for this kind of bibliographic tool is evident on all levels of library research. As elementary and secondary schools, businesses and industries, and colleges and universities develop an awareness of the value of government documents, it becomes even more essential to develop better means of bibliographic control.

Best known of the current guides to government publications is the *Monthly Catalog*. It lists nearly 20,000 publications annually, most of them available from the Government Printing Office. The National Technical Information Service (formerly Clearinghouse for Federal Scientific and Technical Information) has the responsibility for collecting, announcing, and disseminating business, statistical, and technical reports and similar data. It announces over 50,000 publications annually, primarily in *Government Reports Announcements* (formerly *U.S. Government Research and Development Reports*), a semimonthly abstracting service. The 1,055 entries in this bibliography, out of 140,000 publications issued over the past two years, should help reference librarians and researchers pinpoint governmental reference resources in a wide variety of subjects.

The types of reference materials included are bibliographies, directories, indexes, dictionaries, statistical guides, handbooks, almanacs, catalogs, and biographical sources. Descriptive annotations state purpose, scope, arrangement, details of coverage, and special features of each. The complete bibliographical citations provide price, Library of Congress card order number, if any, stock number, and Superintendent of Documents classification number. Access to these citations is facilitated by the detailed personal author, subject, and title index.

Stock numbers (designated S/N) are eight-digit numbers assigned to new documents sold by GPO. The first four digits represent the issuing agency (e.g., 1780 for the Office of Education) and the last four, the publication itself. This sytem was initiated in late 1970 to speed up the processing of orders. The Government Printing Office is notoriously slow in this respect; if this new system works (in conjunction with the new distribution centers in Philadelphia and Pueblo, Colorado), GPO orders should be processed much more quickly than in the past.

Entries are arranged under five broad areas: social sciences, science and technology, humanities, general reference, and periodicals. Parts one through four are further subdivided by specific subjects, arranged alphabetically. The periodicals section, arranged by title, is new in this edition. It lists works of reference value published more frequently than twice a year. The information in these entries includes title, year of first publication, frequency, subscription price, LC card number, and SuDocs number. For all periodicals not available from GPO, the complete address of the issuing agency is provided in the entry. This new section, to be included in future biennial editions, is a concise guide to important periodicals. It also records new periodicals as well as those which have ceased publication in the past two years. Subject access to this section is through the index.

Government publications go out of print more quickly than privately published materials; the biennial publication of this guide, however, insures its value as a selection aid for even the smallest libraries. Depository libraries will find it useful for selection of non-depository materials as well as for answering reference questions. Additionally, it should be helpful as a reference aid for researchers, local, state and national government employees and officials, educators, businessmen, and interested individuals.

TABLE OF CONTENTS

PART ONE—SOCIAL SCIENCES

GENERAL WORKS	17
ECONOMICS AND BUSINESS	19
General Works	19
Bibliographies	19
Directories	21
Indexes	22
Statistics	22
Business and Industry	23
General Works	23
Bibliographies	23
Directories	24
Statistics	24
Inventory and Record Control	25
Marketing	25
Specific Businesses and Industries	26
Chemical and Petroleum Plants	26
Clothing Stores	27
Construction Industry	27
Drugstores	27
Engineering Firms	27
Food Processing and Retailing	28
Hobby Shops	28
Manufacturing	28
Motels	28
Nursery Business	29
Printing	29
Shipbuilding	29
Shopping Centers	29
Utility Companies	29
Wholesale Businesses	30
Communications	30
Mass Media	30
Postal Guides	31
Consumer Information	32
Economic Development Programs	33
Employment and Labor	34
General Works	34
Bibliographies	34
Handbooks and Guides	35
Statistics	36
Labor-Management Relations	37
Labor Organizations	39
Manpower Research and Training	40

Finance and Banking	41
Foreign Trade	42
General Works	42
Bibliographies	42
Dictionaries	42
Directories	42
Indexes	43
Statistics	43
Export/Import Data	44
Transportation	45
Insurance	46
Occupations	47
Real Estate	48
Taxes	49
EDUCATION	51
General Works	51
Bibliographies	51
Dictionaries	52
Directories	52
Statistics	54
Adult Education	54
Elementary and Secondary Education	55
Bibliographies	55
Dictionaries	56
Directories	57
Handbooks and Guides	57
Higher Education	58
Bibliographies	58
Directories	58
Research	60
Special Education	61
Disadvantaged	61
Handicapped	62
Vocational Education	62
GEOGRAPHY	64
Atlases	64
Bibliographies	65
Dictionaries	66
Gazetteers	66
HISTORY AND AREA STUDIES	67
Africa	67
General Works	67
Algeria	67
Burma	67
Congo	68
Ethiopia	68
Ghana	69
Somalia	69

South Africa	69
Tunisia	70
United Arab Republic	70
Asia and the Middle East	71
Asia	71
Ceylon	71
China	71
India	72
Indonesia	72
Korea	72
Malaysia	73
Mongolia	73
Pakistan	74
Thailand	74
Middle East	75
General Works	75
Iran	75
Iraq	76
Israel	76
Saudi Arabia	76
Syria	76
Turkey	77
Europe	77
General Works	77
Albania	78
Cyprus	78
Soviet Union	78
Latin America	79
General Works	79
Brazil	79
Colombia	80
Costa Rica	80
Cuba	81
El Salvador	81
Guatemala	81
Honduras	82
Nicaragua	82
Uruguay	82
Venezuela	83
Oceania	83
General Works	83
Antarctica	84
Indian Ocean	85
United States	85
Archives	85
General History and Area Studies	86

```
            Military History  . . . . . . . . . . . . . . . . . . . . . . . . . . .   87
                Air Force  . . . . . . . . . . . . . . . . . . . . . . . . . . .   87
                Army  . . . . . . . . . . . . . . . . . . . . . . . . . . . . . .   87
                Marine Corps  . . . . . . . . . . . . . . . . . . . . . . . .   87
                Navy  . . . . . . . . . . . . . . . . . . . . . . . . . . . . . .   88
    LAW  . . . . . . . . . . . . . . . . . . . . . . . . . . . . . . . . . . . . . . . . . .   90
        General Works  . . . . . . . . . . . . . . . . . . . . . . . . . . . . . . .   90
            Bibliographies  . . . . . . . . . . . . . . . . . . . . . . . . . . . .   90
            Directories  . . . . . . . . . . . . . . . . . . . . . . . . . . . . . .   90
            Handbooks and Guides  . . . . . . . . . . . . . . . . . . . . .   91
        Treaties  . . . . . . . . . . . . . . . . . . . . . . . . . . . . . . . . . . .   92
    POLITICAL SCIENCE AND INTERNATIONAL RELATIONS  . . . . .   93
        Communism  . . . . . . . . . . . . . . . . . . . . . . . . . . . . . . . . .   93
        International Affairs  . . . . . . . . . . . . . . . . . . . . . . . . . .   93
            General Works  . . . . . . . . . . . . . . . . . . . . . . . . . . . .   93
                Directories  . . . . . . . . . . . . . . . . . . . . . . . . . .   93
                Guides  . . . . . . . . . . . . . . . . . . . . . . . . . . . . .   94
            Military Affairs  . . . . . . . . . . . . . . . . . . . . . . . . . .   94
            Protocol  . . . . . . . . . . . . . . . . . . . . . . . . . . . . . . .   95
            Research  . . . . . . . . . . . . . . . . . . . . . . . . . . . . . .   95
        United States Government  . . . . . . . . . . . . . . . . . . . . . .   96
            Atlases  . . . . . . . . . . . . . . . . . . . . . . . . . . . . . . . .   96
            Bibliographies  . . . . . . . . . . . . . . . . . . . . . . . . . . . .   96
            Directories  . . . . . . . . . . . . . . . . . . . . . . . . . . . . . .   96
            Indexes  . . . . . . . . . . . . . . . . . . . . . . . . . . . . . . . .   98
            Manuals  . . . . . . . . . . . . . . . . . . . . . . . . . . . . . . .   98
    RECREATION AND TRAVEL  . . . . . . . . . . . . . . . . . . . . . . . . .  100
        General Works  . . . . . . . . . . . . . . . . . . . . . . . . . . . . . . .  100
        Arts and Crafts  . . . . . . . . . . . . . . . . . . . . . . . . . . . . . .  100
        Outdoor Recreation  . . . . . . . . . . . . . . . . . . . . . . . . . . .  100
            Assistance Programs  . . . . . . . . . . . . . . . . . . . . . . . .  100
                Government Assistance Programs  . . . . . . . . . . . . .  100
                Private Assistance Programs  . . . . . . . . . . . . . . . .  101
            National Parks and Recreation Areas  . . . . . . . . . . . . . .  102
            Research  . . . . . . . . . . . . . . . . . . . . . . . . . . . . . . . .  102
            Statistics  . . . . . . . . . . . . . . . . . . . . . . . . . . . . . . .  103
        Stamp Collecting  . . . . . . . . . . . . . . . . . . . . . . . . . . . .  103
        Travel Guides  . . . . . . . . . . . . . . . . . . . . . . . . . . . . . . .  103
    SOCIOLOGY  . . . . . . . . . . . . . . . . . . . . . . . . . . . . . . . . . . . .  105
        General Works  . . . . . . . . . . . . . . . . . . . . . . . . . . . . . . .  105
        Minority Group Relations  . . . . . . . . . . . . . . . . . . . . . . . .  105
            General Works  . . . . . . . . . . . . . . . . . . . . . . . . . . . .  105
            American Indians  . . . . . . . . . . . . . . . . . . . . . . . . . .  106
            Negroes  . . . . . . . . . . . . . . . . . . . . . . . . . . . . . . . .  106
            Spanish Americans  . . . . . . . . . . . . . . . . . . . . . . . . .  107
        Social Conditions  . . . . . . . . . . . . . . . . . . . . . . . . . . . . .  107
            Aging  . . . . . . . . . . . . . . . . . . . . . . . . . . . . . . . . . .  107
            Children and Youth  . . . . . . . . . . . . . . . . . . . . . . . . .  108
```

Social Problems	110
Behavior	110
Criminology	110
Drug Abuse	111
Bibliographies	111
Dictionaries	112
Directories	112
Filmographies	114
Family Planning	114
Poverty	114
STATISTICS AND DEMOGRAPHY	115
Bibliographies	115
Compendia	115
Directories	116
Handbooks	117
Indexes	118
URBANOLOGY	119
General Works	119
Bibliographies	119
Dictionaries	119
Directories	120
Laws	120
Statistics	120
Housing and Planning	121
Urban Transportation	121

PART TWO—SCIENCE AND TECHNOLOGY

GENERAL WORKS	125
Bibliographies	125
Directories	127
Guides	128
Indexes	128
Statistics	129
AGRICULTURAL SCIENCES	130
Agriculture	130
General Works	130
Bibliographies	130
Directories	130
Laws	131
Statistics	132
Yearbooks	133
Farm Products	133
Soil Management	133
Forestry	134
Atlases	134
Bibliographies	134

Directories	135
Guides	135
Home Economics	135
Wildlife Management	136
ASTRONOMY	137
General Works	137
Atlases	137
Ephemerides	137
Navigation	138
BIOLOGICAL SCIENCES	139
Botany	139
Zoology	140
CHEMISTRY	142
DATA PROCESSING	144
Abstracts	144
Dictionaries	144
Equipment	144
Handbooks and Guides	145
EARTH SCIENCES	146
Geology	146
Bibliographies	146
Catalogs	147
Geologic Names	147
Hydrology	147
Bibliographies	147
Dictionaries	148
Directories	149
Indexes	149
Meteorology	150
General Works	150
Climatology	151
Mineralogy	151
Oceanography	153
General Works	153
Atlases, Maps and Charts	153
Bibliographies	153
Directories	154
Manuals	154
Oceanographic Ships	154
Tides	155
Paleontology	156
Seismology	156
ENGINEERING	158
General Works	158
Aeronautical and Space Engineering	158
Bibliographies	158
Chronologies and Histories	159

Civil and Public Safety Engineering	160
Civil Defense	160
Fire Sciences	161
Law Enforcement	162
Transportation	162
Aviation	162
Boating	164
Highways and Traffic Safety	164
Electrical and Electronic Engineering	166
Military Engineering	166
Nuclear Engineering	166
Abstracts and Indexes	166
Bibliographies	167
Classification	169
Dictionaries	169
Directories	169
Tables	170
ENVIRONMENTAL SCIENCES	171
General Works	171
Bibliographies	171
Directories	171
Guides	172
Air Pollution	172
Bibliographies	172
Directories	173
Pesticides	174
Waste Disposal	175
Water Pollution	175
MATHEMATICS	177
MEDICAL SCIENCES	178
General Medicine	178
Abstracts and Indexes	178
Almanacs and Yearbooks	179
Atlases	180
Audio-visual Guides	180
Bibliographies	181
General	181
Diseases and Handicaps	183
Health Testing	185
Public Health Service Agencies' Catalogs	185
Dictionaries	186
Directories	186
Health Occupations	188
Laws	188
Statistics	189
Dentistry	189

    Mental Health and Psychiatry 190
        Bibliographies 190
        Directories 191
    Mental Retardation 192
        Bibliographies 192
        Directories 193
    Nursing 194
    Pharmacology 194
    Public Health 195
        Bibliographies 195
        Directories 196
        Guides 196
    Toxicology 196
    Veterinary Medicine 197
PHYSICS 198

PART THREE—HUMANITIES

ART AND ARCHITECTURE 201
LANGUAGES 201
LITERATURE 202
MOTION PICTURES AND DRAMA 202
MUSIC 203
RELIGION 203

PART FOUR—GENERAL REFERENCE

GENERAL BIBLIOGRAPHIES 207
GOVERNMENT PUBLICATIONS 207
LIBRARY SCIENCE 209
MICROFORMS 209
PERIODICALS AND SERIALS 210

PART FIVE—PERIODICALS

PERIODICALS (alphabetically by title) 213

INDEX 227

PART ONE

SOCIAL SCIENCES

GENERAL WORKS

1. U.S. Department of Health, Education, and Welfare. **Catalog: Department of Health, Education, and Welfare Publications: July 1970—June 1971.** Cumulative Issue. Washington, HEW Office of Public Affairs, 1971. 124p. Free. (HE 1.18/3:971)

HEW's new computerized Departmental Publications Management Information System was inaugurated with the publication of this catalog. It lists all available HEW publications produced from July 1, 1970, through June 30, 1971, with some imprints prior to 1970. Entries are by title within chapters for each agency. Bibliographic information is not complete—e.g., year of publication is omitted. However, price, SuDocs number, ordering information, and frequency are all listed. The biggest asset of this catalog is the lengthy annotations; the greatest drawback is the omission of any index.

2. U.S. Department of Health, Education, and Welfare. **Catalog of HEW Assistance: 1970 Supplement.** Washington, GPO, 1970. 203p. $1.75. LC Card No. 78-604100. (HE 1.6/6:969/supp. 970)

See *Government Reference Books 68/69* (entry number 67) for main volume. This supplement provides information on programs initiated since 1969.

3. U.S. Department of Health, Education, and Welfare. **Field Directory.** 21st edition. Washington, GPO, 1970. 68p. $0.75. LC Card No. 53-61399. S/N 1700-0048. (HE 1.17:970)

Offices of the Department of Health, Education, and Welfare are located throughout the United States. This directory shows what is located where, provides an organization chart of the entire department and a map of HEW regions, and also lists field units alphabetically by state and city.

4. U.S. Office of Economic Opportunity. **Catalog of Federal Domestic Assistance: Description of Federal Government's Domestic Programs to Assist the American People in Furthering Their Social and Economic Progress.** Washington, GPO, 1970. 1034p. $15.00 (looseleaf). LC Card No. 74-600920. (PrEx 10.2:P 94/970)

5. U.S. Office of Economic Opportunity. **Update of 1970 Catalog.** Comp. by the Office of Management and Budget. Washington, GPO, 1970. 198p. $15.00. (PrEx 10.2:P 94/970/Ch.)

6. U.S. Office of Management and Budget. **1971 Catalog of Federal Domestic Assistance.** Washington, GPO, 1971. 944p. $7.25. LC Card No. 78-613743. (PrEx 2.20:971)

Provides "a description of the federal government's domestic programs to assist the American people in furthering their social and economic progress." The summary description for each program provides specific information, its nature and purpose, availability, authorizing legislation and the administering agency, and where additional information may be found. Programs are arranged alphabetically by departments. Thoroughly indexed.

7. U.S. Social and Rehabilitation Service. **Characteristics of General Assistance in the United States.** Washington, GPO, 1970. 122p. $1.25. S/N 1760-0091. (HE 17.19:39)

In addition to a good introductory chapter on general assistance (i.e., both social and economic) programs, this directory provides information about specific programs. The data are arranged by states and grouped in five categories: general description, conditions of eligibility, standards, administration, and other aid.

ECONOMICS AND BUSINESS

GENERAL WORKS

BIBLIOGRAPHIES

8. U.S. Civil Service Commission. **Federal Civil Service: History, Organization, and Activities.** Washington, GPO, 1971. 55p. (Personnel Bibliography Series, No. 43) $0.60. LC Card No. 72-600592. S/N 0600-0619. (CS 1.61/3:43)

The main volume of this bibliography was published in 1962 and a supplement was issued in 1968. The present volume covers material received by the Civil Service Commission library during 1969 and 1970. The bibliography, arranged by broad subjects, is international in scope, lists periodical articles, government documents and books, and contains detailed annotations. Not indexed.

9. U.S. Civil Service Commission. **Fifty United States Civil Service Commissioners: Biographical Sketch, Biographical Sources, Writings.** Washington, GPO, 1971. 275p. Free from the Commission. LC Card No. 78-614566. (CS 1.61:C 73)

This is a very thorough work. The name of each former Civil Service Commissioner is followed by a biographical sketch and bibliographies of biographical sources, of unpublished sources and manuscripts, and of writings by the commissioner. The work is arranged in order of tenure with a name index. There is also a bibliography of standard reference sources cited, and of additional sources of information on Civil Service commissioners, and a guide to organizations and collections listed.

10. U.S. Congress. Joint Economic Committee. **Committee Publications and Policies Governing Their Distribution, 87th–92d Congresses, 1961-1971.** Washington, GPO, 1971. 27p. Issuing agency. LC Card No. 78-613786. (Y 4.Ec7:P 96/961-71)

This committee print lists all publications of the Joint Economic Committee from 1961 to 1971. Note is made of out-of-print materials. Not indexed or annotated. Arranged chronologically by Congress.

11. U.S. Department of Commerce. **United States Department of Commerce Publications: Catalog and Index, 1969 Supplement.** Comp. by E. Nell Sawyer. Washington, GPO, 1970. 59p. $0.35. (C 1.2:P 96/supp. 969)

12. U.S. Department of Commerce. **United States Department of Commerce Publications: Catalog and Index, 1970 Supplement.** Comp. by E. Nell Sawyer. Washington, GPO, 1971. 81p. $0.75. LC Card No. 52-60731. S/N 0300-0328. (C 1.2:P 96/supp. 970)

Business Service Checklist is a weekly list of new Department of Commerce publications; it is cumulated into these annual volumes. These volumes are also supplements to a basic bibliography entitled *United States Department of Commerce Publications*, which lists works published from 1790 to 1950.

The first section in each of these volumes lists U.S. government documents depository libraries and Department of Commerce field offices. Section two is the bibliography, arranged by issuing agency. Thoroughly indexed.

13. U.S. Department of Labor. **Publications of the U.S. Department of Labor: Subject Listing, 1965 to June 1970.** Washington, GPO, 1971. 78p. Issuing agency. LC Card No. L56-151. (L 1.34:P 96/965-970)

14. U.S. Department of Labor. **Publications of the U.S. Department of Labor: Subject Listing 1966 to June 1971.** Washington, GPO, 1971. 72p. Issuing agency. LC Card No. L56-151. (L 1.34:P 96/966-971)

Each issue of this departmental catalog contains an overview of publications issued during a five-year period. Within each subject heading publications are listed alphabetically by title, with the following information given for each: year of publication, number of pages, price (or o.p.), issuing agency, type of publication, and its number. Not annotated or indexed.

15. U.S. House of Representatives. Select Committee on Small Business. **List of Publications and Committee Membership of the Select Committee on Small Business, House, 77th–91st Congresses (1941-1970).** Washington, GPO, 1971. Issuing agency. LC Card No. 75-611803. (Y 4.Sm 1:P 96/941-70)

16. U.S. Small Business Administration. **Basic Library Reference Sources.** By Elizabeth G. Janezeck. Rev. ed. Washington, GPO, 1970. 11p. (Small Business Bibliographies, No. 18) Issuing agency. LC Card No. 70-608262. (SBA 1.3:18)

This bibliography lists books, pamphlets, and periodicals which form the nucleus of a basic library of business reference sources. It includes federal, state, and nongovernmental publications and services. Complete addresses of publishers and prices are provided in citations. Brief informative annotations accompany each entry.

17. U.S. Small Business Administration. **Small Business Administration Publications: For-Sale Booklets.** Washington, GPO, 1970. 6p. Issuing agency. (SBA 1.18:970-2)

18. U.S. Small Business Administration. **Small Business Administration Publications: For-Sale Booklets.** Washington, GPO, 1970. 6p. Issuing agency. (SBA 1.18:970-4)

19. U.S. Small Business Administration. **Small Business Administration Publications: For-Sale Booklets.** Washington, GPO, 1971. 6p. Issuing agency. (SBA 1.18:971)

These three booklets are checklists of currently available publications. They are not annotated or indexed.

20. U.S. Women's Bureau. **Publications of the Women's Bureau Currently Available.** Washington, GPO, 1970. 8p. Issuing agency. (L 13.11:10)

21. U.S. Women's Bureau. **Publications of the Women's Bureau Currently Available.** Washington, GPO, 1970. 8p. Issuing agency. (L 13.11:10/22)

22. U.S. Women's Bureau. **Publications of the Women's Bureau.** Washington, GPO, 1971. 6p. Issuing agency. (L 13.11:10)

23. U.S. Women's Bureau. **Publications of the Women's Bureau.** Washington, GPO, 1971. 8p. Issuing agency. (L 36.110:10)
These four bibliographies list business and economic publications of interest to women.

DIRECTORIES

24. U.S. Civil Service Commission. **Directory, Federal Job Information Centers.** Washington, GPO, 1970. 8p. Issuing agency. (CS 1.48:BRE-9)
Lists offices throughout the United States where interested persons can obtain, from one place, information about federal government employment opportunities anywhere in the United States.

25. U.S. Department of Commerce. **National Roster of Minority Professional Consulting Services.** Prep. by the Government Programs Coordination Division, Office of Minority Business Enterprise. Washington, GPO, 1971. 200p. Issuing agency. LC Card No. 79-614404. (C 1.57/3:971)

26. U.S. Department of Housing and Urban Development. **Minority Business Opportunities: A Manual on Opportunities for Small and Minority Group Businessmen and Professionals in HUD Programs.** Washington, GPO, 1970. 398p. $3.00. S/N 2300-0155. (HH 1.6/3:M66)
Describes U.S. government-sponsored housing, development, planning, construction, and related business and economic programs.

27. U.S. General Services Administration. **Federal Buying Directory.** Washington, GPO, 1971. 14p. (Counseling Guides, No. 6) Issuing agency. (GS 1.6/6-2:6/2)
Of limited value, this directory is designed to serve as a guide for businessmen in the Washington, D.C., area. Lists government personnel who either buy or have knowledge of the buying done by their agencies.

28. U.S. Securities and Exchange Commission. **Directory of Companies Filing Annual Reports with the Securities and Exchange Commission under the Securities Exchange Act of 1934.** Washington, GPO, 1970. 334p. $2.50. LC Card No. 59-61379. (SE 1.27:969)

29. U.S. Securities and Exchange Commission. **Directory of Companies Filing Annual Reports with the Securities and Exchange Commission under**

the Securities Act of 1934. Washington, GPO, 1971. 401p. (Office of Policy Research) $3.00. S/N 4600-0081. (SE 1.27:970)

These two directories list companies whose stocks are listed on national exchanges and which have registered under the Securities Act of 1934. Part one lists companies alphabetically by name with code numbers to industrial groups and Securities Exchange docket numbers. Part two lists companies by nine major industrial groups and subgroups.

30. U.S. Travel Service. **United States Conventions and Trade Shows, 1971-1972.** Washington, GPO, 1970. 62p. Issuing agency. (C 47.2: C 76/971-72)

Previous editions were entitled: *Major Conventions, Exhibitions and Trade Shows Held in the United States; United States Conventions and Exhibitions.* Intended as a guide only, these directories do not purport to be comprehensive. They include only those organizations' conventions which responded to a U.S. Travel Service questionnaire by saying that they welcome attendance from abroad at their meetings. Index by classifications and a chronological listing. Main body of the directory is by subject. Executive officer and address are listed, with a brief statement about the organization itself. Place and dates of conventions are provided for current year and for forthcoming years when possible.

INDEXES

31. U.S. House of Representatives. Judiciary Committee. **Index of Antitrust Subcommittee Publications, 81st Congress (January 1949) through 91st Congress, 2nd Session (December 1970).** Washington, House, 1971. 81p. Issuing agency. LC Card No. 70-611377. (Y 4.J 89/1:An 8/11/949-70)

32. U.S. Patent Office. **Index of Trademarks, 1969.** Washington, GPO, 1970. 327p. $4.25(cloth). LC Card No. 30-26199. (C 21.5/3:969)

33. U.S. Patent Office. **Index of Trademarks, 1970.** Washington, GPO, 1971. 303p. $4.25(cloth). (C 21.5/3:970)

These indexes include "the registrants of all trademark registrations issued during the year; and also registrants of trademarks published in the *Official Gazette* . . . , and registrants of trademark registrations renewed, canceled, surrendered, amended, disclaimed, corrected, etc., during the year . . . ." Arranged alphabetically by name of registrant with address and registration information.

STATISTICS

34. U.S. Agency for International Development. **Selected Economic Data for Less Developed Countries, Data Based on the Most Recent Information Available, General for the Years 1968 and 1969.** Washington, GPO, 1970. 8p. (Office of Statistics and Reports, Bureau of Program and Policy Coordination) $0.10. (S 18.2:Ec 7/2/970)

35. U.S. Agency for International Development. **Selected Economic Data for Less Developed Countries, Data Based on the Most Recent Information Available, General for the Years 1969 and 1970.** Washington, GPO, 1971. 8p. (Office of Statistics and Reports, Bureau for Program and Policy Coordination) $0.10. LC Card No. 78-614783. S/N 4401-0032. (S 18.2:Ec 7/2/971)

The statistical data in these compendia cover population, area, gross national product, exports, transportation, education, and health for countries in Latin America, East, Near East, and South Asia, and Africa. Regional comparisons are included.

36. U.S. Office of Business Economics. **1969 Business Statistics: Supplement to the Survey of Current Business.** Prep. by the Current Business Analysis Division. 17th biennial ed. Washington, GPO, 1970. 264+187p. $3.00. LC Card No. 21-26819. (C 43.8/4:969)

A "basic reference volume designed to provide historical perspective to the numerous economic statistics reported currently in the monthly magazine *Survey of Current Business*," this current issue provides data for approximately 2,500 series from 1939 through 1968. When appropriate, annual totals are shown for all years. Series compiled quarterly are shown on that basis; those compiled monthly are also shown. The appendix provides monthly or quarterly data for approximately 350 of the more important economic series. All materials are made easy to locate through the edge index on the back cover and the detailed alphabetical subject index.

BUSINESS AND INDUSTRY

GENERAL WORKS

BIBLIOGRAPHIES

37. U.S. Department of the Air Force. **Management (Excluding Personnel).** Prep. by Susan McEnally. San Francisco, Pacific Air Force, 1970. 51p. (PACAF Basic Bibliographies for Base Libraries) Available from CINCPACAF, (DPSR)/Director, PACAF Libraries, APO, San Francisco, Calif. 96553. LC Card No. 58-61790. (D 301.62:M 31/2/970)

38. U.S. National Aeronautics and Space Administration. **Management: Continuing Literature Survey with Indexes; Selection of Annotated References to Unclassified Reports and Journal Articles Entering NASA and DoD Information Systems in 1969.** Springfield, Va., CFSTI, 1970. $3.00. (NASA SP Series) $3.00. LC Card No. 71-608868. [NAS 1.21:7500(04)]

39. U.S. National Aeronautics and Space Administration. **Management: Continuing Literature Survey with Indexes; Selection of Annotated References to Unclassified Reports and Journal Articles Entering NASA and DoD Information Systems in 1970.** Springfield, Va., NTIS, 1971. 67+60p. (NASA SP Series) $3.00. [NAS 1.21:7500(05)]

These two works supplement two earlier volumes, which were published in 1968 and which covered the years 1962 to 1967. See *Government Reference Books 68/69*, entry number 227.

40. U.S. Small Business Administration. **Small Business Administration Publications: Classification of Management Publications.** Washington, GPO, 1970. 8p. Issuing agency. (SBA 1.18/3:970)

    A checklist of available publications without annotations or index.

41. U.S. Small Business Administration. **Small Business Administration Publications: Free Management Assistance Publications.** Washington, GPO, 1971. 4p. Issuing agency. (SBA 1.18:971-2)

    Checklist of available publications. Updated frequently.

DIRECTORIES

42. U.S. Travel Service. **Plant Tours for International Visitors to the United States.** 1971-72 ed. Washington, GPO, 1971. 154p. $1.00. S/N 0312-0011. (C 47.2:P 69/971-72)

    All information was supplied by Travel Service liaisons in the various states. Arranged alphabetically by state, city and name of the plant. A number beside each entry keys that entry to the "Industrial Classification Index," which lists plants by particular industry.

STATISTICS

43. U.S. Bureau of Domestic Commerce. **Industry Profiles, 1958-68.** Washington, GPO, 1970. 297p. $2.25. LC Card No. 73-603430. (C 41.2: In 2/25/958-68)

44. U.S. Bureau of Domestic Commerce. **Industry Profiles, 1958-69.** Washington, GPO, 1971. 298p. $2.25. (C 41.2:In 2/25/958-69)

    These two works provide statistical data on the economic development of selected manufacturing industries. Designed to "provide users of industrial data with a convenient single source of comparable basic industry statistics."

45. U.S. Bureau of Domestic Commerce. **U.S. Industrial Outlook, 1971, with Projections Through 1980.** Washington, GPO, 1971. 495p. $5.00. LC Card No. 60-60662. (C 41.42/4:971)

    "Presents narrative and statistical trend analyses on an industry-by-industry basis for major areas in the U.S. economy." Each industry section contains information on recent developments, effects of new technology, international trade and prospects for the coming year. Includes a detailed subject index.

46. U.S. Bureau of the Census. **Alphabetical Index of Industries and Occupations; 1970 Census of Population.** Washington, GPO, 1971. 189p. $3.00. S/N 0301-2283. (C 3.223:Oc 1/970)

    This publication lists approximately 19,000 industry and occupation titles in alphabetical order. Industry titles denote the nature of business of the person's employer; occupation titles denote the type of work in which the person is engaged.

47. U.S. Bureau of the Census. **Classified Index of Industries and Occupations: 1970 Census of Population.** Washington, GPO, 1971. 265p. $2.00. LC Card No. 74-179488. (C 3.223:Oc 1/2/970)

Contains the same type of information as in the previous publication. Here, the information is classified according to type of industry or occupation.

INVENTORY AND RECORD CONTROL

48. U.S. National Archives and Records Service. Office of the Federal Register. **Guide to Record Retention Requirements.** Rev. ed. Washington, GPO, 1971. 92p. $1.00. S/N 2203-0246. (GS 4.107/a:R245/971)

This handy guide for industry, business, and the general public contains over 1,000 summaries of record retention regulations, which were compiled from laws in the U.S. Statutes and rules of various federal agencies. The guide explains what records must be kept, who must keep them, and how long they must be kept. Each summary contains a reference to the full text of the law or regulation. The index lists the categories of persons, companies, and products affected by federal record retention requirements.

49. U.S. Small Business Administration. **Automation for Small Offices.** By Frank J. Carberry. Rev. ed. Washington, GPO, 1971. 12p. (Small Business Bibliographies, No. 58) (SBA 1.3:58/3)

Lists books and periodical articles which relate to office automation as it pertains to small companies.

50. U.S. Small Business Administration. **Inventory Management.** By Donald F. Mulvihill. Washington, GPO, 1970. 8p. (Small Business Bibliography No. 75) Issuing agency. LC Card No. 77-606965. (SBA 1.3:75/2)

Contains separate sections for government and nongovernment publications. Government publications are arranged by department; nongovernment by publisher. Descriptive annotations are provided. A list of periodicals and a "sample" list of relevant articles are also provided.

MARKETING

51. U.S. Agricultural Research Service. **Bibliography of Insect-Resistant Packaging, 1913-69.** By Henry A. Highland and C. E. Metts. Washington, the Service, 1970. 16p. (ARS Series No. 51-36) Issuing agency. LC Card No. 74-608929. (A 77.15:51-36)

52. U.S. Bureau of Domestic Commerce. **Business Machine Market Information Sources.** Washington, GPO, 1971. 41p. $0.50. S/N 0308-0140. (C 41.2:M 18/4)

This is a guide to non-technical sources of information in the business machine industry. It includes, but is not limited to, electronic computer and data processing equipment.

53. U.S. Bureau of Domestic Commerce. **Marketing and the Low Income Consumer.** Rev. ed. Washington, GPO, 1971. 65p. $0.65. LC 77-613862. S/N 0308-0142. (C 41.12:M 34/4/971)
   This is an enlarged edition of a bibliography published in 1969 entitled *Bibliography on Marketing to Low-Income Consumers.* Included are materials which deal with the characteristics of the market system serving low income consumers and with programs designed to improve the market system. Brief annotations are provided.

54. U.S. Consumer and Marketing Service. **Federal-State Market News Reports: Directory of Services Available.** Rev. ed. Washington, GPO, 1970. 50p. Issuing agency. LC Card No. 70-610025. (A 88.40/2:21)
   Designed to aid farmers in deciding what to grow and where to sell. Lists market news reports and offices which issue them, describes the market news wire network and contains an alphabetical tabulation of cities from which news reports are issued.

55. U.S. Small Business Administration. **National Directories for Use in Marketing.** By Lloyd M. De Boer. Rev. ed. Washington, GPO, 1971. 18p. (Small Business Bibliographies, No. 13) Issuing agency. LC Card No. 75-614411. (SBA 1.3:13/4)
   Directories are listed alphabetically under subjects, e.g., apparel, jobbers, warehouses. Prices and addresses are given for those wanting to purchase the directories listed. Annotated.

SPECIFIC BUSINESSES AND INDUSTRIES

CHEMICAL AND PETROLEUM PLANTS

56. U.S. Bureau of Mines. **Bibliography of Investment and Operating Costs for Chemical and Petroleum Plants, January—December 1969.** By Sidney Katell and John R. Duda. Washington, GPO, 1970. 162p. $1.25. LC Card No. Int 59-53. (I 28.27:8478)
   In addition to investment and operating costs, other subjects, such as cost-estimating methods and theory, developments in the United States and abroad, and nuclear science, are covered.

57. U.S. Bureau of Mines. **Petroleum Refineries in the United States and Puerto Rico.** Pittsburgh, Pa., Bureau of Mines, 1971. 15p. Issuing agency. (I 28.17/2:971)
   This directory lists names and addresses of petroleum refineries in the United States and Puerto Rico.

58. U.S. Department of the Interior. **Desalting Plants Inventory Report.** By Milton S. Sachs. Washington, GPO, 1970. 25p. $0.35. LC Card No. 76-606875. (I 1.87/4:2)

59. U.S. Department of the Interior. **Desalting Plants Inventory Report No. 3.** By Frank O'Shaughnessy. Washington, GPO, 1971. 28p. $0.35. S/N 2400-0705. (I 1.87/4:3)

These reports contain an inventory of world-wide land based desalting plants in operation or under construction. Only those plants capable of producing 25,000 gallons or more of fresh water daily are listed.

CLOTHING STORES

60. U.S. Small Business Administration. **Apparel and Accessories for Women, Misses, and Children.** By Karen R. Gillespie. Rev. ed. Washington, GPO, 1971. 23p. (Small Business Bibliographies, No. 50) Issuing agency. (SBA 1.3: 50/3)

This bibliography was prepared for persons interested in any phase of the apparel and accessories industry. Through the sources cited, persons may find information on advertising, distribution, fabric, fashion, laws, machinery, and much more.

CONSTRUCTION INDUSTRY

61. U.S. Department of Labor. **Construction Industry. Selected References, 1960-69.** Washington, Department of Labor, 1970. 13p. (Current Bibliographies Prepared by the Library, No. 2) Issuing agency. LC Card No. 73-607062. (L 1.34/4:2)

Limited to items in the Department of Labor library.

DRUGSTORES

62. U.S. Small Business Administration. **Drugstores.** By Joseph D. McEvilla. Rev. ed. Washington, GPO, 1970. 8p. (Small Business Bibliographies, No. 33) LC Card No. 73-608725. (SBA 1.3:33/3)

Provides general information on managing a retail drugstore and an annotated list of relevant publications.

ENGINEERING FIRMS

63. U.S. Bureau of Domestic Commerce. **Engineers' Overseas Handbook.** Prep. by Gwen Parsons Benjamin. Rev. ed. Washington, GPO, 1971. 250p. $1.50. S/N 0308-0138. (C 41.6/9:En 3/971)

Engineering firms attempting to develop business overseas will find this condensed source of information very useful. It contains data on market conditions in 114 countries in the free world, including current conditions and requirements which affect the ability of engineers to work on overseas projects.

FOOD PROCESSING AND RETAILING

64. U.S. Consumer and Marketing Service. **List of Equipment Approved for Use in Federally Inspected Meat and Poultry Plants as of December 5, 1970.** Washington, GPO, 1971. 26p. $0.25. (A 88.2:Eq 5)

65. U.S. Consumer and Marketing Service. **List of Plants Operating Under USDA Poultry and Egg Grading and Egg Products Inspection Programs.** Washington, GPO, 1971. 44p. Issuing agency. (A 88.15/23:971)

    Plants are listed alphabetically by state. Includes an index of 1,552 official plant identification numbers.

66. U.S. Small Business Administration. **Soft-Frozen Dessert Stands.** By Karl Kern. Rev. ed. Washington, GPO, 1971. 11p. (Small Business Bibliographies, No. 47) Issuing agency. LC Card No. 77-611072. (SBA 1.3:47/2)

    Provides information for prospective and already-active dessert stand operators, including both privately-owned and franchised operations.

HOBBY SHOPS

67. U.S. Small Business Administration. **Hobby Shops.** By Milton K. Grey. Rev. ed. Washington, GPO, 1971. 8p. (Small Business Bibliographies, No. 53) Issuing agency. (SBA 1.3:53/3)

    This bibliography lists general works on retail hobby and craft stores, plus how-to books on specific activities.

MANUFACTURING

68. U.S. Small Business Administration. **Manufacturers' Sales Representative.** By John C. Warren. Rev. ed. Washington, GPO, 1970. 11p. (Small Business Bibliographies, No. 67) Issuing agency. LC Card No. 75-609500. (SBA 1.3:67/3)

    An introductory chapter explains the job of a sales representative, the method of beginning a sales agency and the outlook for future work in this field. The bibliography, well-annotated, lists government documents, directories, periodicals, and monographs. A list of associations and consultants is appended.

MOTELS

69. U.S. Small Business Administration. **Motels.** By Albert E. Kudrle. Rev. ed. Washington, GPO, 1971. 11p. (Small Business Bibliographies, No. 66) Issuing agency. (SBA 1.3:66/3)

    "In determining whether the motel business is for him, a person should start by making a careful study of the books and other publications listed in this bibliography."

NURSERY BUSINESS

70. U.S. Small Business Administration. **Nursery Business.** By John J. Pinney. Rev. ed. Washington, GPO, 1971. 12p. (Small Business Bibliographies, No. 14) Issuing agency. (SBA 1.3:14)
  This bibliography is aimed at both the current and the prospective nurseryman.

PRINTING

71. U.S. Congress. Joint Committee on Printing. **Bibliography on Electronic Composition.** Washington, Committee, 1970. 58p. Issuing agency. LC Card No. 79-609465. (Y 4.P93/1:El 2/2)
  Accompanies a volume entitled *Electronic Composition Cost Comparison* (Y 4.P93/1:El 2).

SHIPBUILDING

72. U.S. Naval Ship Systems Command. **Ship Metallic Material Comparison and Use Guide.** Washington, GPO, 1971. 305p. $3.25. S/N 0852-0024. (D 211.6/2:M 56)
  This handbook is a ready reference source for information on metals commonly used in shipbuilding. It is divided into 11 sections, with materials grouped according to similarities in chemistry and in fabrication characteristics.

SHOPPING CENTERS

73. U.S. Small Business Administration. **Suburban Shopping Centers.** By Robert H. Myers. Rev. ed. Washington, GPO, 1970. 12p. (Small Business Bibliographies, No. 27) Issuing agency. LC Card No. 70-610818. (SBA 1.3:27/3)
  Designed to assist the businessman who is considering location in a suburban shopping center.

UTILITY COMPANIES

74. U.S. Federal Power Commission. **Statistics of Interstate Natural Gas Pipeline Companies, 1969.** Washington, GPO, 1970. 139p. $1.25. S/N 1500-0178. (FP 1.21:205)

75. U.S. Federal Power Commission. **Statistics of Interstate Natural Gas Pipeline Companies, 1970.** Washington, GPO, 1971. 181p. $1.50. S/N 1500-0214. (FP 1.21:213)
  Financial and operating statistics were compiled from annual reports filed with the Federal Power Commission by the natural gas pipeline companies.

76. U.S. Federal Power Commission. **Statistics of Privately Owned Electric Utilities in the United States, 1969.** Washington, GPO, 1970. 424p. $3.75. S/N 1500-0179. (FP 1.21:206)

77. U.S. Federal Power Commission. **Statistics of Privately Owned Electric Utilities in the United States, 1970.** Washington, GPO, 1971. 804p. $3.25. S/N 1500-0217. (FP 1.21:214)
    Contains comprehensive financial and operating data on all large privately owned electric utility companies operating in the United States.

78. U.S. Federal Power Commission. **Statistics of Publicly Owned Electric Utilities in the United States, 1968.** Washington, GPO, 1970. 137p. $1.50. (FP 1.21:200)

79. U.S. Federal Power Commission. **Statistics of Publicly Owned Electric Utilities in the United States, 1969.** Washington, GPO, 1971. 193p. $1.75. (FP 1.21:210)
    Compiled from annual reports filed with the Federal Power Commission, these compendia provide comprehensive data on finances and operations of publicly owned electric utility companies.

WHOLESALE BUSINESSES

80. U.S. Small Business Administration. **Wholesaling.** By Theodore N. Beckman, Alton F. Doody, and Daniel J. Seeney. Rev. ed. Washington, GPO, 1971. 23p. (Small Business Bibliographies, No. 55) (SBA 1.3:55/5)
    Entries in this bibliography were chosen "with the intent of aiding the independent wholesale manager to remain a viable and vital link in the American distributive system." Part one lists government documents; part two, arranged by subject, lists privately published books.

COMMUNICATIONS

MASS MEDIA

81. U.S. Department of Commerce. **World Maps of Atmospheric Radio Noise in Universal Time by Numerical Mapping.** By Donald H. Zacharisen and William B. Jones. Washington, GPO, 1970. 31p. (Telecommunications Research Reports, No. 2) $0.40. LC Card No. 70-612109. (C 1.60:2)

82. U.S. Federal Communications Commission. **Directory of Field Contacts for Coordination of Use of Radio Frequencies.** Washington, FCC, 1971. 191p. Issuing agency. (CC 1.2:R 11/14)
    This publication was issued jointly with the Office of Telecommunication Police, Executive Office of the President.

83. U.S. Foreign Broadcast Information Service. **Broadcasting Stations of the World.** Washington, GPO, 1971. 4v. $8.50. LC Card No. 47-32798. (PrEx 7.9:971/pt.)

Published biennially before 1965, this work is now annual, in four parts. It covers broadcast stations all over the world but excludes those in the United States which broadcast on local channels. The four parts are: 1) Amplitude Modulation Broadcasting Stations by Country and City; 2) Amplitude Modulation Broadcasting Stations by Frequency; 3) Frequency Modulation Broadcasting Stations; and 4) Television Stations.

POSTAL GUIDES

84. U.S. Postal Service. **Directory of Post Offices.** Washington, GPO, 1970. 488p. $4.25. S/N 3900-0076. (P 1.10/4:970)

85. U.S. Postal Service. **Directory of Post Offices.** Washington, GPO, 1971. 491p. $4.25. S/N 3900-0232. (P 1.10/4:971)

These directories include the following: A list of all post offices, branches, and stations arranged alphabetically by states with ZIP codes as an aid in determining parcel post zones (only the first three digits are given for larger cities which have more than one ZIP code); an alphabetical list of all post offices, named stations, and branches; lists of sectional centers and major cities by states; a list of post offices by states and counties showing the number of box holders on rural routes, star routes, and in post offices; a numerical list of post offices by ZIP code; a list of post offices, named stations, and branches discontinued or with names changed during the past two years; a list of Army posts, camps, and stations; Air Force bases, fields, and installations; APO's; and FPO's.

86. U.S. Postal Service. **International Mail.** Washington, GPO, 1971. 574p. $2.50 (looseleaf). (P 1.10/5:971)

Formerly called *Directory of International Mail.* Contains detailed information about postage rates, services available, prohibitions, import restrictions, and other conditions governing mail to other countries.

87. U.S. Postal Service. **National ZIP Code Directory, 1970-71.** Washington, GPO, 1970. 1733p. $10.00. LC Card No. 66-60919. S/N 3900-0080. (P 1.10/8:970-71)

88. U.S. Postal Service. **National ZIP Code Directory, 1971-72.** Washington, GPO, 1971. 1773p. $10.00. S/N 3900-0233. (P 1.10/8:971-72)

This directory enables the user to determine the ZIP code for every mailing address in the United States. Code listings are arranged alphabetically by state. Within each state, a complete listing is given of all post offices, stations, and branches with the appropriate five-digit ZIP code for each delivery area. An appendix after each state gives the ZIP code for each address in the larger cities. Also in these directories are: a ZIP code area map; a listing of two-letter state abbreviations; a listing of sectional center facilities; ZIP code prefixes by state; a numerical list of post offices by ZIP code; and a listing of postal units discontinued.

CONSUMER INFORMATION

89. U.S. Bureau of Labor Statistics. **Consumer Prices in the United States, 1959-68: Trends and Indexes.** Washington, GPO, 1970. 73p. $0.70. (L 2.3: 1647)

    The trend of consumer prices for the ten-year period 1959 to 1968 is analyzed in this bulletin. Tables of indexes and related data for the years 1964 to 1968 and technical notes describing changes made in index pricing and calculation procedures since the completion of the comprehensive revision in January 1964 are also included.

90. U.S. Consumer Product Information Coordinating Center. **Consumer Product Information: Index of Selected Federal Publications on How to Buy, Use, and Take Care of Consumer Products.** Washington, GPO, 1971. 15p. Issuing agency. (GS 11.9:971)

91. U.S. Consumer Product Information Coordinating Center. **Consumer Product Information: Index of Selected Federal Publications of Consumer Interest.** 2nd ed. Washington, GPO, 1971. 15p. Issuing agency. (GS 11.9: 971-2)

92. U.S. Consumer Product Information Coordinating Center. **Consumer Product Information: Index of Selected Federal Publications on How to Buy, Use, and Take Care of Consumer Products.** 3rd ed. Washington, GPO, 1971. 16p. Issuing agency. (GS 11.9:971-3)

    These works briefly annotate publications from many federal agencies, covering consumer education topics such as how to buy and use consumer products, repairing and financing houses, child care, family budgeting. The list is arranged by subject: appliances, automobiles, clothing, food, and miscellaneous. Orders for pamphlets listed in the Index should be sent to Consumer Product Information Coordinating Center. Complete order information and forms are included in the index.

93. U.S. Office of Consumer Affairs. **Consumer Education Bibliography.** Rev. ed. Washington, GPO, 1971. 192p. $1.00. S/N 4000-0251. (PrEx 16.10:Ed 8)

    Prepared jointly by the Office of Consumer Affairs and the New York Public Library, this bibliography will be useful to anyone concerned with consumer affairs, but particularly to educators, librarians, and researchers. It lists over 4,000 books, pamphlets, periodical articles, audiovisual aids, and teachers' materials relating to consumer interest and education.

94. U.S. Office of Consumer Affairs. **Guide to Federal Consumer Services.** Washington, GPO, 1971. 151p. $1.00. LC Card No. 73-616122. S/N 4000-0073. (PrEx 16.8:Se 6)

    The first edition of this work was published in 1967. This new work reflects the growing governmental concern with consumer problems. The vast number of services and programs offered by the government to aid the consumer are not always easy to locate. This directory pulls it all together in one helpful volume. It is arranged by agency, giving general information about each agency followed by data on consumer programs, how they are carried out and enforced, information on how consumers can use these services, and selected publications. Includes a glossary of agency initials and a subject index.

ECONOMIC DEVELOPMENT PROGRAMS

95. U.S. Department of Commerce. **Directory of Private Programs Assisting Minority Business.** 2nd ed. Prep. by the Office of Minority Business Enterprise. Washington, GPO, 1970. 364p. $2.50. LC Card No. 72-603592. (C 1.56:970)

This directory identifies the type of private assistance available for minority business enterprises and provides information covering activities currently underway, together with specialized federal government and municipally-sponsored programs. The information is grouped in chapters by private assistance programs, municipal programs, national organizations, national technical and management assistance programs and minority owned financial institutions. A synopsis of the work of each organization or program is furnished along with name, address, phone, and names of administrative officials. Indexed by names.

96. U.S. Department of Commerce. **Higher Education Aid for Minority Business: A Directory of Assistance Available to Minorities by Selected Collegiate Schools of Business.** Washington, GPO, 1970. 103p. $1.00. LC Card No. 78-607539. (C 1.2:M 66/4)

This is the first compilation listing the opportunities open specifically to minorities in business schools across the country which will aid them in acquiring the necessary training. It was published to help the minority person "sharpen his means of competition" in the business field. The first section is an alphabetical list of schools which indicated an offering of some type of financial aid specifically set aside for minority students interested in business careers. The second section is a narrative description of 44 schools which have special programs for minority groups in such areas as recruitment, management assistance, or special sources. The third section lists schools by states.

97. U.S. Department of Commerce. **Special Catalog of Federal Programs Assisting Minority Enterprise 1971.** Washington, GPO, 1971. 89p. $1.00. LC Card No. 77-614023. S/N 0300-0324. (C 1.2:M 66/6)

This catalog describes programs of many federal agencies which provide various kinds of help to minority business.

98. U.S. Department of Labor. **Directory of Job Corps Centers, Civilian Conservation Centers, Men's Centers, Residential Manpower Centers, Women's Centers, Residential Support Centers.** Washington, GPO, 1971. 20p. Issuing agency. LC Card No. 70-611704. (L 1.2:J 57/12)

99. U.S. Economic Development Administration. **Directory for Economic Development Districts.** Washington, EDA, 1970. 51p. Issuing agency. (C 46.2: D 62)
    This directory shows the location of EDA districts in the United States.

100. U.S. Economic Development Administration. **EDA Directory of Approved Projects, as of June 30, 1971.** Washington, GPO, 1971. 245p. Issuing agency. (C 46.19/2:971)
    This directory lists all projects approved for Economic Development Administration assistance under PL 89-136 (1965).

EMPLOYMENT AND LABOR

GENERAL WORKS

BIBLIOGRAPHIES

101. U.S. Bureau of Labor Standards. **Selected Publications of the Bureau of Labor Standards.** Washington, GPO, 1970. 23p. Issuing agency. (L 16.17: P 96/2/970)
    Lists publications available from both GPO and the Bureau. Publications are under broad headings—safety, labor legislation, youth employment standards. Most entries are annotated. A chronological list of publications is included, with page references to the main entry.

102. U.S. Bureau of Labor Statistics. **BLS Publications on Productivity and Technology.** Washington, GPO, 1971. 16p. Issuing agency. (L 2.34/2: P 94/6)
    Publications are grouped according to the following: productivity studies, technology studies, international comparisons, and construction labor requirements studies. A list of studies in progress is appended.

103. U.S. Bureau of Labor Statistics. **Publications of the Bureau of Labor Statistics, July-December 1969.** Washington, GPO, 1970. 44p. Issuing agency. LC Card No. 14-10111. (L 2.34:969/2)

104. U.S. Bureau of Labor Statistics. **Publications of the Bureau of Labor Statistics, January-June, 1970.** Washington, GPO, 1971. 56p. Issuing agency. LC Card No. 14-10111. (L 2.34:970/1)

105. U.S. Bureau of Labor Statistics. **Publications of the Bureau of Labor Statistics, July-December 1970.** Washington, GPO, 1971. 53p. Issuing agency. (L 2.34:970/2)

106. U.S. Bureau of Labor Statistics. **Publications of the Bureau of Labor Statistics, January-June 1971.** Prep. by Sarah B. Perry. Washington, GPO, 1971. 42p. Issuing agency. (L 2.34:971/1)
    This semi-annual catalog is a classified list of publications issued during the

preceding six months. Brief summaries accompany many of the entries. Includes information for ordering publications.

107. U.S. Civil Service Commission. **Equal Opportunity in Employment.** Washington, GPO, 1971. 135p. (Personnel Bibliography Series, No. 38) $1.25. LC Card No. 72-600588. S/N 0600-0614. (C 1.61/3:38)

   Lists materials received in the Civil Service Commission library during 1969 and 1970. Chapters are on minority groups, the handicapped, older workers and women. Each chapter contains a list of bibliographies first. All entries are annotated.

108. U.S. National Bureau of Standards. **Man, His Job, and the Environment: A Review and Annotated Bibliography of Selected Research on Human Performance.** By William G. Mather, III, and others. Washington, GPO, 1970. 101p. $1.00. LC Card No. 77-604124. (C 13.10:319)

   Recent scientific literature was searched to review procedures currently being used to study human reactions to work and environmental stress. Task variables, environmental conditions, individual variations in subjects, and physiological, psychophysical, psychological and sociological responses were considered. The different types of research reviewed included analysis of on-the-job performance, simulations of real-life situations, laboratory experiments with human and nonhuman subjects, and clinical studies. In addition to an extensive bibliography, detailed abstracts of 190 research reports are included.

HANDBOOKS AND GUIDES

109. U.S. Civil Service Commission. **Handbook of Selective Placement in Federal Civil Service Employment of the Physically Handicapped, the Mentally Restored, the Mentally Retarded, the Rehabilitated Offender.** Washington, GPO, 1970. 48p. $0.60. (CS 1.7/4:Se 4/970)

   Of interest to employers within the federal government and to prospective employees.

110. U.S. Department of Agriculture. Personnel Office. **Guides for Supervisors.** Prep. by Cameron C. Smith. Rev. Washington, GPO, 1970. 118p. $1.25. (A 49.8:Eu 7/2)

   This supersedes *Guide Posts for Supervisors* published in 1952.

111. U.S. Department of Labor. **Handbook for Job Restructuring.** By J. Edmund Phillips and others. Washington, GPO, 1970. 46p. $0.55. (L 1.7/2: J 57/4)

   This handbook was developed to provide a basic guide for use in restructuring job systems in order to utilize available manpower resources more efficiently.

112. U.S. Veterans' Reemployment Rights Office. **Veterans' Reemployment Rights Handbook.** Washington, GPO, 1970. 196p. $1.00. (L 25.6/2:V 64/970)

This handbook will be of interest to veterans, their counselors, their former employers, their unions, and others who may be affected by questions in this field. It covers such subjects as an explanation of who is eligible for reemployment rights; applying for reemployment; applicant's qualifications; change in employer's circumstances; position and rate of pay to be offered; seniority rights; and more.

113. U.S. Wage and Labor Standards Administration. **Handy Reference Guide to the Fair Labor Standards Act.** Washington, GPO, 1971. 16p. $0.25. S/N 2905-0019. (L 22.5:F 15/3/971)

Contains general information concerning the Fair Labor Standards Act, including basic wage and hour standards, exemptions to minimum wage and overtime requirements, etc.

STATISTICS

114. U.S. Bureau of Labor Statistics. **Employment and Earnings, States and Areas, 1939-1969.** Washington, GPO, 1970. 607p. $4.50. (L 2.3:1370-7)

115. U.S. Bureau of Labor Statistics. **Employment and Earnings, States and Areas, 1939-1970.** Washington, GPO, 1971. 646p. $4.50. S/N 2901-0681. (L 2.3:1370-8)

This series groups together information available as a result of the Current Employment Statistics Program, presenting comprehensive historical reference for state and local area employment and earnings statistics. Each issue includes data from 1939 to the current year in 214 major labor areas. Agricultural, domestic and self-employed workers are not included in this statistical survey.

116. U.S. Bureau of Labor Statistics. **Employment and Earnings, United States, 1909-70.** Washington, GPO, 1971. 602p. $4.25. (L 2.3:1312-7)

Contains historical national statistics for individual nonagricultural industries from the earliest date of each series, with summary tables. Includes monthly and annual averages on employment covering all employees, women, production workers in manufacturing and mining, construction workers in private companies, and nonsupervisory workers in the remaining private nonmanufacturing industries.

117. U.S. Bureau of Labor Statistics. **Handbook of Labor Statistics, 1970.** Washington, GPO, 1970. 400p. (Bulletin No. 1666) $3.50. LC Card No. L 27-328. (L 2.3:1666)

118. U.S. Bureau of Labor Statistics. **Handbook of Labor Statistics, 1971.** Washington, GPO, 1971. 369p. (Bulletin No. 1705) $3.25. S/N 2901-0641. (L 2.3:1705)

Each edition of this handbook is in two major parts: "Technical notes," which describes major statistical programs and identifies the tables, and "Tables" which are arranged consecutively under major subject headings. Each table is historically complete, beginning with the earliest reliable and consistent data. Related data from other U.S. government agencies and from foreign countries are included.

119. U.S. Bureau of Labor Statistics. **Indexes of Output Per Man-Hour, Selected Industries, 1939 and 1947-69.** Washington, GPO, 1970. 112p. $1.00. (L 2.3:1680)

120. U.S. Bureau of Labor Statistics. **Indexes of Output Per Man-Hour, Selected Industries, 1939 and 1947-70.** Washington, GPO, 1971. 158p. $1.25. S/N 2901-0661. (L 2.3:1692)

    Updates earlier industry indexes. Indexes are for output per man-hour, output per employee, and unit labor requirements of the industries currently included in the government's productivity measurement program.

121. U.S. Bureau of Labor Statistics. **Occupational Employment Statistics, 1960-1967.** Washington, GPO, 1970. 42p. $0.50. (L 2.3:1643)

    This is a handy reference to the various sources of occupational employment statistics and makes available, in one place, the more recent figures on major occupations. This information should prove useful to anyone concerned with the changing occupational composition of the labor force and its implications for training programs, counseling, and manpower policy.

122. U.S. Equal Employment Opportunity Commission. **Spanish Surnamed American Employment in the Southwest.** By Fred H. Schmidt. Prep. for the Colorado Civil Rights Commission under the auspices of the Equal Employment Opportunity Commission. Washington, GPO, 1970. 247p. $2.00. LC Card No. 79-607436. (Y 3.Eq 2:2Sp 2)

    Provides statistical information on the job patterns that prevail for this minority group in the southwestern part of the United States, where they are most heavily settled. Also gives the historical background of these people, showing how and why the discriminatory job patterns have evolved.

123. U.S. Social Security Administration. **Earnings Distributions in the United States, 1967.** Washington, GPO, 1971. 318p. $2.50. S/N 1770-0164. (HE 3.2:Ea 7/967)

    This is the first volume in a new series. It is based on social security earnings record data and provides a comprehensive accounting of earned income in the United States. The data are classified by age, sex, race, and geographic location.

LABOR-MANAGEMENT RELATIONS

124. U.S. Bureau of Labor Statistics. **Municipal Labor-Management Relations: Chronology of Compensation Developments in Milwaukee, 1960-70.** Washington, GPO, 1971. 118p. $1.25. S/N 2901-0702. (L 2.3:1720)

    This bulletin presents a summary of the major changes in salaries and supplementary (fringe) benefits that have taken place during the period 1960 to 1970 for municipal employees subject to the regulation of the Milwaukee Common Council, the city's governing body.

125. U.S. Civil Service Commission. **Employee Benefits and Services.** Washington, GPO, 1970. 150p. (Personnel Bibliography Series, No. 33) $1.25. LC Card No. 74-608657. (CS 1.61/3:33)

Includes materials received in the Civil Service Commission library from 1964 to 1969. "Material has been selected on the basis of its application and usefulness in research on federal government programs." Arranged by benefits or services. Annotated.

126. U.S. Civil Service Commission. **Employee-Management Relations in Public Service.** Washington, GPO, 1970. 62p. (Personnel Bibliography Series, No. 36) $0.60. LC Card No. 74-610105. (CS 1.61/3:36)

Updates number 7 in this series and its first supplement. Covers materials from 1967 to 1969. Works on grievances and appeals, strikes, employee participation in management, among others, are included.

127. U.S. Civil Service Commission. **Executive Manpower Management.** Washington, GPO, 1971. 113p. (Personnel Bibliography Series, No. 40) $1.00. LC Card No. 72-600589. S/N 0600-0616. (CS 1.61/3:40)

This bibliography updates number ten in this series, *Staffing the Higher Federal Civil Service* (1962), number 23, *Executive Manpower Management* (1968), and number 26, *Supervisory Responsibilities, Selection, and Evaluation.* Three primary chapters are "The Federal Executive," "Public Executives," and "Political Executives." The bibliography cites research reports, journal articles, and government publications.

128. U.S. Civil Service Commission. **Managing Human Behavior.** Washington, GPO, 1970. 177p. (Personnel Bibliography Series, No. 35) $1.50. LC Card No. 71-610115. (CS 1.61/3:35)

Updates number 16 in this series, *Productivity, Motivation and Incentive Awards*, and cites works published or received in the Civil Service Commission library from 1965 through 1969. Materials excluded are those on general aspects of personnel management and research and special areas of training and evaluation because these are covered in other bibliographies. Includes an author index.

129. U.S. Civil Service Commission. **Managing Overseas Personnel.** Washington, GPO, 1970. 86p. (Personnel Bibliography Series, No. 37) $0.75. LC Card No. 78-610106. (CS 1.61/3:37)

This compilation brings together a number of shorter bibliographies prepared by the Civil Service Commission library for internal use. It includes materials received through 1969. Arranged by broad subject areas. Annotated.

130. U.S. Civil Service Commission. **Personnel Management Function—Organization, Staffing, and Evaluation.** Washington, GPO, 1971. 55p. (Personnel Bibliography Series, No. 42) $0.60. LC Card No. 72-600593. S/N 0600-0618. (CS 1.61/3:42)

This bibliography updates three earlier issues in this series (Nos. 2, 27, and 28). Coverage is generally for 1969-1970, with some 1971 publications included. Organization is by type of management function, with separate chapters for research activities and textbooks and handbooks. Annotated.

131. U.S. Civil Service Commission. **Personnel Policies and Practices.** Washington, GPO, 1970. 106p. (Personnel Bibliography Series, No. 32) $1.00. LC Card No. 73-609016. (CS 1.61/3:32)

Updates and consolidates numbers 8, 12, 20-22 in this series. Cross references to related bibliographies are given at the beginning of each section. Includes such topics as employment tests in general and group oral tests; qualification rating; federal government and public service examining programs; certification and probation; veterans preference; selection and placement; promotion; disciplinary problems and absenteeism and tardiness. Annotated but not indexed.

132. U.S. Civil Service Commission. **Position Classification and Pay in the Federal Government.** Washington, GPO, 1970. 63p. (Personnel Bibliography Series, No. 31) $0.65. LC Card No. 78-608832. (CS 1.61/3:31)

Supplements a 1965 bibliography with the same title. It includes works received in the Civil Service Commission library from 1965 to 1969.

133. U.S. Department of Labor. **Important Events in American Labor History, 1778-1971.** Washington, GPO, 1971. 35p. $0.25. S/N 2900-0132. (L 1.2:H 62/2/778-971)

This chronology briefly describes the major events in labor history.

134. U.S. Department of the Air Force. **Personnel Management.** Prep. by Mary Louise Sauer. San Francisco, Pacific Air Forces, 1970. 71p. (PACAF Basic Bibliographies for Base Libraries) Available from Commander-in-Chief, Pacific Air Forces, Attn: DPSR, Commander Librarian, APO, San Francisco, Calif. 96553. LC Card No. 58-61777. (D 301.62:P 43/970.

A 52-page supplement was issued in 1971.

LABOR ORGANIZATIONS

135. U.S. Bureau of Labor Statistics. **Analysis of Work Stoppages, 1968.** Washington, GPO, 1970. 61p. $0.65. (L 2.3:1646)

This is a detailed statistical analysis of work stoppages in 1968. To expand the scope of this report, a breakdown of stoppages by industry group and duration for 1968, and a historical record by industry group for the period from 1937 to 1968 are included. There is also a chapter analyzing major strikes in 1968 which covered 10,000 workers or more.

136. U.S. Bureau of Labor Statistics. **Directory of National and International Labor Unions in the United States, 1969.** Prep. by Lucretia Dewey and others. Washington, GPO, 1970. 121p. $1.25. LC Card No. L44-36. (L 2.3:1665)

Lists unions and principal officers, including state labor organizations. Appendices list acronyms and index of names.

137. U.S. Maritime Administration. **Seafaring Guide and Directory of Labor-Management Affiliations.** Rev. ed. Washington, GPO, 1970. 85p. $1.00. LC Card No. 72-606586. (C 39.206/3:S 31/969)

Lists U.S. flag shipowners, operators and/or agents who are parties to collective bargaining agreements with maritime labor, seafaring unions, longshore unions, shipyard unions, and shipowner associations.

MANPOWER RESEARCH AND TRAINING

138. U.S. Civil Service Commission. **Directory of Studies and Reports Related to Training and Education: Aid to Federal Trainers and Managers in Planning, Developing, and Evaluating Their Own Programs.** Rev. ed. Washington, GPO, 1971. 111p. $1.00. (CS 1.48:T-6)

"The purpose of this directory is to promote and coordinate an exchange of the training related information that agencies obtain as they conduct studies of their training needs, problems, and courses and as they prepare reports on special programs or courses." Arranged by types of studies or reports, with names, addresses, and brief abstract. Indexed by title.

139. U.S. Civil Service Commission. **Guide to Training Resources and Information Publications.** Prep. by the Bureau of Training. Washington, GPO, 1971. 8p. $0.20. S/N 0600-0593. (CS 1.48:T 10/2)

Describes training resources such as courses and programs offered by agencies in a variety of subject areas. Also included is information about long-term non-government training opportunities and publications about training media and technology.

140. U.S. Civil Service Commission. **Planning, Organizing, and Evaluating Training Programs.** Washington, GPO, 1971. 140p. (Personnel Bibliography Series, No. 41) $1.25. LC Card No. 72-600591. S/N 0600-0617. (CS 1.61/3:41)

This bibliography updates three others published in 1968: No. 18, Supplement 1, with the same title; No. 24, *Executive Development Programs*; and No. 25, *Supervisory Development Practices*. Most works cited were published in 1969 and 1970.

141. U.S. Civil Service Commission. **Self Development Aids for Supervisors and Middle Managers.** Washington, GPO, 1970. 1v. (various paging) (Personnel Bibliography Series, No. 34) $1.75. (CS 1.61/3:34)

This bibliography includes works received in the Civil Service Commission library through 1969. It is a consolidation of several earlier reading lists and is designed to aid training officers and individual employees interested in self development.

142. U.S. Department of Labor. **Index to Publications of the Manpower Administration, January 1969 to June 1971.** Washington, GPO, 1971. 26p. Issuing agency. LC Card No. 74-614723. (L 1.34:M 31/4:969-71)

Lists all works published by the Manpower Administration during the period. Includes over 600 publications, not annotated, arranged by subject. Not indexed.

FINANCE AND BANKING

143. U.S. Administrative Office of United States Courts. **Tables of Bankruptcy Statistics.** Washington, the Office, 1971. 1v. (various paging) Issuing agency. LC Card No. 41-50534. (Ju 10.9:969)
    These tables contain references to bankruptcy cases commenced and terminated in U.S. District courts during FY 1969.

144. U.S. Department of Housing and Urban Development. **Bibliography on Mortgage Finance.** Washington, GPO, 1971. 3p. (HUD International Information Sources Series) Issuing agency. (HH 1.40/4:M 84)
    Lists books and periodicals which discuss, in detail, the various ways in which a borrower can obtain financing, the institutions involved, and the procedures followed by both lenders and borrowers. Entries are annotated and ordering information is provided.

145. U.S. Department of the Treasury. **Statistical Appendix to the Annual Report of the Secretary of the Treasury.** Washington, GPO, 1971. $1.50. LC Card No. 79-603508. (T 1.1:970/app.)

146. U.S. Economic Research Service. **Index of Deposits of Country Banks.** Prep. by Carson D. Evans. Washington, GPO, 1970. 3p. (A 93.9/7:970)

147. U.S. Federal Reserve System. Board of Governors. **Historical Chart Book, 1970.** Washington, the Board, 1970. 123p. Issuing agency. LC Card No. 50-13379. (FR 1.2:C 38)

148. U.S. Federal Reserve System. Board of Governors. **Historical Chart Book, 1971.** Washington, the Board, 1971. 123p. $0.60 (from the issuing agency). (FR 1.30/2:971)
    This annual publication contains long-range charts that supplement the monthly *Federal Reserve Chart Book* on financial and business statistics. Covers such topics as bank reserves and reserve bank credit, liquid assets and money supply, commercial banks, government finance, business finance, agriculture, consumer financing, and prices. Some charts show figures as far back as 1900.

149. U.S. House. Committee on Banking and Currency. **List of Publications Issued by the Committee on Banking and Currency: Hearings, Reports, and Committee Prints, 39th-91st Congresses (1865-1970).** Washington, the Committee, 1970. 151p. Issuing agency. LC Card No. 71-610927. (Y 4.B 22/1:P 96/2/865-970)

FOREIGN TRADE

GENERAL WORKS

BIBLIOGRAPHIES

150. U.S. Bureau of International Commerce. **Checklist, International Business Publications.** Washington, GPO, 1970. 21p. Issuing agency. (C 42.15:C 41/970)

151. U.S. Bureau of International Commerce. **Checklist of International Business Publications.** Washington, GPO, 1971. 34p. Issuing agency. (C 42.15:C 41/971)
　　This checklist was published semiannually until 1970. It lists publications available from the Bureau of International Commerce and covers the following series: Trade Lists, Market Share Reports, World Trade Directories, Export/Import Summaries, and others. There is a list by country of all publications in the checklist.

152. U.S. Bureau of International Commerce. **Sources of Information on American Firms for International Buyers.** Washington, GPO, 1971. 37p. $0.30. S/N 0309-0197. (C 42.2:Am 3/971)
　　This bibliography lists sources from which names, addresses, and commercial information on business firms in the United States are available. The directories listed are limited to those which are revised periodically or kept up to date with supplements.

153. U.S. Maritime Administration. **Publications of the Maritime Administration.** Washington, GPO, 1970. 16p. Issuing agency. (C 39.227:P 96/970)
　　This bibliography of Maritime Administration publications is frequently revised.

DICTIONARIES

154. U.S. Department of Agriculture. **Dictionary of International Agricultural Trade.** Comp. by Harry W. Henderson. Washington, GPO, 1971. 170p. (Agriculture Handbooks, No. 411) $1.50. LC Card No. 76-612219. (A 1.76:411)
　　Identifies terms which are uniquely connected with trade, those which are standard economic terms, and those which relate to regions, official agencies, weights and measures, etc. Acronyms and abbreviations are also included.

DIRECTORIES

155. U.S. Bureau of International Commerce. **List of Foreign Firms with Some Interest/Control in American Manufacturing and Petroleum Companies.** Washington, Bureau, 1971. 59p. Issuing agency. (C 42.2:F 76/7)

INDEXES

156. U.S. Bureau of International Commerce. **Cumulative Index to Foreign Market Surveys Available in Foreign Production and Commercial Reports, December 1968–August 1970.** Washington, GPO, 1970. 35p. Issuing agency. (C 42.15/3-3:F 76/968-70)

STATISTICS

157. U.S. Bureau of the Census. **Foreign Commerce and Navigation of the United States, 1965.** Washington, GPO, 1970. 3v. $7.00 (cloth, vol. 1); $8.25 (cloth, vol. 2); $9.00 (cloth, vol. 3). LC Card No. 7-19228. (C 3.159: 965/v.)
    Volume 1: Standard International Trade Classification (SITC): Commodity by Country.
    Volume 2: Area and Country by Standard International Trade Classification (SITC).
    Volume 3: Schedule A and Schedule B: Commodity by Country.
    Contains summary data on foreign trade by year; exports and general imports by month, by continent, world area, and country of destination or country of origin.

158. U.S. Bureau of the Census. **Guide to Foreign Trade Statistics, 1970.** Washington, GPO, 1970. 175p. $1.50. LC Card No. A68-7732. (C 3.6/2: F 76/970)

159. U.S. Bureau of the Census. **Guide to Foreign Trade Statistics, 1971.** Washington, GPO, 1971. 182p. $1.50. S/N 0301-2276. (C 3.6/2:F 76/971)
    "Intended to serve as a guide to the various sources of foreign trade statistics, to inform users of the content and arrangement of data . . . and to assist in the location of particular information and make it possible to utilize the sources to better advantage." Explains the coverage of statistics with sample illustrations of the content and arrangement of material in individual publications and foreign trade reports.

160. U.S. Bureau of the Census. **U.S. Foreign Trade Statistics: Classifications and Cross-Classifications.** Washington, GPO, 1971. 579p. $6.00. (C 3.2: F 76/2/970)
    "This publication brings together all schedules of commodity and geographic trade classifications and cross-classifications currently being used in the compilation and publication of U.S. foreign trade statistics." It permits ready reference to classifications and cross-classifications for better use and interpretation of commodity and geographic trade statistics.

161. U.S. Department of Commerce. **United States Foreign Trade, Annual 1964-70.** Washington, GPO, 1971. 24p. (Overseas Business Reports, No. 71-009) $0.15. LC Card No. 66-97329. (C 1.50:71-009)
    This statistical compendium is part of the irregularly issued "Overseas Business Reports" series.

162. U.S. Foreign Direct Investments Office. **Foreign Affiliate Financial Survey, 1966-69.** By Philip D. Berlin. Washington, the Office, 1971. 52p. Issuing agency. (C 54.2:F 49/966-69)

    The statistical data were collected by the Office of Foreign Direct Investments. The volume includes interpretive analysis of the data.

EXPORT/IMPORT DATA

163. U.S. Agricultural Research Service. **Geographical Guide to Summaries of Plant Quarantine Import Requirements of Foreign Countries.** Washington, ARS, 1971. 9p. Issuing agency. (A 77.306/3:G 29)

    Arranged by country with brief statements about their plant quarantine regulations.

164. U.S. Bureau of International Commerce. **Foreign Business Practices, Materials on Practical Aspects of Exporting, Investing, and Licensing Abroad.** Washington, GPO, 1971. 75p. $0.60. S/N 0309-0198. (C 42.8/a:F 761/971)

165. U.S. Bureau of International Commerce. **Introductory Guide to Exporting.** Washington, GPO, 1970. 47p. $0.35. LC Card No. 75-601892. (C 42.6/2:Ex 7/3/970)

166. U.S. Department of Commerce. **National and Regional Export Expansion Councils Directory, 1969-71.** Washington, GPO, 1970. 83p. Issuing agency. (C 1.42/3:D 62/969-71)

    This directory lists members of the National and Regional Export Expansion Council and the National Export Expansion Council Executive Board.

167. U.S. Foreign Agricultural Service. **Food and Agricultural Export Directory, 1970.** Washington, GPO, 1970. 44p. Issuing agency. (A 67.26: 201/2)

168. U.S. Foreign Agricultural Service. **Food and Agricultural Export Directory, 1971.** Washington, GPO, 1971. 57p. Issuing agency. (A 67.26: 201/3)

    Lists sources of information for firms with agricultural products to sell in the export market. Principal export agencies of the federal and state governments and trade associations are given. An annotated bibliography of government export publications is also included.

169. U.S. Tariff Commission. **Tariff Schedules of United States Annotated (1971) for Use in Classification of Imported Merchandise for Rate of Duty and Statistical Purposes.** Washington, GPO, 1970. 920p. $8.00 (includes supplements for an indefinite period). LC Card No. 70-610147. (TC 1.35/2:971)

    Contains the legal text of the tariff schedules together with annotations prescribing statistical information to be listed on customs forms.

TRANSPORTATION

170. U.S. Civil Aeronautics Board. **Handbook of Airline Statistics, Data for Individual Carriers, 1959-68, Data for Carrier Groups, 1926-68.** 1969 ed. Washington, GPO, 1970. 544p. $8.00. LC Card No. 44-40873. (C 31.249:969)

This is a comprehensive current statistical view of the various airlines and carrier groups. Includes historical statistics of U.S. airlines, traffic statistics of certificate route air carriers, income statements and other statistics.

171. U.S. Coast Guard. **Merchant Vessels of the United States, 1969 (Including Yachts).** Washington, GPO, 1970. 1590p. $12.50 (cloth). S/N 5012-0019. (TD 5.12/2:969)

172. U.S. Coast Guard. **Merchant Vessels of the United States, 1970 (Including Yachts).** Washington, GPO, 1971. 1680p. $13.00 (cloth). S/N 5012-0022. (TD 5.12/2:970)

Lists American merchant vessels and yachts which had uncancelled documents (i.e., register, license or enrollment and licenses) on January 1 of each year. Provides for each the official number, signal and radio call letters, rig information, name of vessel, symbols used for signal, classification, gross and net tonnage, dimensions, year of build and place, trade or business in which the vessel is engaged, horsepower, name of owner, and home port.

173. U.S. Interstate Commerce Commission. **Transport Statistics in the United States—Year Ended December 31, 1969.** Washington, GPO, 1971. 6 pts. (IC 1.25:969/pts.)

Published in separate volumes for railroads, electric railways, water carriers, oil pipe lines, motor carriers, freight forwarders, and private car lines.

174. U.S. Maritime Administration. **Essential United States Foreign Trade Routes.** Washington, GPO, 1970. 81p. $1.00. LC Card No. 60-62459. (C 39.202:F 76/969)

Provides descriptions and map of foreign trade routes. Lists U.S. steamship lines and the commodities moving over them.

175. U.S. Maritime Administration. **Index of Current Regulations of the Maritime Administration, Maritime Subsidy Board, National Shipping Authority.** Washington, GPO, 1970. 38p. $0.30. (D 1.13/2-2:2/2)

176. U.S. Maritime Administration. **Index of Current Regulations of the Maritime Administration, Maritime Subsidy Board, National Shipping Authority.** Washington, GPO, 1971. 38p. $0.50. S/N 0307-0020. (C 39.206/4:971)

This is a guide to the regulations of the Maritime Administration and related boards. It contains the regulations in numerical order, alphabetically by subject and by symbol.

177. U.S. Maritime Administration. **Merchant Fleets of the World: Ocean-going Steam and Motor Ships of 1,000 Gross Tons and Over, as of December 31, 1970.** Washington, GPO, 1971. 19p. $0.30. (C 39.212:970)

    Data includes that from nations acquiring national maritime fleets since 1946, changes in major maritime fleets of the world by number of ships and data on individual countries' fleets.

178. U.S. Maritime Administration. **Statistical Analysis of the World's Merchant Fleets Showing Age, Size, Speed and Draft by Frequency Groupings as of December 31, 1968.** Prep. by the Office of Subsidy Administration. Washington, GPO, 1970. 114p. $1.00. LC Card No. 58-60323. (C 39.224:968)

    Shows age, size, speed and draft by frequency groupings.

179. U.S. Naval Oceanographic Office. **World Port Index.** 4th ed. Washington, GPO, 1971. 333p. $3.00. S/N 0842-0051. (D 203.22:150/971)

    Gives the location, characteristics, facilities and available services of ports and shipping docks throughout the world. Sailing direction is given for each place listed.

INSURANCE

180. U.S. Bureau of Labor Statistics. **Digest of Selected Pension Plans.** 1970 ed. Prep. by Dorothy R. Kittner and Majella A. Leary. Washington, GPO, 1971. 362p. $5.00 (looseleaf). (L 2.99:970)

    Summarizes, in separate sections, the principal features of selected pension plans for employees under collective bargaining and selected pension plans for salaried employees. For each plan the information on the following topics is provided: participation requirements, normal retirement, early retirement, benefit options, disability retirement, vesting, involuntary retirement, death benefits, financing, medium of funding, and administration. Indexed by companies. Supplements are issued in separate pages and are substituted in the main volume for superseded sections.

181. U.S. Social Security Administration. **Basic Readings in Social Security.** Washington, GPO, 1970. 181p. $0.75. LC Card No. 61-61469. (HE 3.38:R 22)

    This is an annotated bibliography of recent and standard works in the field of social security and social welfare. Indexed by author.

182. U.S. Social Security Administration. **Directory, Medicare Providers and Suppliers of Services.** Washington, GPO, 1970. 684p. $4.75. LC 72-605972. (HE 3.51/5:969)

    Until the fourth edition, 1969, this was published in the following volumes: 1) Home Health Agencies, 2) Hospitals, 3) Extended Care Facilities, and 4) Independent Laboratories. These services, plus those for outpatient physical therapy, are now listed in a single annual volume.

183. U.S. Social Security Administration. **The Impact of Medicare: An Annotated Bibliography of Selected Sources.** Prep. by Mary McGee. Washington, GPO, 1970. 70p. $0.40. LC Card No. 70-604540. (HE 3.38:M 46/2)

An annotated bibliography of selected references from periodicals, reports, and books published between August 1965 and December 1968. Entries within each of nine broad subject categories are arranged alphabetically according to authors and annotated in detail. Indexed by authors.

184. U.S. Social Security Administration. **Social Security Programs in the United States.** Washington, GPO, 1971. 134p. $0.60. LC Card No. 75-174-756. S/N 1770-0161. (HE 3.2:So 13/21/971)

Reports on social security programs including not only old-age, survivors, disability, and health insurance, but also the railroad retirement program, retirement systems for government employees, and veterans' compensation and pensions. It covers also the state and railroad unemployment insurance, temporary disability insurance programs, and workmen's compensation; gives a summary of the state-federal public assistance programs; and provides a brief discussion of private pension and other employee benefits plans.

185. U.S. Social Security Administration. **Social Security Programs Throughout the World, 1969.** Prep. by the International Staff, Office of Research and Statistics. Washington, GPO, 1970. 249p. $2.75. LC Card No. HEW62-40. (HE 3.49:31)

This is an analysis of the principal provisions of social security programs in all countries of the world. Countries are listed alphabetically and a separate summary is given for each. The larger part of the programs covered are social insurance measures, but several related types of social security programs are also included.

OCCUPATIONS

186. U.S. Bureau of Labor Statistics. **Occupational Outlook Handbook.** Prep. in the Division of Manpower and Occupational Outlook. 1970-71 ed. Washington, GPO, 1970. 859p. $6.25. LC Card No. L49-6. (L 2.3:1650)

This comprehensive listing of over 700 occupations is particularly useful for guidance counselors and persons seeking a field of employment. Occupational summaries include trends, working conditions, salary range, and references to additional sources of information. The index contains an alphabetical list of occupations and industries. Kept up to date by *Occupational Outlook Quarterly* (L 2.70/4:vols.; $1.50/yr.).

187. U.S. Civil Service Commission. **Guide to Federal Career Literature.** Washington, GPO, 1971. 28p. $0.40. S/N 0600-0600. (CS 1.48:BRE-24)

This bibliography is designed to serve as a convenient reference guide to federal recruiting literature. It contains brief descriptions of 224 pamphlets and brochures from 46 different departments and agencies.

188. U.S. Department of Commerce. **Careers in the U.S. Department of Commerce.** Washington, GPO, 1970. 100p. $1.00. (C 1.2:C 18/970)

Lists the wide variety of employment opportunities within the Department. Economists, patent examiners, statisticians, engineers, oceanographers and meteorologists are among the almost 1,000 college-trained people employed annually. Career fields are described briefly; also describes what this Department does, explains the role of offices and bureaus, and indicates where and how the Department uses specific degree majors.

189. U.S. Department of the Interior. **Careers in the United States Department of the Interior.** Washington, GPO, 1970. 71p. $0.50. (I 1.73/2:3/2)

190. U.S. Department of the Interior. **Careers in the United States Department of the Interior.** Washington, GPO, 1971. 63p. $0.45. S/N 2400-0587. (I 1.73/2:3/3)

This directory, aimed at college students, shows the functions of the Department, and its employment and career opportunities.

REAL ESTATE

191. U.S. Bureau of Land Management. **Public Land Statistics, 1969.** Washington, GPO, 1970. 188p. $0.75. LC Card No. 49-46739. (I 53.1/2:969)

192. U.S. Bureau of Land Management. **Public Land Statistics, 1970.** Washington, GPO, 1971. 182p. $0.75. LC Card No. 49-46739. (I 53.1/2:970)

"The U.S. has 2.3 billion acres in its gross area, including about 755 million acres which are federally owned. Title to some 1.1 billion acres has been transferred from federal ownership under various land laws. This useful compendium of public statistics tells of the acreage involved in these transfers, present ownership by state and agency of the remainder; and describes the management of today's public lands."

193. U.S. Department of the Interior. Territories Office. **Territorial Areas Administered by the United States.** Washington, GPO, 1971. 25p. $0.20. S/N 2407-0002. (I 35.2:T 27/2/971)

This directory gives brief descriptions of the offshore areas administered by the Interior Department, with references to other outlying areas administered by other federa agencies (including islands of disputed ownership).

194. U.S. General Services Administration. **Inventory Report on Real Property Owned by the United States Throughout the World as of June 30, 1969.** Washington, GPO, 1970. 90p. illus. $0.55. LC Card No. 57-44028. (GS 1.15:969)

195. U.S. General Services Administration. **Inventory Report on Real Property Owned by the United States Throughout the World as of June 30, 1970.** Washington, GPO, 1971. 92p. $0.60. LC Card No. 57-44028. (GS 1.15:970)

Summarizes detailed data on all land, buildings, and other structures and facilities owned by the United States (including wholly owned government corporations) throughout the world.

TAXES

196. U.S. Department of the Air Force. Judge Advocate General. **All States Income Tax Guide: Information for Service Personnel.** Washington, GPO, 1970. 113p. $1.25. (D 302.8:In 2/971)

The purpose of this pamphlet is to furnish information to personnel in the armed services about their possible liability for income tax to the several states of the United States. Contains outlines of the tax laws of those states imposing income taxes on individuals. The outlines have been prepared primarily from information furnished by several states, and reflect, in matters of interpretation, the views of the state tax authorities. States which do not have income tax laws have been so set forth, but personnel should check the tax statutes of subordinate jurisdictions.

197. U.S. Department of the Navy. Judge Advocate General. **Federal Income Tax Information for Armed Forces Personnel.** Washington, GPO, 1970. 62p. $0.30. (D 205.9:971)

This guide, published with approval of the Internal Revenue Service, is primarily for active duty armed services personnel. Contains information on their income tax rights, benefits, obligations, and for their assistance in the preparation of federal income tax returns and declarations of estimated tax. Its purpose is to supplement, but not replace, instructions for preparing returns, and to highlight provisions especially applicable to Navy and military personnel.

198. U.S. Internal Revenue Service. **Catalogue of Forms, Form Letters, and Notices.** Washington, GPO, 1971. 149p. $1.25. S/N 4804-0397. (T 22.2: F 76/6/971)

This booklet is intended as an aid for those interested in knowing the purpose and use of the various forms and form letters used by the Internal Revenue Service to communicate with the public. Contains identifying information about the Service's form letters, computer generated bills, information notices, and many miscellaneous forms concerning tax matters. Includes a list of forms in use as of May 31, 1971.

199. U.S. Internal Revenue Service. **Comprehensive Tax Guide to U.S. Civil Service Retirement Benefits.** Washington, GPO, 1970. 88p. $0.70. LC Card No. 76-610423. (T 22.19/2:R 31/2)

200. U.S. Internal Revenue Service. **Employer's Tax Guide.** Washington, GPO, 1970. 46p. Issuing agency. LC Card No. 55-4793. (T 22.20/2: E/971)

Information on withholding, deposit, payment, and reporting of federal income tax, social security taxes, and federal unemployment tax.

201. U.S. Internal Revenue Service. **Farmer's Tax Guide.** Washington, GPO, 1970. 48p. Issuing agency. LC Card No. 56-61352. (T 22.19/2:F 22/971)

Explains special tax rules for income and self-employment as they pertain to farmers.

202. U.S. Internal Revenue Service. **A Guide to Federal Estate and Gift Taxation.** Washington, GPO, 1971. 41p. $0.50. S/N 4804-0388. (T 22.19/2:Es 8/971)

Presents a general explanation of the federal estate and gift tax laws. It is written in relatively nontechnical language, and covers both legal provisions and practical matters, such as how to file a return. Intended for use by taxpayers desiring general information in this area, as well as by Internal Revenue officials.

203. U.S. Internal Revenue Service. **Tax Guide for Small Business.** 1970 ed. Washington, GPO, 1970. 158p. $0.60. LC Card No. 57-60150. (T 22.19/2:Sm 1/970)

This book provides details on Internal Revenue Service rules for small business, individuals, sole proprietorships, partnerships, and small corporations concerning income, excise and employment taxes.

204. U.S. Internal Revenue Service. **United States Tax Guide for Aliens.** Washington, GPO, 1970. 34p. $0.30. (T 22.44/2:519/3)

205. U.S. Internal Revenue Service. **Your Federal Income Tax for Individuals.** Washington, GPO, 1970. 160p. $0.75. (T 22.44:971)

This publication is designed to help persons file federal income tax returns. It explains how to prepare forms, what exemptions and deductions are allowed, what income is taxable, how to determine income and deductions from investment properties, how to determine capital gains and losses, and other regulations. Examples are provided to make rules more easily understood, and explanations are written clearly and concisely. A detailed index facilitates the use of this handy publication.

EDUCATION

GENERAL WORKS

BIBLIOGRAPHIES

206. U.S. Bureau of Health Professions and Manpower Training. **Educational Technology and the Teaching-Learning Process: A Selected Bibliography.** Prep. by Jeanne Saylor Berthold, Mary Alice Curran, and Diana Y. Barhyte. Rev. ed. Washington, GPO, 1970. 61p. Issuing agency. LC Card No. 73-608611. (HE 20.3113:T 22/969)

This bibliography, like the first edition published in 1968, is "intended to serve as an introduction to the literature on the teaching-learning process and on the various new approaches in the field of teaching technology." Recent books and journal articles are cited under major subject headings.

207. U.S. House of Representatives. Committee on Science and Astronautics. **New Technology in Education: Selected References.** Prep. for the Subcommittee on Science, Research, and Development by Lilla M. Pearce and Helen A. Miller. Washington, the Committee, 1971. 140p. Issuing agency. LC Card No. 74-614790. (Y 4.Sci 2:92-1/F)

208. U.S. Office of Education. **Education, Literature of the Profession: A Bibliography.** Comp. by Eunice von Ende. Washington, GPO, 1970. 41p. $0.50. S/N 1780-0079. (HE 5.210:10060-A)

Contains a bibliography of the acquisitions of the Educational Materials Center from January 1, 1969, through June 30, 1970. Entries are by subject under "Books and Monographs" or by format, including indexes, periodicals, and newsletters.

209. U.S. Office of Education. **Outdoor Education: A Selected Bibliography, Supplement No. 1.** Comp. by David M. Altus. Washington, GPO, 1971. 254p. (ERIC. Clearinghouse on Rural Education and Small Schools) $2.00. S/N 1780-0832. (HE 5.10:Ou 8/supp. 1)

Part one of this bibliography contains citations and abstracts which appeared in *Research in Education* from January through July 1971. Part two includes citations which appeared in *Current Index to Journals in Education* from its first issue (January 1969) through July 1971. Citations in both sections are in numerical order of accession. Entries in part one give publication date, list of descriptors, abstract, publisher, address, and price. Citations in part two include publication date, personal author, descriptors, annotation if title is not descriptive, and journal citation. Subject index refers to accession numbers.

210. U.S. Office of Education. **Publications of the Office of Education, 1970.** Prep. by Bobbie Lonergan. Washington, GPO, 1970. 77p. $0.40. LC Card No. HEW 64-37. (HE 5.211:11000-70)

Lists publications from the Office of Education which are currently available, regardless of publication date. Arranged by type of educational specialty. Within each category, arranged by OE number. Annotated with title index.

DICTIONARIES

211. U.S. Office of Education. **The State Education Agency: A Handbook of Standard Terminology and Guide for Recording Information About State Education Agencies.** Comp. and ed. by Yeuell Y. Harris and Ivan N. Seibert. Washington, GPO, 1971. 168p. $1.75. S/N 1780-0822. (HE 5.223:23054)

Classifies and defines terms concerned with state education authorities, the functions of state departments of education, the personnel and property of state education authorities and state departments of education, and the financial operations of state departments of education.

DIRECTORIES

212. U.S. Office of Education. **Education Directory, 1969-70: State Governments.** Prep. by Madeline G. Hagermann. Washington, GPO, 1970. 163p. $1.00. LC Card No. E 13-213. (HE 5.25:969-70/pt. 1)

Arranged alphabetically by states, listing principal people in state agencies dealing with elementary and secondary education and vocational-technical education. Professional members of state education departments are included and other state service organizations are described. Professional members of state library extension agencies are also listed.

213. U.S. Office of Education. **Education Directory, Part 2, 1969-70: Public School Systems.** By John P. Sietsema and Beatrice O. Mongello. Washington, GPO, 1970. 313p. $2.50. LC Card No. E 13-213. (HE 5.25:969-70/pt. 2)

214. U.S. Office of Education. **Education Directory, Part 2, 1970-71: Public School Systems.** By John P. Sietsema, Beatrice O. Mongello, and Jacqueline Montague. Washington, GPO, 1971. 298p. $2.25. LC Card No. E 13-213. S/N 1780-0757. (HE 5.25:970-71/pt. 2)

All school districts, regardless of size, are included in this section. Arranged alphabetically by state and then by school system. Gives location of the superintendent, ZIP code, county name, enrollment, and grade span. Also lists any administrative units for each state.

215. U.S. Office of Education. **Education Directory, 1969-70: Higher Education.** Washington, GPO, 1970. 529p. $4.50. LC Card No. E 13-213. (HE 5.25:969-70/pt. 3)

216. U.S. Office of Education. **Education Directory, 1970-71: Higher Education.** Washington, GPO, 1971. 515p. $3.75. LC Card No. E 13-213. S/N 1780-0648. (HE 5.25:970-71/pt. 3)

Lists those institutions of higher education in the United States which offer at least a two-year program of college-level or occupational studies in residence and which submitted the information required for listing. Editions previous to that of 1968-69 had accreditation criteria for inclusion; now, through the use of computers, all schools are included. A symbol denotes accreditation, if any, and name of accrediting agency. Lists schools alphabetically within each state with the following information for each: address, control or affiliation, coed or not, calendar system, highest degree offered, type of program, enrollment, and names and titles of administrative officials. Includes supplementary material such as a list of higher education associations, schools now listed under new names, and those in new locations.

217. U.S. Office of Education. **Education Directory, 1969-70, Part 4: Education Associations.** Prep. by Bobbie D. Lonergan. Washington, GPO, 1970. 109p. $1.25. LC Card No. E 13-213. (HE 5.25:969-70/pt. 4)

Lists associations alphabetically, providing for each the address of headquarters, name and address of the chief officer, name and address of the secretary, and title or titles of official periodical publications and their frequency. Divided into broad headings such as State Education Association, Religious Education Associations, Foundations. Indexed by subjects with names of associations listed under each.

218. U.S. Office of Education. **Everyman's Guide: An ERIC Search System for Social Studies Teachers, Consultants and Librarians.** By Sharon Ervin. Washington, GPO, 1971. 15p. (ERIC. Clearinghouse for Social Studies/Social Science Education. Reference Series, No. 1) $0.30. S/N 1780-0828. (HE 5.6/2:Ev 2)

Provides information for social studies teachers, consultants and librarians on how to use ERIC's products and research tools, especially *Research in Education* and *Current Index to Journals in Education.* This guide offers manual search shortcuts that simulate a computer search system and will simplify and maximize a review of the literature.

219. U.S. Office of Education. **Opportunities Abroad for Teachers, 1971-72.** Washington, GPO, 1970. 28p. $0.20. (HE 5.214:14047-72)

220. U.S. Office of Education. **Opportunities Abroad for Teachers, 1972-73.** Washington, GPO, 1971. 28p. $0.25. S/N 1780-0829. (HE 5.214:14047-73)

Opportunities are available under the International Educational and Cultural Exchange Program for qualified American teachers either to teach for an academic year in elementary and secondary schools abroad or to attend summer seminars abroad. This bulletin describes the U.S. government grants to be offered to American teachers. Arranged alphabetically by countries which have positions.

221. U.S. Office of Education. **Foreign Curriculum Consultant Program, 1972-73, for American Schools, Colleges, and State Departments of Education.** Washington, GPO, 1971. 20p. $0.20. S/N 1780-0805. (HE 5.214:14143-73)

The Foreign Curriculum Consultant Program brings specialists from foreign countries to the United States for assistance in planning and developing local curriculums (from high schools through colleges) in foreign languages and area studies. This directory details the operation of this program.

STATISTICS

222. U.S. Office of Education. **Digest of Educational Statistics.** By Kenneth A. Simon and W. Vance Grant. Washington, GPO, 1970. 140p. $1.25. LC Card No. HEW 62-154. S/N 1780-0718. (HE 5.210:10024-70)

An abstract of statistical information covering the entire field of American education from kindergarten through the graduate school. Contains data broken down by state on the number of schools and colleges, enrollments, teachers, graduates, educational attainment, finances, federal funds for education, libraries, international education, and research and development.

223. U.S. Office of Education. **Selected Statistics on Educational Personnel.** By Leslie J. Silverman and Stafford Metz. Washington, GPO, 1970. 59p. $0.65. LC Card No. 75-606793. (HE 5.258:58041)

This is an appraisal of the nation's existing and future personnel needs in the field of education, including preschool programs, elementary and secondary education, vocational and technical education, adult and higher education, and the adequacy of the nation's efforts to meet these needs.

ADULT EDUCATION

224. U.S. Office of Education. **Adult Basic Education Program Statistics: Student and Staff Data.** By Nicholas A. Osso. Washington, GPO, 1971. 52p. $0.60. S/N 1780-0858. (HE 5.213:13037-70)

Provides statistical information on the Adult Basic Education Program for the years 1966 to 1970.

225. U.S. Office of Education. **Books Related to Adult Basic Education and Teaching English to Speakers of Other Languages, A Bibliography.** Comp. by Myra H. Thomas, Thelma M. Knuths, and Sidney E. Murphy. Washington, GPO, 1970. 18p. $0.30. LC Card No. 73-610058. S/N 1780-0708. (HE 5.213:13039)

This is a bibliography of acquisitions of the Educational Materials Center as of May 1, 1970, in the area of adult education, specifically, materials for teaching adults the first essential skills of reading, writing, arithmetic, community living, and citizenship.

226. U.S. Women's Bureau. **Continuing Education Programs and Services for Women.** Prep. by Jean A. Wells. Rev. ed. Washington, GPO, 1971. 167p. $0.70. S/N 2902-0042. (L 36.112:10)

Lists programs designed by educational institutions and related organizations, for adult women seeking educational opportunities adapted to their needs and interests. Includes an alphabetical list of colleges, by state; a list of miscellaneous organizations, by state; a guide to selected features of programs and services reported; and a resume of federal funds for continuing education programs.

ELEMENTARY AND SECONDARY EDUCATION

BIBLIOGRAPHIES

227. U.S. Library of Congress. **Children's Books, 1969, A List of Books for Preschool through Junior High School.** Comp. by Virginia Haviland and Lois B. Watt. Washington, GPO, 1970. 16p. $0.15. LC Card No. 65-60014. (LC 2.11:969)

228. U.S. Library of Congress. **Children's Books, 1970, A List of Books for Preschool through Junior High School.** Comp. by Virginia Haviland and Lois Watt. Washington, GPO, 1971. 16p. $0.15. LC Card No. 65-60014. S/N 3001-0039. (LC 2.11:970)

This is an annual graded list of about 200 books, including picture books, stories for older children, folklore, biography, poetry, plays, Bible stories, histories, and science books published during the year in the United States. Information for each work includes author, title, publisher, number of pages, price, grade level, and a brief synopsis.

229. U.S. Office of Education. **Aids to Media Selection for Students and Teachers.** Comp. by Yvonne Carter and others. Washington, GPO, 1971. 82p. $0.75. LC Card No. 78-614373. S/N 1780-0810. (HE 5.234:34045)

Designed as an aid to book selection, this bibliography describes selected book lists and periodicals which review books, audiovisual materials, and multiethnic instructional materials. Entries are annotated; indexed by author and title.

230. U.S. Office of Education. **Books Related to English Language and Literature in Elementary and Secondary Schools: A Bibliography from the Educational Materials Center.** Comp. by Lois B. Watt, Delia Goetz, and Caroline Stanley. Washington, GPO, 1970. 24p. $0.35. LC Card No. 77-607134. (HE 5.230:30024)

This bibliography was compiled to "answer questions from educators concerning new books related to English language and literature programs in elementary and secondary schools." It includes trade and textbooks which were received in the Educational Materials Center between January 1968 and October 1969. Entries are arranged by publishing company in the textbook section and by author in the section of trade books. Annotations include grade levels. Not indexed.

231. U.S. Office of Education. **Environmental-Ecological Education: A Bibliography of Fiction, Nonfiction, and Textbooks for Elementary and Secondary Schools.** Comp. by Lois B. Watt and Myra H. Thomas. Washington, GPO, 1971. 34p. (ERIC. Clearinghouse for Social Studies/Social Science

Education. Reference Series, No. 5) $0.40. S/N 1780-0886. (HE 5.10: En 8)

    Bibliography of materials added to the Educational Materials Center from January 1, 1969, through May 25, 1971. It includes juvenile literature, textbooks for elementary and secondary school students, and professional resources for teachers which have been favorably reviewed in at least two professional journals or in a major evaluative bibliography representing committee selection. Brief annotations; author and subject indexes.

232. U.S. Office of Education. **Rural Education and Small Schools: A Selected Bibliography, Supplement 1.** Comp. by David M. Altus. Washington, GPO, 1971. 486p. (ERIC. Clearinghouse on Rural Education and Small Schools) $3.50. S/N 1780-0833. (HE 5.10:R 88/2/supp. 1)

    Provides access to some of the latest research findings and developments in the realm of rural education and small schools. Contains citations and abstracts which have appeared in *Research in Education* and *Current Index to Journals in Education* from January 1969 through July 1971. Entries include complete bibliographical data, a list of descriptors, and an abstract. Subject index refers to accession numbers by which the work is arranged.

233. U.S. Office of Education. **Science and Mathematics Books for Elementary and Secondary Schools: A Bibliography Based on Acquisitions of the Educational Materials Center.** Comp. by Lois B. Watt, Delia Goetz, and Eunice von Ende. Washington, GPO, 1970. 19p. $0.30. LC Card No. 74-608070. (HE 5.229:29071)

    Lists science and mathematics text and trade books received in the Educational Materials Center between January 1969 and February 1970. It was prepared as a means of "answering questions from educators about the nature and availability of new books for possible use in science and mathematics education programs in elementary and secondary schools in the United States."

DICTIONARIES

234. U.S. Office of Education. **Standard Terminology for Curriculum and Instruction in Local and State School Systems.** Comp. and ed. by John F. Putnam and W. Dale Chismore. Washington, GPO, 1970. 319p. (State Educational Records and Reports Series, Handbook No. 6) $3.00. LC Card No. 79-611252. S/N 1780-0721. (HE 5.223:23052)

    This is a guide for state and local school systems to use in keeping records and making reports about curriculum and instruction. It is concerned with the terminology for describing curriculum and instruction in elementary schools, middle schools, secondary schools, junior colleges, and adult schools or other adult education organizational arrangements.

DIRECTORIES

235. U.S. Department of Health, Education, and Welfare. **Directory of Public Elementary and Secondary Schools in Selected Districts, Enrollment and Staff by Racial/Ethnic Group, Fall 1968.** Washington, GPO, 1970. 1703p. $11.00. LC Card No. 71-608762. (HE 1.38:968)

    This directory contains reported information, as of the beginning of the 1968-69 school year, on the racial/ethnic composition of pupils and full-time classroom teachers (assigned to one school) in approximately 8,500 school districts in the continental United States including Alaska and the District of Columbia.

236. U.S. Office of Education. **Directory, Public and Nonpublic Elementary and Secondary Day Schools, 1968-69.** Washington, GPO, 1970. 5v. LC Card No. 70-607482. (HE 5.220:20126/vol.)
    Vol. 1: **North Atlantic Region.** 232p. $2.00.
    Vol. 2: **Great Lakes and Plains Region.** 358p. $3.25.
    Vol. 3: **Southeast Region.** 264p. $2.50.
    Vol. 4: **West and Southwest.** 316p. $2.00.
    Vol. 5: **Nonpublic Elementary and Secondary Day Schools.** 252p. $2.50. (HE 5.220:20127)

    This is the "first comprehensive listing of every elementary and secondary day school, both public and nonpublic, in the nation." The five-volume directory lists 114,000 schools, including 18,718 nonpublic. Data for each school include: state and post office, ZIP code, name of school, street address, grade span, number of pupils and teachers by grade levels, graduates, type of program, district name. Schools for which data are not presented are listed in the appendixes.

237. U.S. Office of Education. **Follow Through Project Directory, School Year 1970-71.** Washington, GPO, 1970. 48p. Issuing agency. (HE 5.237:37065)

    The Follow Through Project is a program designed to help children in early primary grades build on the foundation provided by full-year Head Start or similar preschool programs. It provides special programs of instruction as well as support services such as medical and dental care, nutrition, etc. This directory lists programs by state and city with a separate section listing program sponsors.

HANDBOOKS AND GUIDES

238. U.S. Office of Education. **Career Education in the Environment: A Handbook.** Washington, GPO, 1971. 407p. $3.00. S/N 1780-0892. (HE 5.6/2:En 8/2)

    This handbook is designed to be used in high school classes as an aid in exploring environmental problems and solutions. It also provides information on existing and emerging career opportunities in this field.

239. U.S. Office of Education. **Handbook of Statistical Procedures for Long-Range Projections of Public School Enrollment.** By A. J. Jaffe. Washington, GPO, 1970. 118p. $1.25. LC Card No. 70-610179. (HE 5.224: 24017)

    This handbook describes a number of statistical procedures which can be used for making projections on future enrollment of public schools.

HIGHER EDUCATION

BIBLIOGRAPHIES

240. U.S. Office of Education. **Higher Education Administration: An Annotated Bibliography of Research Reports Funded by the Cooperative Research Act, 1956-1970.** Washington, GPO, 1971. 12p. $0.30. S/N 1780-0791. (HE 5.212:12054)

    This list of research reports in higher education administration includes studies on communication facilities, financing, institutional management, instructional programs, and students.

DIRECTORIES

241. U.S. Cabinet Committee on Opportunity for the Spanish Speaking. **Spanish Surnamed American College Graduates, 1970.** Washington, GPO, 1970. 331p. Issuing agency. LC Card No. 76-607253. (Y 3.Sp 2/7:2Am 3/970)

242. U.S. Cabinet Committee on Opportunity for the Spanish Speaking. **Spanish Surnamed American College Graduates, 1971-72.** Washington, GPO, 1971. 2 pts. (pt. 1, 589p.; pt. 2, 314p.). Issuing agency. LC Card No. 76-607253. (Y 3.Sp 2/7:2Am 3/971-72/pt.)

    Lists college juniors and seniors alphabetically by state and college, with home addresses, college major, and expected date of graduation. Also lists students alphabetically by major discipline and chronologically by date of graduation. It is designed for use by businesses recruiting Spanish- or Mexican-Americans.

243. U.S. Department of Health, Education, and Welfare. **A Guide for Colleges and Universities: Cost Principles and Procedures for Establishing Indirect Cost Rates for Grants and Contracts with the Department of Health, Education, and Welfare.** Washington, GPO, 1971. 66p. $1.00. S/N 1700-0090. (HE 1.6/3:C 68)

    Describes the cost principles under which federal grants and contracts are awarded, the process of indirect cost rate determination, and the methods of submitting rate proposals by grantees and contractors.

244. U.S. House of Representatives. **Guide to Student Assistance.** Prep. by the Committee on Education and Labor. Washington, GPO, 1970. 129p. $0.60. LC Card No. 77-606417. (91-2:H.doc.221)

Lists and describes the major federal programs to financially assist students. Selected federal graduate fellowship programs, and other selected programs available to undergraduates are discussed, along with other major non-federal undergraduate scholarships and loans.

245. U.S. National Science Foundation. **Inventory of Computers in U.S. Higher Education, 1966-67: Utilization and Related Degree Programs.** Washington, GPO, 1970. 440p. $3.00. (NS 1.2:C 73)

This report presents the results of a survey sponsored by the National Science Foundation. Since many colleges are now adding computers for the first time and many universities and colleges which already have computers are adding or replacing computer systems, the inventory of computers and computer science curricula for 1966-67 provides much useful information for guidance in making related decisions.

246. U.S. Office of Education. **Accredited Postsecondary Institutions and Programs, Including Institutions Holding Preaccredited Status.** Washington, GPO, 1971. 136p. $1.25. S/N 1780-0897. (HE 5.250:50066)

This new annual publication replaces the quadrennial *Accredited Higher Institutions* (FS 5.250:50012-yr.). It differs in that 1) the scope is broader (it includes vocational and other specialized institutions accredited by nationally recognized accrediting agencies), and 2) institutions approved or licensed by state agencies only are not included.

Part one lists colleges and universities alphabetically by state; part two lists professional, technical, occupational and specialized schools or departments by subject; and part three lists schools and programs with pre-accreditation status.

247. U.S. Office of Education. **Directory of Graduate Deans at United States Universities, 1872-1970.** 2nd ed. By John L. Chase. Washington, GPO, 1970. 47p. Issuing agency. LC Card No. HEW 66-140. (HE 5.2: D 34/872-970)

First edition was published in 1966. The purpose of this directory is to provide certain historical and biographical information about the administration of graduate work at U.S. colleges and universities. Institutions are listed alphabetically by state. Each entry shows the year the first doctorate was conferred, the year in which a separate unit for administration of the graduate program was established, and, from then, a chronological list of people in charge. For each administrator it provides his academic field and years of tenure. Includes an alphabetical list of deans.

248. U.S. Office of Education. **Eligible Institutions: Guaranteed Student Loan Program, Higher Education Act of 1965 as Amended.** Washington, GPO, 1971. 131p. $1.25. (HE 5.255:55059)

Lists eligible institutions for students who seek loans through the Guaranteed Loan Program. Arranged alphabetically by state.

249. U.S. Office of Education. **Index of Institutions of Higher Education by State and Congressional District.** By the Educational Services Section, Higher Education Surveys Branch. Washington, GPO, 1971. 47p. Issuing agency. LC Card No. 70-612122. (HE 5.250:50060-71)

    Arranged by states and congressional districts, this directory lists members of the House of Representatives followed by the institutions of higher education in their districts. Information about each school includes city, control (private/public), and student body (male/female/coed).

250. U.S. Office of Education. **National Defense Graduate Fellowships, Graduate Programs 1971-72.** Washington, GPO, 1971. 26p. Issuing agency. LC Card No. HEW 61-25. (HE 5.255:55017-72)

    Contains a directory of participating institutions, statistics on fellowships awarded, and a general description of the program.

251. U.S. Office of Education. **Research and Training Opportunities Abroad, 1972-73: Higher Education Programs in Foreign Language and Area Studies.** Washington, GPO, 1971. 32p. $0.25. S/N 1780-0815. (HE 5.214:14134-73)

    Discusses opportunities for American educators at all levels and graduate and undergraduate students in foreign languages, area studies, and world affairs to participate in well-planned research activities and training programs abroad.

252. U.S. Senate. **Federal and State Student Aid Programs.** Prep. by Colleen A. Campbell. Washington, GPO, 1970. 82p. $0.40. (91-2:S.doc.73)

    A list of federal programs grouped according to the level of study of the recipient and further subdivided by area of study; a selected listing of career and training opportunities available through various federal agencies; descriptions of state programs of student assistance; a brief listing of other sources of information on colleges, career opportunities, and private programs of student financial aid.

RESEARCH

253. U.S. Office of Education. **ERIC Products, 1967-68: A Bibliography of Information and Analysis Publications of the ERIC Clearinghouse, July 1967-June 1968.** Washington, Bureau of Research, ERIC, 1970. 18p. Issuing agency. LC Card No. 70-608002. (HE 5.77/2:967-68)

254. U.S. Office of Education. **Research in Education, Annual Index, January-December 1970.** Washington, GPO, 1970. 913p. (ERIC. National Center for Educational Communications) $6.00. LC Card No. HEW 68-45. S/N 1780-0742. (HE 5.77:970-2/ind.)

255. U.S. Office of Education. **Research in Education, Annual Index, January-December 1971.** Washington, GPO, 1971. 1101p. (ERIC. National Center for Educational Communications) $7.00. LC Card No. HEW 68-45. S/N 1780-0891. (HE 5.77:971-2/ind.)

Cumulates the indexes in each monthly issue of *Research in Education*. The four indexes are by subject, author, institution, and clearinghouse accession number/ED number cross reference.

SPECIAL EDUCATION

DISADVANTAGED

256. U.S. Civil Service Commission. **Catalog of Basic Education Systems.** Washington, GPO, 1971. 118p. $1.50. LC Card No. 77-612088. (CS 1.2: Ed 8/2)

"This catalog is intended for use of training officers in need of prescribing basic learning programs for use by educationally disadvantaged employees, such as high school dropouts...." Materials are under the headings of reading, language arts, mathematics, world of work, consumer education, and multi-subject programs. Specific criteria for inclusion were that no programs listed begin above a sixth-grade level, that the programs be geared to hold the interest of at least a 16- or 17-year-old, and that objective measurement of progress be possible. Information for each program includes title, publisher, subject, purpose, entry level, readability, reader orientation, format, feedback and recordkeeping, remediation, flexibility and supervision, time required, validation (proven results), cost, related material. Indexed by subject.

257. U.S. Department of Health, Education, and Welfare. Project Head Start. **Directory of Full Year Head Start Programs.** Washington, GPO, 1971. 95p. Issuing agency. LC Card No. 70-611701. (HE 21.202:P 94)

Lists program supervisors and addresses. Arranged alphabetically by state and city. Includes approximately 700 summer programs in addition to those in operation all year.

258. U.S. Office of Education. **American Indian Education, A Selected Bibliography, Supplement No. 2.** Comp. by David M. Altus and Albert D. Link. Washington, GPO, 1971. 286p. (ERIC. Clearinghouse on Rural Education and Small Schools) $2.25. S/N 1780-0872. (HE 5.10:In 2/2/supp.2)

This bibliography provides access to some of the latest research findings and developments on American Indian education. It is in two main sections: first, citations from *Research in Education*, and second, from *Current Index to Journals in Education*. Indexed by subject.

259. U.S. Office of Education. **Directory of Consultants on Migrant Education: National and State Lists for Migrant Education under Title I, Elementary and Secondary Education Act, Public Law 89-10, as Amended.** Washington, GPO, 1970. 91p. Issuing agency. LC Card No. 74-610357. (HE 5.2:M 58/7/970)

Lists consultants who are knowledgeable in the field of migrant education and available to help state and local education agencies to plan, develop, and implement new approaches to improve migrant education. Each consultant listed has been recommended by a state education agency. Consultants are listed by state with a separate section for national consultants. Areas of specialization are noted for each person included.

260. U.S. Office of Education. **Migrant Education, A Selected Bibliography, Supplement No. 2.** Comp. by David M. Altus. Washington, GPO, 1971. 129p. (ERIC. Clearinghouse on Rural Education and Small Schools) $1.25. S/N 1780-0850. (HE 5.10:M 58/supp. 2)

Provides access to some of the latest research findings and developments on migrant education. Part one lists citations from *Research in Education*, with lengthy abstracts; part two contains citations from *Current Index to Journals in Education*, with a brief annotation if titles are not definitive. Indexed by subject.

261. U.S. Office of Education. **Upward Bound, Ideas and Techniques, Reference Manual.** Washington, GPO, 1970. 116p. $1.75. (HE 5.250:50061)

This manual is designed to provide project staffs with a quick reference to ideas and source materials used in Upward Bound programs throughout the country. Capsule summaries of program techniques make up the major part of the book and were compiled from project staffs over the past four years. Includes chapters on such things as recruiting students, curriculum, counseling, and parental involvement. Appendixes include lists of bibliographic sources, addresses of Upward Bound programs, and other relevant supplemental information.

HANDICAPPED

262. U.S. Department of Health, Education, and Welfare. **A Review of Selected Program Activities in the Education of the Deaf.** Washington, GPO, 1971. 15p. $0.30. S/N 1700-0085. (HE 1.2:D 34/3)

Describes educational and cultural opportunities available for the deaf.

263. U.S. Office of Education. **Directory of Special Education Personnel in State Education Agencies.** Prep. by the Bureau of Education for the Handicapped. Washington, GPO, 1970. 81p. $1.00. LC Card No. 78-611678. S/N 1780-0748. (HE 5.235:35098)

Arranged alphabetically by state with address of the state department of education and special education personnel listed by rank.

VOCATIONAL EDUCATION

264. U.S. Office of Education. **Guidelines for Health Occupations Education Programs.** By Robert M. Tomlinson, Lois M. Laugdon, and Chester S. Rzonca. Washington, GPO, 1971. 49p. $0.55. S/N 1780-0801. (HE 5.6/2:H 34)

Designed to promote planning and cooperation among health and related associations, health facilities, educational programs and government agencies. The focus is on educational programs which require less than a baccalaureate degree. Arranged by type of system. Appendixes list agencies and organizations, information sources, and reference books.

265. U.S. Office of Education. **Inventory of Vocational Educational Statistics Available in Federal Agencies.** By Evelyn R. Kay. Washington, GPO, 1970. 59p. $0.65. LC Card No. 71-608143. (HE 5.280:80069)

Statistical reports are listed under the agency which compiled them. Project titles, dates, research directors, and types of data are listed.

266. U.S. Office of Education. **Vocational Education for Handicapped Persons: A Handbook for Program Implementation.** Washington, GPO, 1971. 92p. $0.50. LC Card No. 75-611523. (HE 5.235:35096)

The majority of the information concerns mentally handicapped vocational education programs. Special sections deal with the hearing impaired, the visually impaired, and the physically handicapped.

267. U.S. Office of Education. **Vocational Instructional Materials Available from Federal Agencies: For Agriculture.** Washington, GPO, 1971. 74+50p. $1.50. S/N 1780-0386. (HE 5.10:V 85 ag)

268. U.S. Office of Education. **Vocational Instructional Materials Available from Federal Agencies: For Distributive Education.** Washington, GPO, 1971. 43+50p. $1.25. S/N 1780-0837. (HE 5.10:V 85 ed)

269. U.S. Office of Education. **Vocational Instructional Materials Available from Federal Agencies: For Health Occupations Education.** Washington, GPO, 1971. 26+50p. $1.00. S/N 1780-0838. (HE 5.10:V 85 he)

270. U.S. Office of Education. **Vocational Instructional Materials Available from Federal Agencies: For Home Economics.** Washington, GPO, 1971. 33+50p. $1.25. S/N 0780-0839. (HE 5.10:V 85 ec)

271. U.S. Office of Education. **Vocational Instructional Materials Available from Federal Agencies: For Office Occupations.** Washington, GPO, 1971. 27+50p. $1.00. S/N 0780-0840. (HE 5.10:V 85 of)

272. U.S. Office of Education. **Vocational Instructional Materials Available from Federal Agencies: For Technical Education.** Washington, GPO, 1971. 48+50p. $1.25. S/N 0780-0841. (HE 5.10:V 85 te)

273. U.S. Office of Education. **Vocational Instructional Materials Available from Federal Agencies: For Trade and Industrial Occupations.** Washington, GPO, 1971. 84+50p. $1.50. S/N 0780-0842. (HE 5.10:V 85 tr)

These seven publications are annotated listings of printed materials produced by various federal agencies, which are relevant to particular vocational-technical education programs. Together they list over 1,600 training and curriculum documents and provide information for over 400 instructional programs. Each citation includes title, date published, number of pages, source and price, and relevant instructional programs and descriptive information. The section "Related Career Education Materials" in each volume contains a list of curriculum materials with general applications to all seven areas of vocational education.

GEOGRAPHY

ATLASES

274. U.S. Central Intelligence Agency. **People's Republic of China Atlas.** Washington, GPO, 1971. 82p. $5.25. S/N 4115-0001. (PrEx 3.10/4:C 44)
    Comparisons between the United States and China are graphically presented in this atlas. Subject areas covered include geography, economics, history, and the cultural aspects. The atlas is "designed as an introduction and general reference aid" but the scope of areas covered makes it more than that. It will be valuable for more in-depth research than is indicated. The illustrations include regional and thematic maps, charts and photographs. This publication is also available from Rand McNally.

275. U.S. Department of Agriculture. **The Look of Our Land: An Airphoto Atlas of the Rural United States; The East and South.** Comp. by Simon Baker and Henry W. Dill, Jr. Washington, GPO, 1971. 99p. (Agriculture Handbooks) $1.25. LC Card No. 72-612234. S/N 0100-1279. (A 1.76:406)

276. U.S. Department of Agriculture. **The Look of Our Land: An Airphoto Atlas of the Rural United States; The Far West.** Comp. by Simon Baker and Henry W. Dill, Jr. Washington, GPO, 1970. 48p. (Agriculture Handbooks) $0.60. (A 1.76:372)

277. U.S. Department of Agriculture. **The Look of Our Land: An Airphoto Atlas of the Rural United States; The Mountains and Deserts.** Comp. by Simon Baker and Henry W. Dill, Jr. Washington, GPO, 1971. 68p. (Agriculture Handbooks) $1.00. LC Card No. 72-612234. (A 1.76:409)

278. U.S. Department of Agriculture. **The Look of Our Land: An Airphoto Atlas of the Rural United States; North Central States.** Comp. by Simon Baker and Henry W. Dill, Jr. Washington, GPO, 1970. 64p. (Agriculture Handbooks) $0.75. LC Card No. 72-609746. S/N 0100-1104. (A 1.76:384)

279. U.S. Department of Agriculture. **The Look of Our Land: An Airphoto Atlas of the Rural United States; The Plains and Prairies.** Washington, GPO, 1971. 84p. (Agriculture Handbooks) $1.00. S/N 0100-1473. (A 1.76:419)
    These volumes contain airphoto index sheets and contact prints to illustrate land resource areas, characteristics, and use patterns. Descriptive annotations, which accompany each photograph, discuss climate, soils, and topography.

280. U.S. Geological Survey. **National Atlas of the United States.** Washington, Geological Survey, 1970. 417p. $100.00 (cloth). Order from Washington Distribution Center, U.S. Geological Survey, 1200 South Eads Street, Arlington, Virginia 22202. LC Card No. 79-654043. (I 19.2:N 21a)
    This is one of the most significant reference works published by the

United States government. It is also the first national atlas of the United States. Prepared by the Geological Survey, with the cooperation of more than 80 agencies and more than two dozen colleges, universities, and commercial firms, this atlas is designed to be of "practical use to decision makers in government and business, planners, research scholars, and others needing to visualize country-wide distributional patterns and relationships between environmental phenomena and human activities."

It contains 756 maps, and hundreds of insets, under the following headings: General Reference, Physical, Historical, Economic, Socio-Cultural, Administrative Mapping and Charting, and The World. Of particular interest for businessmen engaged in international commerce are maps showing foreign service areas and U.S. foreign trade routes. The section entitled "Administrative Maps" shows the changing face of regional administration of the federal government as well as public lands such as national parks, forests, and wilderness areas.

A detailed subject index is included at the beginning of the atlas and an index of over 41,000 place names is at the end.

BIBLIOGRAPHIES

281. U.S. National Archives and Records Service. **Cartographic Records of the Bureau of Agricultural Economics.** Comp. by William J. Heynen. Washington, GPO, 1971. 110p. (Special Lists, No. 28) Issuing agency. LC Card No. 70-182578. (GS 4.7:28)

282. U.S. National Archives and Records Service. **Guide to Cartographic Records in the National Archives.** Prep. by Charlotte Ashby and others. Washington, GPO, 1971. 444p. (National Archive Publication No. 71-16) $3.25 (cloth). LC Card No. 76-611061. S/N 2202-0032. (GS 4.6/2:C 24)

This is actually a guide to the cartographic records in the Cartographic Branch of the National Archives, and a note in the introduction explains that many maps are filed with related textual documents in other divisions of the National Archives. The guide was planned as a "central source of information about the cartographic holdings of the National Archives." Arrangement is by agency and then by record group. Brief statements about the mapping activities of the various agencies generally precede the listing of cartographic records. The maps listed reflect a wide range of governmental activity: topography, geology, weather and climate, agriculture, demography and ethnography, housing and planning, transportation, and military affairs. A very detailed (165-page) subject index refers to entry numbers or pages.

283. U.S. National Archives and Records Service. **Pre-Federal Maps in the National Archives: An Annotated List.** Comp. by Patrick D. McLaughlin. Washington, National Archives, 1971. 42p. (Special Lists, No. 26) Issuing agency. LC Card No. 73-175628. (GS 4.7:26)

DICTIONARIES

284. U.S. Department of Defense. **Glossary of Mapping, Charting, and Geodetic Terms.** 2nd ed. Washington, GPO, 1970. 281p. Issuing agency. LC Card No. 73-604750. (D 1.2:M 32)

Prepared to "satisfy the need for effective communication and mutual understanding of the terminology used in mapping, charting, and geodesy" and as a standard throughout the Department of Defense. The terms and definitions were selected from existing glossaries and dictionaries, military and civilian sources, and technical publications dealing with the various disciplines. In peripheral areas such as photography, math, etc., only the basic terms relevant to mapping, charting, and geodesy were included. Cross references to related terms are provided. A list of bibliographic sources is appended. A one-page errata sheet was issued in 1971.

GAZETTEERS

285. U.S. Department of the Interior. Board on Geographic Names. **Gazetteers.** Washington, GPO. (I 33.8: nos.)

All gazetteers are available from The Army Topographic Command, 6500 Brooks Lane, Washington, D.C. 20315, Attn.: Geographic Names Division, 53600. The following were issued in 1970 and 1971:

    Number 10. **Malaysia, Singapore, and Brunei.** 2nd ed. 1971. 1014p. LC Card No. 70-611500.
    Number 42. **U.S.S.R.** 2nd ed. 1970. 7v. LC Card No. 78-608761.
    Number 58. **South Vietnam and the South China Sea.** 2nd ed. 1971. 337p. LC Card No. 70-613599.
    Number 112. **Morocco.** 1970. 923p. LC Card No. 72-608974.
    Number 113. **Malawi.** 1970. 161p. LC Card No. 70-607550.
    Number 114. **Israel.** 1970. 123p. LC Card No. 76-608758.
    Number 115. **Lebanon.** 1970. 676p. LC Card No. 77-610513.
    Number 116. **Mongolia.** 1970. 256p. LC Card No. 72-611367.
    Europe and U.S.S.R. Gazetteer Supplement. 1971. 151p. LC Card No. 79-614822. (I 33.8/2:Eu 7)
    Americas, Gazetteer Supplement. 1971. 86p. LC Card No. 76-616041. (I 33.8/2:Am 3)

HISTORY AND AREA STUDIES

AFRICA

GENERAL WORKS

286. U.S. Library of Congress. General Reference and Bibliography Division. **Sub-Saharan Africa: A Guide to Serials.** Comp. by the African Section, Reference Department. Washington, GPO, 1970. 409p. $5.25 (cloth). LC Card No. 70-607392. (LC 2.8:Af 8/2)

The publications listed in this guide relate to Africa south of the Sahara; they are issued either in Western languages or in African languages which use the Roman alphabet. Monographic serials and many annual publications are included; however, periodic reports of government agencies are not.

Serials are listed alphabetically by title with place, publisher and frequency. Library of Congress holdings are listed for those in its collection; for others, National Union Catalog symbols are used to show location. Some serials included are not devoted exclusively to sub-Saharan Africa, but because they frequently carry pertinent articles they are therefore significant for research purposes.

Additional information in this guide makes it especially useful: several hundred entries (out of a total of 4,670) contain a list of abstracting or indexing services (up to four) which regularly include those journals.

Indexed by subject and by organization.

ALGERIA

287. U.S. Department of the Army. **Area Handbook for Algeria.** Washington, GPO, 1965 (repr. 1970). 519p. $3.50 (cloth). (D 101.22:550-44)

The purpose of this *Area Handbook for Algeria* is to describe briefly and in general terms the political, economic and social bases of Algerian society, to outline its domestic and foreign policies, and to evaluate its strengths and weaknesses. The present study represents a thorough revision of the *Area Handbook for Algeria*, prepared by Human Relations Area Files in 1958.

Because of the date of this work and the subsequent events in Algeria, it is questionable whether the handbook was worth reprinting.

BURMA

288. U.S. Department of the Army. **Area Handbook for Burma.** By John W. Henderson and others. Washington, GPO, 1971. 341p. $3.00. LC Card No. 75-612066. (D 101.22:550-61)

Some of the data in this area handbook was taken from a three-volume study on Burma by Frank N. Trager (Human Relations Area Files, 1956). Because of the country's policy of isolation from world affairs, there were very few primary or secondary sources available to the researchers of this volume.

Chapters cover general characteristics, physical features, history, population, ethnic groups, social structure, education, cultural setting, religion and more. Spelling of Burmese terms and proper names conforms to local usage. A short glossary, which does not attempt to be comprehensive, and a bibliography are other noteworthy features.

CONGO

289. U.S. Department of the Army. **Area Handbook for Congo (Kinshasa).** By Gordon McDonald and others. Washington, GPO, 1971. 587p. $3.75 (cloth). LC Card No. 79-608680. (D 101.22:550-67)

This book is an attempt to provide, in compact, convenient, balanced and objective form, an integrated exposition and analysis of the dominant social, political, and economic aspects of the Congolese society. It is designed to provide an understanding of the dynamics of the component elements of the society and an insight into the ideas and feelings of its people.

Sources of information have included scholarly texts and journals, official reports by governmental and international organizations, local and foreign newspapers and periodicals, and other documents. Much political, economic, and other information was relatively up to date, but no recent population figures were available. The spelling of other proper names conforms to current usage in the country or to the most authoritative available sources.

290. U.S. Department of the Army. **Area Handbook for the People's Republic of the Congo (Congo Brazzaville).** By Gordon C. McDonald and others. Washington, GPO, 1971. 255p. $2.50 (cloth). LC Card No. 76-608679. S/N 0820-0346. (D 101.22:550-91)

Sources of information for this handbook have included scholarly texts and journals, official reports by governmental and international organizations, local and foreign newspapers and periodicals, and other documents. Because of Congolese government restrictions on the distribution of news and official data and the breakdown of diplomatic relations with the United States, relatively little up-to-date, useful information was available directly from official Congolese sources.

Place names have been given as published in 1962 by the United States Board on Geographic Names, unless official Congolese government changes have been announced. The spelling of other proper names conforms to current usage in the country or to the most authoritative available sources.

ETHIOPIA

291. U.S. Department of the Army. **Area Handbook for Ethiopia.** 2nd ed. By Irving Kaplan and others. Washington, GPO, 1971. 543p. $3.75 (cloth). LC Card No. 79-609351. (D 101.22:550-28/2)

The first area handbook for Ethiopia was published in 1960. This handbook seeks to provide a compact and objective exposition and analysis of the dominant social, political, and economic aspects of Ethiopian society. It is designed to give readers an understanding of the forces operating in the society and an insight into the goals and values of the people. The Ethiopian calendar system is explained, as are the relationships between the Ethiopian calendar year, the Gregorian calendar year, the Ethiopian trade year, and the Ethiopian fiscal year.

Because there is no standardized or universally acceptable system for the transliteration of Amharic, the handbook cites the *Statistical Abstract* (Ethiopia Central Statistical Office, 1964) as its primary source.

GHANA

292. U.S. Department of the Army. **Area Handbook for Ghana.** 2nd ed. By Irving Kaplan and others. Washington, GPO, 1971. 449p. $3.25 (cloth). LC Card No. 74-611338. (D 101.22:550-153)

This handbook is shorter and more compact that the first edition, published in 1962. It is designed to give readers an understanding of the dominant forces (social, political and economic) operating in the society. A bibliography and a short glossary of terms are provided. The work is thoroughly indexed.

SOMALIA

293. U.S. Department of the Army. **Area Handbook for Somalia.** By Irving Kaplan and others. Washington, GPO, 1970. 455p. $3.25 (cloth). LC Card No. 73-607519. (D 101.22:550-86)

This book is an attempt to provide, in compact, convenient, balanced and objective form, an integrated exposition and analysis of the dominant social, political, and economic aspects of Somali society. Many questions posed, however, could not be answered, since much of the information sought was not available. Thus, some parts of the total picture are missing. This is a result of the military coup which occurred in October 1969, after the research and writing of this handbook were completed.

Because of the dual British and Italian colonial heritage, the spelling of Somali terms and proper names has sometimes been problematic. Official documents and maps show variant spellings. Generally, spelling of place names in the area formerly under Italian rule conforms to Italian usage—for example, Mogadiscio rather than Mogadishu. The spelling of other words and names follows English usage. A glossary is provided, as is a bibliography for more detailed research.

SOUTH AFRICA

294. U.S. Department of the Army. **Area Handbook for the Republic of South Africa.** By Irving Kaplan and others. Washington, GPO, 1971. 845p. $4.75 (cloth). LC Card No. 75-608712. (D 101.22:550-93)

Descriptions and analyses of South African society often conflict and are characterized by varying degrees of distortion. This book, based on a wide sampling of the many published sources, attempts to provide in compact, convenient, and balanced form an exposition and analysis of the dominant social, political, and economic features of South African society.

South Africa has two official languages—Afrikaans and English. All laws and other government documents are published in both. This book has generally used the English version of official usage. In the case of nongovernmental institutions, Afrikaans has been used if the institution is of Afrikaner origin and English if it is of English origin. There are many terms for different segments of South Africa's population. Wherever possible, the preference of the group named has been ascertained and used even if it is not the official term. Thus, the word *African*, rather than the official word *Bantu*, has been used for the indigenous black population. On the other hand, when a term has become thoroughly entrenched in the language, it has been used for convenience even if scholars do not now consider it accurate. Thus, *Hottentot* is employed instead of the term *Khoikhoin* for these people.

Contains a summary of pertinent data such as government, population, climate, topography, etc., and an extensive bibliography.

TUNISIA

295. U.S. Department of the Army. **Area Handbook for the Republic of Tunisia.** By Howard C. Reese and others. Washington, GPO, 1970. 415p. $3.25 (cloth). LC Card No. 70-607904. (D 101.22:550-89)

This book is an attempt to provide, in compact, convenient, balanced and objective form, an integrated exposition and analysis of the dominant social, political, and economic aspects of the Tunisian society. It is designed to give readers an understanding of the dynamics of the component elements of the society and an insight into the ideals and feelings, the goals, and the hopes and fears of its people.

The main reliance has been on secondary sources, but a number of consultants have provided recent first-hand information on particular phases of the study. Extensive use has been made of official and semiofficial reports and studies currently published in Tunis.

Spellings of Arabic words are based on forms judged to be most convenient to the American reader, and most diacritical marks have been omitted. The guiding principle has been to follow current usage in standard periodicals and books in English. A glossary is included as an appendix for the reader's convenience, and there is a bibliography for further research.

UNITED ARAB REPUBLIC

296. U.S. Department of the Army. **Area Handbook for the United Arab Republic (Egypt).** By Harvey H. Smith and others. Washington, GPO, 1970. 555p. $3.75. LC Card No. 71-608841. (D 101.22:550-43/2)

This is a revision of *U.S. Army Area Handbook for the United Arab Republic (Egypt)* published in December 1964. When research and writing for this volume were completed in December 1969, President Gamal Abdul Nasser had been in power for over 12 years. His sudden death of a heart attack on September 28, 1970, significantly increased the uncertainties of the Middle Eastern situation.

An attempt was made in this study to indicate the significant patterns of change and to point out the clearly discernible trends likely to have an effect in the near future. Consultants and all available materials were used in an effort to analyze the dominant sociological, political, and economic aspects of a society in transition and to identify the patterns of thought and behavior of its members.

An effort was made to establish a common, simple system that will allow the general reader to understand the Arabic word and approximate its pronunciation. Symbols and diacritical marks which are uncommon in English usage were not used. The spelling of Arabic words and names follows the transliteration system of *Webster's Third New International Dictionary* (unabridged). Conventional spelling, however, was retained for some personal and place names.

ASIA AND THE MIDDLE EAST

ASIA

CEYLON

297. U.S. Department of the Army. **Area Handbook for Ceylon.** By Richard F. Nyrop and others. Washington, GPO, 1971. 525p. $3.50 (cloth). LC Card No. 71-609526. (D 101.22:550-96)

Located 18 miles off the southeastern tip of the Indian subcontinent, Ceylon has long had a strategic importance with respect to the Bay of Bengal and the Indian Ocean. After 145 years of British rule as a British crown colony, Ceylon achieved independence in 1948.

This book is an attempt to provide a comprehensive study of the dominant social, political, and economic aspects of the society, to present its strengths and weaknesses, and to identify the patterns of behavior characteristic of its members. It does not, however, pretend to be exhaustive.

Sources used included scholarly studies, official reports, local newspapers, and current journals. A considerable body of up-to-date information exists, although some of the data, which should be considered as provisional or as estimates, should be used with caution.

This volume also includes a bibliography for further research and a glossary of terms.

CHINA

298. U.S. Department of the Army. **Communist China: A Bibliographic Survey.** Washington, GPO, 1971. 253p. $7.50. LC Card No. 72-613755. S/N 0820-0351. (D 101.22:550-9)

Updates two earlier bibliographies published by the Army: *Communist China: Ruthless Enemy or Paper Tiger: A Bibliographic Survey* (1962) and *Communist China: A Strategic Survey, A Bibliography* (1966).

This bibliography covers a wide range of source materials on a number of subjects including China's nuclear threat, global ambitions and objectives, foreign policy and international relations, the cultural revolution, the political, sociological, and economic aspects, and military posture.

A chapter is devoted to works on the Republic of China on Taiwan. There are more than 800 entries with detailed annotations, but no index. Supportive material in the appendixes includes statistics, texts of documents (U.S. and Chinese), and organization charts. There are also 17 maps, four in an envelope inside the back cover.

INDIA

299. U.S. Department of the Army. **Area Handbook for India.** Rev. ed. By Rinn-Sup Shinn and others. Washington, GPO, 1970. 791p. $4.50 (cloth). LC Card No. 76-608601. (D 101.22:550-21/2)

This revision of the *U.S. Army Handbook for India*, prepared in 1963, is an attempt to provide a compact, balanced, and objective exposition and analysis of the dominant social, political, and economic aspects of Indian society. It is designed to give readers an understanding of the dynamic forces operating in the society and an insight into the aspirations and goals, needs and achievements of its people. It represents an effort not only to deal with post-1963 developments in India, but also to bring to the study the benefit of recent research and writing by specialists in Indian affairs.

INDONESIA

300. U.S. Department of the Army. **Area Handbook for Indonesia.** By John W. Henderson and others. Washington, GPO, 1970. 569p. $4.00 (cloth). LC Card No. 73-608279. (D 101.22:550-39/2)

Since 1964, when the last edition of the *Area Handbook for Indonesia* was published, the end of the Sukarno era has produced profound changes in the political, economic, social, and military life of the country. Consequently, almost at a stroke, much of the content of the previous edition of the handbook became obsolete. This volume describes Indonesia as it had emerged by 1969 under President Suharto.

In general, the official Indonesian government names are used in this book, in some cases with an English equivalent in parentheses. For certain cities and islands, where international usage has made English names exceptionally well-known, the reverse practice has been adopted arbitrarily.

KOREA

301. U.S. Department of the Air Force. **Korea.** Prep. by Constance R. Johnson. San Francisco, Pacific Air Forces, 1970. 55p. (Basic Bibliographies for Base Libraries) Available from Commander-in-Chief, Pacific Air Forces, Attn: DPSR, Command Librarian, APO, San Francisco, California 96553. Issuing agency. LC Card No. 72-607035. (D 301.62:K 84)

302. U.S. Department of the Army. **Communist North Korea: A Bibliographic Survey.** Washington, GPO, 1971. 130p. $3.25. LC Card No. 71-614453. (D 101.22:550-11)

This annotated bibliography of articles, books, and pamphlets on North Korea is concerned with subjects that are basic to the knowledge of the nation and its people. The materials listed, including both Western literature and that originating in North Korea and other Communist countries, are pertinent to the strategic, political, economic, and sociological aspects of the country. Information is contained in five chapters: Whither Korea; The North Korean State; North Korea and the World; Korea's Historic Past; and Aids to Further Research. Appendixes include statistics, organization charts, and a bibliography of the Korean War. Several maps are included in a pocket in the back of the book.

A companion volume for South Korea is planned.

MALAYSIA

303. U.S. Department of the Army. **Area Handbook for Malaysia.** By John W. Henderson and others. Washington, GPO, 1970. 639p. $4.00 (cloth). LC Card No. 71-608971. (D 101.22:550-45/2)

Fundamental changes have taken place in the structure of Malaysia, as well as in its foreign relations, since the *Area Handbook for Malaysia and Singapore* was prepared in 1965. Among the major developments that have required a revision of the original handbook have been Singapore's separation and its establishment as an independent state, the end of the so-called Confrontation between Indonesia and Malaysia, and the first moves toward reduction of the British and other Commonwealth defense presence in the area.

English usage in the revised edition follows *Webster's Third New International Dictionary* (unabridged). Malay language usage has followed Wilkinson's *Malay-English Dictionary*, 8th edition, 1961. Malaysian place names and official names are transliterated in accordance with Malaysian official usage, whenever this could be determined from available sources.

MONGOLIA

304. U.S. Department of the Army. **Area Handbook for Mongolia.** By Trevor N. Dupuy and others. Washington, GPO, 1970. 500p. $3.75 (cloth). (D 101.22:550-76)

Since 1921, the Mongolian People's Party or its successor, the Mongolian People's Revolutionary Party, has constantly endeavored to transform the area known sometimes as Outer Mongolia into a model Communist state. The nature and development of this transformation are the explicit theme of every chapter of this book, a book of and about people as individuals and as members of the society, and how they live. It is designed to give readers an understanding of the dynamics of the component elements of the society and an insight into the ideas and feelings, the goals, and the hopes and fears of its people. This work includes a brief reference summary of data on Mongolia, a detailed bibliography, and a glossary.

PAKISTAN

305. U.S. Department of the Army. **Area Handbook for Pakistan.** By Richard F. Nyrop and others. Washington, GPO, 1971. 691p. $4.25 (cloth). LC Card No. 79-608677. (D 101.22:550-48/2)

The present *Area Handbook for Pakistan* is a second revision of the 1958 *Area Handbook for Pakistan*, which was researched and written by a team at the Human Relations Area Files, Inc. The first revision, done by a team under the chairmanship of Harvey H. Smith at the Foreign Area Studies of The American University, was published in October 1965. Although the present handbook incorporates some of the material from the earlier studies, it is a substantial revision.

This book is an attempt to provide a comprehensive study of the dominant social, political, and economic aspects of Pakistani society and to identify the pattern of behavior characteristic of its members. Sources of information used included scholarly studies, official reports of governments and of international organizations, local newspapers, and current journals. Relatively up-to-date economic data were available, but because the most recent census report available was that of the 1961 census, the demographic statistics are based on estimates and are subject to considerable revision when the results of the 1971 census become available.

The handbook includes an extensive bibliography, a glossary, and a detailed index.

THAILAND

306. U.S. Department of the Army. **Area Handbook for Thailand.** By John W. Henderson and others. Washington, GPO, 1971. 413p. $3.25 (cloth). LC Card No. 72-611403. (D 101.22:550-53)

Swiftly moving events in Southeast Asia have brought many changes to Thailand within the last few years. This revision of the *Area Handbook for Thailand* has been prepared to take account of the altered scene and attempts to be current to 1970. Its purpose is to provide in a compact, convenient, balanced, and objective form an integrated exposition and analysis of the dominant social, political, and economic aspects of Thai society.

There are some inconsistencies in the transliteration of Thai words, particularly names. The practice was to follow, in most cases, the spelling used in the *Thai Official Yearbook, 1968* and in other Thai official publications. Spelling of most place names has followed official United States government maps and the *Thailand Gazetteer* of the Board on Geographic Names, United States Department of Interior, April 1966. In some cases romanized spelling in general international use by English publications was used, even when it was in conflict with local Thai usage. English usage follows *Webster's Third New International Dictionary* (unabridged). English weights and measures are used, except that all tons are metric tons unless otherwise noted.

MIDDLE EAST

GENERAL WORKS

307. U.S. Department of the Army. **Area Handbook for the Peripheral States of the Arabian Peninsula.** Prep. by the Stanford Research Institute. Washington, GPO, 1971. 201p. $2.50 (cloth). LC Card No. 76-608679. S/N 0820-0347. (D 101.22:550-92)

The purpose of the *Area Handbook for the Peripheral States of the Arabian Peninsula* is to acquaint the reader with the principal economic, political, and sociological elements governing the development of these 13 societies. Special emphasis has been placed on those forces for continuity and change which are most important in shaping contemporary life in the Peripheral States: religious schisms, a tradition of tribalism, the historical influence of Great Britain, the advent of petroleum production, and the rise of Arab nationalism.

An effort has been made to adhere to a common simple system of transliteration. In most instances the spelling of Arab words and names has followed the transliteration system of *Webster's Third New International Dictionary*. Familiar spelling has been used, however, for well-known personal and place names. A glossary has been compiled for the convenience of the reader.

308. U.S. Library of Congress. **American Doctoral Dissertations on the Arab World, 1883-1968.** Comp. by George Dimitri Selim. Washington, GPO, 1970. 103p. $0.55. LC Card No. 79-607590. (LC 1.12/2:Ar 1/883-968)

This bibliography covers "as comprehensively as possible doctoral dissertations on all subjects related to the Arab world accepted by universities in the United States and Canada from 1883 through the academic year 1967-68." It includes dissertations in science and technology, humanities, and the social sciences, and it covers all Arabic-speaking countries of the Near East and North Africa and all communities where Arabic is spoken. There are dissertations on minorities living in Arabic-speaking countries, as well as all titles related to Islam as a religion regardless of the part of the world involved. Coverage extends roughly from 610 A.D. to the present. An appendix lists dissertations dealing with the Near East as a unit. Entries are alphabetical by author and include title, name of the university and year of acceptance. There is a detailed author-subject index.

IRAN

309. U.S. Department of the Army. **Area Handbook for Iran.** By Harvey H. Smith and others. Washington, GPO, 1971. 653p. $4.00 (cloth). LC Card No. 72-608678. (D 101.22:550-68)

This is a revision of the *U.S. Army Area Handbook for Iran*, published in May 1963. Subsequent developments within the country and within the Middle Eastern area in general have indicated the advisability of bringing up to date the 1963 handbook.

This handbook attempts to describe the social, political, and economic bases of Iranian society and to explain the developments in the main features of the government's reform program occurring as late as mid-1970, pointing out discernible trends. Fieldwork has not been possible, but consultants and all available materials have been used in an effort to explain the dominant social, political, and economic aspects of a society in transition and to identify the patterns of thought and behavior of its members.

A glossary is included as an appendix for the reader's convenience. Terms in the glossary are not in every case defined explicitly in the text but may be encountered frequently in reading collateral subject material.

IRAQ

310. U.S. Department of the Army. **Area Handbook for Iraq.** By Harvey H. Smith and others. Washington, GPO, 1971. 413p. $3.25 (cloth). LC Card No. 73-610216. (D 101.22:550-31)

First published in 1969, this handbook contains only one new section— a summary of events from May 1968 through November 1970. No other revisions were made.

ISRAEL

311. U.S. Department of the Army. **Area Handbook for Israel.** By Harvey H. Smith and others. Washington, GPO, 1970. 457p. $3.50 (cloth). LC Card No. 78-608713. (D 101.22:550-25)

This book is an attempt to provide, in compact, convenient, balanced, and objective form, an integrated exposition and analysis of the dominant social, political, and economic aspects of the Israeli society. It is designed to give readers an understanding of the dynamics of the component elements of the society, and an insight into the ideas and goals of its people.

Modern Israel is a predominantly Jewish state in the midst of Arab neighbors. Geographically and topographically, the country is a segment of the Middle East, but in most other respects its people are oriented toward the West.

A glossary of terms used in the text, an extensive bibliography, and a detailed index complete the volume.

SAUDI ARABIA

312. U.S. Department of the Army. **Area Handbook for Saudi Arabia.** By Norman C. Walpole and others. Washington, GPO, 1966 (repr. 1971). 373p. $3.25 (cloth). LC Card No. 74-614218. (D 101.22:550-51)

This area handbook was reprinted without revision, but there is a new section entitled "Summary of Events: January 1966—December 1970."

SYRIA

313. U.S. Department of the Army. **Area Handbook for Syria.** By Richard F. Nyrop and others. Washington, GPO, 1971. 357p. $3.00 (cloth). LC Card

No. 75-177250. (D 101.22:550-47)

This *Area Handbook for Syria* is a revision of a book written in 1965. Research and writing for the present book were completed in May 1971; although it incorporates some of the material in the earlier study, it is a substantial revision.

The book is an attempt to provide a comprehensive study of the dominant social, political, and economic aspects of Syrian society and to identify the pattern of behavior characteristic of its members. Sources of information used included scholarly studies, official reports of governments and of international organizations, local newspapers, and current journals and periodicals. Relatively up-to-date economic data were available but may be subject to substantial margins of error. The census information available was based on the preliminary report of the September 1970 census and may also be subject to revision and refinement.

A glossary is included for the reader's convenience. The transliteration of Arabic names, words, and phrases follows, with some exceptions, the system used by the Library of Congress.

TURKEY

314. U.S. Department of the Army. **Area Handbook for the Republic of Turkey.** By Thomas D. Roberts and others. Washington, GPO, 1970. 438p. $3.50 (cloth). LC Card No. 76-607576. (D 101.22:550-80)

This book is an attempt to provide, in a compact, convenient, balanced, and objective form, an integrated exposition and analysis of the dominant social, political, and economic aspects of the Turkish society. It is designed to give readers an understanding of the dynamics of the component elements of the society and an insight into the ideas and feelings, the goals, and the hopes and fears of its people.

Although the main reliance was on secondary sources, a number of people were consulted for recent firsthand information on particular phases of the study.

Spellings of Turkish words were based on forms judged to be most convenient to the American reader, and most diacritical marks have been omitted. The guiding principle was to follow current usage in standard periodicals and books in English. A glossary is included as an appendix, for the reader's convenience, but most of the terms in the glossary have been defined in the text.

EUROPE

GENERAL WORKS

315. U.S. Department of the Army. **Communist Eastern Europe, An Analytical Survey of Literature.** Washington, GPO, 1971. 367p. $8.00. LC Card No. 78-611513. S/N 0820-0352. (D 101.22:550-8)

This bibliography was prepared "to fill the pressing need for an accurate listing of unclassified source materials on the East European region . . . and to assist both the military analyst and the private researcher in gaining a better understanding of the complex events occurring in this area." The six main divisions are: 1) Communist Eastern Europe and International Communism, 2) Communist Eastern Europe and USSR, 3) USSR and the Communist Bloc, 4) Invasion of Czechoslovakia, 5) Communist Eastern Europe by country, and 6) Source Materials for Research and Reference. Appendixes also contain reference material in statistical tables, charts, and 28 fold-out maps.

ALBANIA

316. U.S. Department of the Army. **Area Handbook for Albania.** By Eugene K. Keefe and others. Washington, GPO, 1971. 223p. $2.50 (cloth). LC Card No. 73-609651. (D 101.22:550-98)

The *Area Handbook for Albania* seeks to present an overview of the various social, political, and economic aspects of the country as they appeared in 1970. The preface states that although the Communist Party leaders "have gone to extremes to maintain an aura of secrecy about their nation and their efforts to govern it, and material on Albania is scanty and sometimes unreliable, the authors have striven for objectivity in this effort to depict Albanian society in 1970."

CYPRUS

317. U.S. Department of the Army. **Area Handbook for Cyprus.** By Eugene K. Keefe and others. Washington, GPO, 1971. 241p. $2.50 (cloth). LC Card No. 79-610125. (D 101.22:550-22)

The authors of this handbook encountered great difficulty in obtaining complete data on many aspects of Cypriot life. Division of the country into two communities resulted in a dearth of information, particularly concerning Turkish Cypriot affairs. No official census had been conducted since 1960, and published statistics often seemed incomplete. Thus, this work should not be considered a final source for statistical research. A bibliography which will lead to further sources of information about Cyprus is included.

SOVIET UNION

318. U.S. Department of the Army. **Area Handbook for the Soviet Union.** By Eugene K. Keefe and others. Washington, GPO, 1971. 827p. $5.25 (cloth). LC Card No. 71-609246. (D 101.22:550-95)

The *Area Handbook for the Soviet Union* is designed to explain the Soviet system. The effort in writing the handbook has been toward objectivity; it does not bring forth unique ideas or new analyses, nor is it exhaustive in any area. In essence, it is an attempt to explore and expose the pertinent aspects of the system that will lead to a better understanding of internal and international Soviet affairs.

Sources used were mostly secondary, although Soviet sources, particularly newspapers, periodicals, and documents, were extensively analyzed.

Transliteration generally follows the rules of the *Romanization Guide* of the United States Board on Geographic Names; however, names of places and persons that have acquired a familiar spelling in the West are given in that spelling—for example, Moscow and Georgia, Trotsky and Podgorny. Acronyms such as USSR, RSFSR, and CPSU, which also have become familiar, are used frequently and are fully explained in the glossary. Russian acronyms are used where necessary and are explained in the text and in the glossary.

319. U.S. Department of the Army. **USSR: Strategic Survey, A Bibliography.** 1969 ed. Washington, GPO, 1970. 237p. $5.25. LC Card No. 77-601689. S/N 0820-0309. (D 101.22:550-6)

The first edition of this bibliography was published in 1963. This edition contains abstracts of unclassified publications and is "intended to serve both the needs of the experts with responsibility for policy and strategy as well as those who simply need descriptive information about the Soviet Union." The 1,000 items included cover the period from the last quarter of 1963 through August 1968. The work is divided into four major sections: 1) Introduction: Fifty Years of Soviet Power, An Overview; 2) National Policy, Strategy and Objectives; 3) The Soviet Nation: The Spectrum of Politics, Sociology and Economics; and 4) Aids to Further Research on the Soviet Union (which lists reference books, primarily bibliographies). Annotations are lengthy and descriptive. Includes maps.

LATIN AMERICA

GENERAL WORKS

320. U.S. Library of Congress. **National Directory of Latin Americanists.** 2nd ed. Comp. by the Hispanic Foundation Reference Department. Washington, GPO, 1971. 683p. (Hispanic Foundation Bibliographical Series; No. 12) $4.25 (cloth). LC Card No. 75-37737. S/N 3013-0004. (LC 24.7:12)

The first edition of this biographical directory was published in 1966 and contained 1,884 biographies. This edition contains biographies of 2,695 Latin American specialists in the social sciences and humanities. Each entry contains the biographee's name, birthplace, birth date, major discipline, degrees (including honoraries), professional career (from earliest to current), fellowships, honors, awards, etc., membership in professional and honorary associations, research specialties and interests, publications (limited to three), language knowledge (on a scale of one to five for each of the following: reading, understanding the spoken language, speaking, and writing), linguistic studies, home and office addresses. Includes indexes of subject specialties and area specialties with biographees' names only under each heading.

BRAZIL

321. U.S. Department of the Army. **Area Handbook for Brazil.** By Thomas E. Weil and others. Washington, GPO, 1971. 645p. $4.00 (cloth). LC Card

No. 73-608516. (D 101.22:550-20/2)

    This book represents an effort to provide a compact and objective exposition and analysis of the dominant social, political, and economic characteristics of Brazilian society. It is designed to give readers an understanding of the dynamics of the component elements of Brazilian society, and an insight into the needs, goals, and achievements of the people. A large number of consultants provided data not available in printed sources.

    English usage follows *Webster's Third New International Dictionary.* Portuguese words and phrases, which have been used only when adequate English equivalents were lacking, are defined at first appearance. If they are employed frequently, they are listed in the glossary. Portuguese is based on James L. Taylor's *A Portuguese-English Dictionary.*

COLOMBIA

322. U.S. Department of the Army. **Area Handbook for Colombia.** By Thomas E. Weil and others. Washington, GPO, 1970. 595p. $3.75 (cloth). LC Card No. 70-608487. (D 101.22:550-26/2)

    In 1969, the Republic of Colombia was engaged in diversifying its economy, carrying out social reforms, improving conditions among the masses, and expanding foreign trade. This handbook represents an effort to provide a compact and objective exposition and analysis of the social, political, and economic characteristics of that society.

    It includes a handy reference summary with basic information on government, population, climate, topography, etc., and an extensive bibliography.

COSTA RICA

323. U.S. Department of the Army. **Area Handbook for Costa Rica.** By Howard L. Blutstein. Washington, GPO, 1970. 323p. $3.00 (cloth). LC Card No. 79-608713. (D 101.22:550-90)

    Costa Rica has long been recognized as a country with a generally high standard of living and a tradition of adherence to democratic principles. This Central American republic, although small in size and population, has managed to achieve and maintain social progress with minimum difficulty because of the unique character of its society, which is basically middle class. It is a country with a high degree of national stability.

    This handbook is an attempt to provide, in compact, convenient, balanced, and objective form, an integrated exposition and analysis of the social, political, and economic aspects of the Costa Rican society. It is designed to give readers an understanding of the component elements of the society and an insight into the ideas and goals of its people.

    Spanish usage is based on *Appleton's New Cuyas Dictionary* (fifth edition). Place names follow the rulings of the Board on Geographic Names, United States Department of the Interior. Spanish words, held to a minimum, are defined at first appearance and, if used frequently, are found in the glossary appended to the book.

CUBA

324. U.S. Department of the Army. **Area Handbook for Cuba.** By Howard L. Blutstein and others. Washington, GPO, 1971. 505p. $3.75 (cloth). LC Card No. 75-610124. (D 101.22:550-152)

In 1970 Cuba celebrated the eleventh anniversary of the Revolution of 1959. The results of that revolution have made what was once a small, relatively unimportant country a center of attention. Many complex changes have taken place domestically and in the country's world situation in the last decade.

This handbook seeks to present an integrated exposition of the society in order to help understand the circumstances and results of the changes that have occurred since 1959.

Spanish usage is based on *Appleton's New Cuyas Dictionary* (fifth edition). Place names follow the rulings of the United States Board on Geographic Names. Spanish words are held to a minimum, are defined at first appearance and, if used frequently, are recorded in the glossary.

EL SALVADOR

325. U.S. Department of the Army. **Area Handbook for El Salvador.** By Howard L. Blutstein. Washington, GPO, 1971. 259p. $2.50 (cloth). LC Card No. 78-609951. (D 101.22:550-150)

El Salvador is the smallest, most densely populated, and most highly industrialized Central American republic. The government is responsibly responding to the pressure of an expanding population for increased social benefits.

This handbook seeks to supply an integrated and comprehensive exposition and analysis of the entire society of El Salvador.

GUATEMALA

326. U.S. Department of the Army. **Area Handbook for Guatemala.** By John Dombrowski and others. Washington, GPO, 1970. 361p. $3.25 (cloth). LC Card No. 79-607286. (D 101.22:550-78)

This book is an attempt to provide a balanced and objective exposition and analysis of the social, political, and economic aspects of Guatemalan society. As a book about the people as individuals and as members of the society and how they live, it is designed to give readers an understanding of the dynamics of the component elements of Guatemalan society and an insight into the feelings and ideas, the goals and the hopes and fears of the people.

English usage in this handbook follows *A Dictionary of Modern English Usage*, by H. W. Fowler (second edition, revised by Sir Ernest Gowers), and *Webster's Third New International Dictionary* (unabridged). Spanish usage is based on *Appleton's New Cuyas Dictionary* (fifth edition). Place names follow the rulings of the United States Board on Geographic Names, United States Department of the Interior. For the Indian languages, both the Mayan derivatives and the Carib dialect, the authors used Guatemalan sources.

HONDURAS

327. U.S. Department of the Army. **Area Handbook for Honduras.** By Howard L. Blutstein and others. Washington, GPO, 1971. 225p. $2.50 (cloth). LC Card No. 72-610126. (D 101.22:550-151)

Honduras, at the close of 1970, was still recovering from the economic and social effects of a brief war with neighboring El Salvador in July 1969. This Central American country, large in size but small in population, was striving to achieve social progress despite difficulties ensuing from a history of political instability.

This handbook seeks to supply an integrated and comprehensive exposition and analysis of the entire society of Honduras. There are several excellent works, in both English and Spanish, concerning the country, but most are either specific studies of one aspect of the society or are broad general descriptions of the situation. The *Area Handbook for Honduras* is not intended to replace any of these studies, but rather to supplement the available material with a unified treatment of the whole society.

It contains a lengthy bibliography, a glossary of words used in the text, and a detailed bibliography.

NICARAGUA

328. U.S. Department of the Army. **Area Handbook for Nicaragua.** By John Morris Ryan and others. Washington, GPO, 1970. 393p. $3.25 (cloth). LC Card No. 79-608283. (D 101.22:550-88)

Nicaragua is one of the smaller countries of the Western Hemisphere. Published sources about it and its people have tended to be fragmentary and sporadic. Although it has a literary tradition, there has been no systematic account of its society. The relatively few survivals of indigenous Indian culture have attracted inadequate attention.

Until recently, economic information was deficient, but lately several organizations have provided good primary sources on many aspects of the national economy. This book is an attempt to provide, in compact, convenient, balanced, and objective form, an integrated exposition and analysis of the major social, political, and economic aspects of the society.

URUGUAY

329. U.S. Department of the Army. **Area Handbook for Uruguay.** By Thomas E. Weil and others. Washington, GPO, 1971. 439p. $3.25 (cloth). LC Card No. 75-609527. (D 101.22:550-97)

In 1970 the Oriental (Eastern) Republic of Uruguay, noted for its dedication to democratic and orderly political processes, its high standard of living, and its comprehensive social welfare system, faced challenging problems involving economic conditions and maintenance of internal security. The government, with the adoption of extraordinary powers, was endeavoring to eliminate threats to the economy and to suppress political enemies who resorted to criminal acts to advance their cause. This handbook provides a compact analysis of sociological, economic and political happenings, including statistics, maps, a bibliography, and a glossary. The detailed index facilitates use of this comprehensive work.

VENEZUELA

330. U.S. Department of the Army. **Area Handbook for Venezuela.** By Thomas E. Weil and others. Washington, GPO, 1971. 525p. $4.00 (cloth). LC Card No. 74-611208. (D 101.22:550-71)

At the end of 1970 Venezuela was enjoying the benefits of increasing national wealth and the strengthening of democratic institutions. These and other significant developments during the late 1960s underlined the need for a revision of the *Area Handbook for Venezuela* which had been published in Feburary 1964.

Government actions reported after completion of research and writing substantially altered conditions affecting foreign investment in Venezuela. In mid-December 1970 the National Congress passed unanimously a banking law that called for all foreign banks to be at least 80 percent Venezuelan-owned. It also approved legislation increasing the tax on profits of the largely foreign-owned petroleum companies from 50 to 60 percent. In January 1971, the minister of mines and hydrocarbons announced that the country's reserves of natural gas would be placed under state control; foreign participation in this industry was to be limited to minority positions.

This handbook attempts to show the effect of these government actions as well as to provide a compact and objective exposition of the social, political and economic characteristics of the country.

OCEANIA

GENERAL WORKS

331. U.S. Department of the Army. **Area Handbook for Oceania.** By John W. Henderson and others. Washington, GPO, 1971. 555p. $4.00 (cloth). LC Card No. 75-609070. (D 101.22:550-94)

Defined in widest terms, Oceania is a group of islands in the Pacific Ocean spread over about a third of the earth's surface. The term Oceania sometimes refers to the land areas of the south-central Pacific. At other times it is considered to include all islands between Asia and North and South America. Usually, however, the Ryukyu and Aleutian islands, as well as the Japanese archipelago, are not thought of as being included. Ordinarily, also, Indonesia, the Philippines, and Taiwan are regarded as a part of the Asian mainland.

In this handbook Australia and New Zealand, the principal large sovereignties of the area, are excluded. The scope therefore is limited mainly to most of Melanesia, most of Polynesia, and a few islands ordinarily grouped as part of Micronesia. Guam, American Samoa, and the Trust Territory of the Pacific are included in supplementary chapters but are not referred to in the reference summary or the glossary.

Characteristics common to several areas have been noted, and major illustrative examples have been described in some detail. The purpose has been to give the reader a feeling for the general nature of the area rather than to furnish a compendium of factual material supported by statistics. One who wishes to learn more in depth about the separate entities will be able to avail himself of the extensive bibliography that the handbook provides.

332. U.S. Department of the Army. **Pacific Islands and Trust Territories: A Select Bibliography.** Comp. by the Army Library. Washington, GPO, 1971. 171p. $5.00. LC Card No. 75-612338. (D 101.22:550-10)

This bibliography attempts to present a "balanced picture of the problems and prospects in the Pacific Islands in general and in the Trust Territories of the Pacific in particular." Emphasis is on materials published between 1965 and 1970. The bibliography contains detailed annotations, but there is no index. Chapters are 1) The Pacific: The Shifting Strategic Picture; 2) The Pacific Islands: An Overview; 3) The Pacific History in Perspective; 4) Micronesia, Melanesia and Polynesia: Political, Economic and Sociological Patterns; and 5) Source Materials for Further Research and Reference. Twenty-six appendixes contain supporting data such as a glossary, texts of other documents, organization charts, lists of treaties, and statistics. There are several maps in an envelope on the back cover.

ANTARCTICA

333. U.S. Library of Congress. **Antarctic Bibliography, 1951-1961.** Comp. by H. Thomas Bowker. Washington, GPO, 1970. 349p. $4.75 (cloth). LC Card No. 65-61825. (LC 33.9:951-61)

This bibliography fills in the gap between the Navy's *Antarctic Bibliography* (published in 1951) and the series with the same title published on an irregular basis by the Library of Congress (see next entry). It covers the literature of the period 1951 to 1961. The scope is international, including significant materials on such subjects as biological sciences, expeditions, geological sciences, ice and snow, logistics, equipment and supplies, etc. Indexed by author, subject, and geographical area.

334. U.S. Library of Congress. Science and Technology Division. **Antarctic Bibliography, Volume 4.** Ed. by Geza T. Thuronyi. Washington, GPO, 1971. 491p. $5.75 (cloth). LC Card No. 65-61825. S/N 3018-0010. (LC 33.9:4)

This is part of a continuing series which abstracts and indexes current (i.e., since 1962) Antarctic literature. The last volume was published in 1968. The bibliography, international in scope, lists significant materials in biological sciences, expeditions, geological sciences, logistics, equipment and supplies, atmospheric physics, and political geography. Indexed by author, title, and geographic area.

INDIAN OCEAN

335. U.S. Department of the Army. **Area Handbook for the Indian Ocean Territories.** Washington, GPO, 1971. 160p. $2.25 (cloth). LC Card No. 73-171984. (D 101.22:550-154)

The gradual withdrawal of British forces from southern Asia beginning in the late 1960s, and the simultaneous appearance of Soviet naval forces in the same region have focused world attention on the strategic importance of the Indian Ocean area. Two of the island territories recently have become independent republics, and political pressures for more autonomy are being felt elsewhere. None of the territories is economically self-sufficient, however, and the need for economic diversification and development is a recurring theme.

Throughout the area people of widely different ethnic backgrounds have been brought together, and they have formed societies that differ substantially from one territory to another. The social, political, and economic factors affecting their lives are described here to the extent that published information permits.

UNITED STATES

ARCHIVES

336. U.S. National Archives and Records Service. **Administration of Modern Archives: A Select Bibliographic Guide.** Comp. by Frank B. Evans. Washington, Office of National Archives, 1971. 213p. Free from issuing agency. LC Card No. 70-609042. (GS 4.17/3:Ad 6)

This bibliography covers many phases of archival management under two main sections: 1) Introduction to Archives Administration, which includes such topics as archival concepts, terminology and principles, archivists, librarians and manuscript curators; and 2) Survey of Archival Functions, which covers, among other topics, preservation and arrangement of archives and problems of archival management as well as specific types of archival records (e.g., sound recordings, oral history, cartographic records, and still pictures). Within each chapter are "recommended," "suggested," and "additional" readings. Includes books, pamphlets, and journal articles. The "additional readings" section of each chapter is in bibliographic essay form, which will aid the user in determining what works would best suit his needs. Includes a subject index but, regrettably, no author/title index.

337. U.S. National Archives and Records Service. **List of Record Groups in the National Archives and Federal Records Centers.** Rev. ed. Washington, GPO, 1971. 40p. Issuing agency. LC Card No. A 61-71.

Lists record groups, in the first section, alphabetically by key word together with the record group number and a symbol for the unit having archival control over the group. The second part lists groups under operating units with control over them, and the third part is by record group number.

338. U.S. National Archives and Records Service. **Select List of Publications of the National Archives and Records Service.** Washington GPO, 1971. 42p. Issuing agency. (GS 4.22:3/2)

Lists all publications of the National Archives and Records Service which have not been superseded or discontinued. An asterisk by an entry denotes out-of-print materials. Entries are not annotated, and there is no index.

339. U.S. National Archives and Records Services. **Select List of Sound Recordings: Voices of World War II, 1937-45.** Washington, National Archives, 1971. 15p. Issuing agency. (GS 4.22:20)

Lists recordings on file in the National Archives.

GENERAL HISTORY AND AREA STUDIES

340. U.S. Library of Congress. General Reference and Bibliography Division. **A Guide to the Study of the United States of America: Representative Books Reflecting the Development of American Life and Thought.** Prep. under the direction of Roy P. Basler by Donald H. Mugridge and Blanche P. McCrum. Washington, GPO, 1960 (repr. 1971). 1193p. $7.00 (cloth). LC Card No. 60-60009. S/N 3001-0011. (LC 2.2:Un 3/4)

This monumental bibliography is concerned with all aspects of American studies. The entries are listed in many chapters which cover the various aspects of a single broad subject and provide extensive treatment in such fields as literature; geography; general, military, intellectual, and local history; periodicals and journalism; population; migration, minorities; society; communications; science and technology; medicine; entertainment; education; religion; music; arts and architecture; economics; government; politics, and many more. In addition to the 6,487 numbered entries, references made in the detailed annotations bring the total to nearly 10,000 works. This work is made even more useful by individual chapter prefaces and a detailed index to authors, subjects, and titles. Cut-off date for inclusion was, in most cases, 1955. The 1972 edition of *Library of Congress Publications in Print* states that a supplement covering 1956-65 imprints is in press.

341. U.S. Library of Congress. **Periodical Literature on the American Revolution, Historical Research and Changing Interpretations, 1895-1970: A Selective Bibliography.** Comp. by Ronald M. Gephart. Washington, GPO, 1971. 93p. $1.00. LC Card No. 74-609228. S/N 3001-0040. LC 2.2:Am 3/3/895-970)

This bibliography was compiled in order to provide students, teachers, scholars, and librarians with a convenient guide to essays and periodical literature about the Revolutionary Period. It is a representative list of studies that have appeared during the past 25 years in periodicals, *festschriften*, and collections of essays or lectures.

342. U.S. National Park Service. **Recording Historic Buildings.** Comp. by Harley J. McKee. Washington, GPO, 1970. 165p. (Historic American Buildings Survey) $3.50 (cloth). LC Card No. 79-606960. (I 29.74:R 24)

States the principles and standards for recording historic architecture by the Historic American Buildings Survey. Two sections are of particular interest: the first describes in detail the process for cataloging historic buildings; the second is a classified bibliography. This work is profusely illustrated and thoroughly indexed.

343. U.S. National Park Service. **Soldier and Brave: Historic Places Associated with Indian Affairs and the Indian Wars in the Trans-Mississippi West.** Washington, GPO, 1971. 453p. $4.00 (cloth). S/N 2405-0236. (I 29.2:H 62/9/v. 12)

The purpose of this volume is to "focus attention on, and stimulate further activities in, the field of historic preservation." Part one is a brief narrative background for the period of early exploration and settlement. The second part consists of evaluations and descriptions of the historic sites and structures of the period. Includes end-notes, a list of selected readings, and a comprehensive index.

MILITARY HISTORY

AIR FORCE

344. U.S. Department of the Air Force. **United States Air Force History: An Annotated Bibliography.** Comp. by Mary Ann Cresswell and Carl Berger. Washington, GPO, 1971. 106p. $0.50. S/N 0870-0307. (D 301.62/2:H 62)

This annotated bibliography on U.S. Air Force history is a sampling of the literature about military aviation and aviators, and their deeds in war and peace. Works are listed under broad subject areas with special chapters on "Reference Works and Guides," "Bibliographies," "Guide to Documentary Collections," and "List of Serial Publications." Indexed by author and subject.

ARMY

345. U.S. Office of the Chief of Military History. **Publications of the Office of the Chief of Military History, United States Army.** Washington, GPO, 1970. 22p. Issuing agency. LC Card No. 76-605851. (D 114.10:970)

346. U.S. Office of the Chief of Military History. **Publications of the Office of the Chief of Military History, United States Army.** Washington, GPO, 1971. 20p. Issuing agency. (D 114.10:971)

This is an annotated bibliography of available publications.

MARINE CORPS

347. U.S. Marine Corps. **United States Marine Corps Ranks and Grades, 1775-1969.** By Bernard C. Nalty and others. Rev. ed. Washington, Marine

Corps, 1970. 62p. (Marine Corps Historical Reference Pamphlet) Issuing agency. LC Card No. 79-609193. (D 214.14/2:R 16)

 Describes the differences or changes in ranks in the Marines from 1775 through 1969.

348. U.S. Marine Corps. **A Concise History of the United States Marine Corps, 1775-1969.** Washington, GPO, 1971. 143p. $1.25. LC Card No. 74-608606. S/N 0855-0050. (D 214.13:M 34/2/775-969)

 This concise history of the Marine Corps contains highlights of significant events and provides an extensive guide for further reading.

349. U.S. Marine Corps. **Annotated Reading List of Marine Corps History.** Comp. by Jack B. Hilliard and Harold A. Bivins. Rev. ed. Washington, Marine Corps, 1971. 55p. (Marine Corps Historical Reference Pamphlet) Issuing agency. LC Card No. 77-614145. (D 214.14/2:H 62/7)

NAVY

350. U.S. Office of Naval Operations. **American Ships of the Line.** Washington, GPO, 1970. 44p. $0.50. LC Card No. 75-605867. (D 207.10/2:Sh 6/4)

 A ship of the line is defined as "a ship of war large enough to have a place in the line of battle." This publication provides an historical narrative on the development of these ships and contains the authorizing legislative acts in chronological order, followed by historical sketches of individual ships.

351. U.S. Office of Naval Operations. **Civil War Naval Chronology, 1861-65.** Prep. by Robert L. Scheina and George K. McCuistion. Washington, GPO, 1971. 1131p. $9.75 (cloth). LC Card No. 71-609471. (D 207.2:C 49/comp.)

 This is a compilation of six earlier volumes published from 1961 to 1966. Each volume contained day-by-day accounts of the Navy's actions in the Civil War for a year. Volume six contained special studies and an extensive index. All volumes contain many maps and photographs. This work is now much easier to use because it is all in one volume.

352. U.S. Office of Naval Operations. **Dictionary of American Naval Fighting Ships; Volume 5, N-Q.** Washington, GPO, 1971. 639p. $6.75 (cloth). LC Card No. 60-60198. S/N 0846-0051. (D 207.10:5)

 Previous volumes were published as follows: Volume 1 (1959), A-B; Volume 2 (1963), C-F; Volume 3 (1968), G-K; Volume 4 (1969), L-M. When complete, this work will make available basic information on every naval ship that has "served its part in shaping the history . . . of the United States." Its purpose is to "give the concise facts about every ship so that it may be a ready reference for those who have served in the ships and for the student, writer, and many others." The descriptions of each ship include tonnage, length, beam, draft, speed, armament, and class; and where known, the builder, sponsor, launching and commission dates, date of acquisition by the Navy, first commanding officer, and a concise operational history. Each volume also includes a bibliography, appendixes for various types of ships in the modern and historic Navy, and illustrations. Expected to be completed by 1976.

353. U.S. Office of Naval Operations. **Naval Documents of the American Revolution: Volume 5.** Edited by William James Morgan. Washington, GPO, 1971. 1486p. $13.25 (cloth). LC Card No. 64-60087. (D 207.12:5)

Covers the American theatre from May 9 through July 31, 1776. The following volumes have also been published:

> Volume 1: American Theatre, December 1, 1774—September 2, 1775; European Theatre, December 6, 1774—August 9, 1775. 1451p. $9.00.
>
> Volume 2: American Theatre, September 3—October 31, 1775; European Theatre, August 11—October 31, 1775; American Theatre, November 1—December 7, 1775. 1463p. $8.00.
>
> Volume 3: American Theatre, December 8—31, 1775; European Theatre, November 1, 1775—January 31, 1776; American Theatre, January 1—February 18, 1776. 1486p. $9.75.
>
> Volume 4: American Theatre, February 19—April 17, 1776; European Theatre, February 1—May 25, 1776; American Theatre, April 18—May 8, 1776. 1580p. $14.25.

In each volume, documents are listed chronologically and bibliographies and indexes are provided.

354. U.S. Office of Naval Operations. **U.S. Naval History Sources in the Washington Area and Suggested Research Subjects.** Comp. by Dean C. Allard and Betty Bern. 3rd ed., rev. and enl. Washington, GPO, 1970. 82p. $1.00. LC Card No. 77-608391. S/N 0846-0044. (D 207.6/2:H 62/970)

Designed to serve as an aid to scholars and other writers working in the field of naval history by identifying archival, manuscript and other special collections in the Washington, D.C., area. This edition includes, for the first time, specific information on the holdings of individual collections. A lengthy list entitled "Some Suggested Research Subjects" is appended. Indexed by institutions, persons, and titles.

LAW

GENERAL WORKS

BIBLIOGRAPHIES

355. U.S. Social and Rehabilitation Service. **Legal Bibliography for Juvenile and Family Courts; Supplement 3, 1969.** By William H. Sheridan and Alice B. Freer. Washington, GPO, 1970. 36p. $0.45. LC Card No. HEW 66-96. (HE 17.17:L 52/supp.3)

    This supplement updates the bibliographies published in 1966, 1967, and 1968 (FS 14.112:L 52 and supp. 1-2). It is designed for use by "judges, probation officers, law enforcement personnel, counsel, and other professional persons in the field of delinquency and the law." Cites journal articles and specific cases. Chapters cover specific subjects, with alphabetical arrangement within each chapter. There are no indexes.

DIRECTORIES

356. U.S. Commission on Civil Rights. Clearinghouse. **Civil Rights Directory.** Rev. ed. Washington, GPO, 1970. 195p. (CHP No. 15) $0.75. LC Card No. 74-610026. (CR 1.10:15)

    Consists of five sections: Section A lists officials of federal agencies who are responsible for monitoring, administering, coordinating, and enforcing various aspects of equal opportunity laws and policies. A name index immediately follows this section. Section B, "Federal officials with liaison responsibility for programs of special interest to Mexican Americans," includes agencies which administer programs "to assist in furthering the social and economic progress of the American people." Section C, "National private organizations with civil rights programs," is a cross section of groups which are concerned almost exclusively with civil rights or those which have developed strong civil rights programs. Section D lists official state agencies with civil rights responsibilities, and Section E, county and municipal agencies.

357. U.S. Department of Justice. **Register of the Department of Justice and the Courts of the United States.** Washington, GPO, 1970. 124p. $4.00. LC Card No. 3-11924. (J 1.7:970)

358. U.S. Department of Justice. **Register of the Department of Justice and the Courts of the United States: First Revision, 1971.** Washington, GPO, 1971. 125p. $4.00. (J 1.7:970/rev. 1)

    Divided into five general sections: 1) "Principal officers of the Department in Washington," arranged by rank with names of officers, date of original appointment and appointment to present position; 2) "Officers of the Administrative Office of the United States Courts"; 3) "The Federal Judiciary: United States Courts" and "Department of Justice: United States Attorneys and Marshals," which first lists the Supreme Court Justices and officials, then gives the "allotment of Supreme Court Justices to circuits," arranged by circuit (five subdivisions are: a) U.S. Courts of Appeals, by circuit; b) U.S. Court of Claims; c) U.S. Court of Customs and Patent Appeals; d) U.S. Customs Court; and e) U.S. District Courts, by districts, which includes attorneys and marshals for each district); 4) "United States penal and correctional institutions" lists wardens and other officials at institutions throughout the U.S.; 5) an appendix lists former officers of the Department of Justice chronologically within each position. Index to all names. Now issued in looseleaf form.

HANDBOOKS AND GUIDES

359. U.S. Department of Justice. **Handbook on the Law of Search and Seizure.** Washington, GPO, 1971. 54p. $0.35. S/N 2700-0067. (J 1.8/2: Se 1/971)

This handbook provides a general set of guidelines for personnel of government agencies performing law enforcement or investigative functions. Its purpose is to provide ready access to the main threads of the law in the area of search and seizure in order to assist agents when confronted with problems requiring quick decisions.

360. U.S. Department of Labor. Wage and Hour and Public Contracts Division. **Handy Reference Guide to the Fair Labor Standards Act (Federal Wage Hour Law).** Washington, GPO, 1970. 16p. $0.25. (L 22.5:F 15/3/970)

361. U.S. Department of Labor. Wage and Hour Division. **Handy Reference Guide to the Fair Labor Standards Act (Federal Wage Hour Law).** Washington, GPO, 1971. 16p. $0.25. (L 22.5:F 15/3/971)

Provides general information concerning the application of the act as amended.

362. U.S. Department of Labor. Wage and Hour Division. **A Guide to Child Labor Provisions of the Fair Labor Standards Act.** Rev. ed. Washington, GPO, 1971. 34p. $0.20. S/N 2905-0017. (L 22.14:101/14)

The Fair Labor Standards Act, in addition to its basic minimum wage and overtime provisions, contains provisions relating especially to child labor. This booklet has been developed as a guide to these provisions.

363. U.S. House of Representatives. **Antitrust Laws, with Amendments, 1890-1970.** Comp. by Gilman G. Udell. Washington, GPO, 1971. 144p. $0.65. LC Card No. 24-26651. S/N 5201-0038. (Y 1.2:An 8/971)

This compilation of laws includes the Sherman Act, Clayton Act, Federal Trade Commission Act, Export Trade Act, Banking Corporations Authorized to do Foreign Banking Business, National Industrial Recovery Act, and Price Discrimination.

364. U.S. House of Representatives. Committee on the Judiciary. **How to Find U.S. Statutes and U.S. Code Citations.** Rev. ed. Washington, GPO, 1971. 8p. $0.10. S/N 5270-1309. (Y 4.J 89/1:St 29/4/971)

This guide has been designed to enable the user to obtain—quickly and easily—an up-to-date and accurate citation to the United States Statutes at Large and the United States Code. A brief description on how to use this guide is given in the introduction. In tabular form, this work will take the user through all steps necessary to find the correct citation. E.g., if user has only the name of the law or date of the law, this guide shows the correct procedure, works to consult and in what order, and final citation, with specific examples of each.

365. U.S. National Labor Relations Board. **A Layman's Guide to Basic Law Under the National Labor Relations Act.** Rev. ed. Washington, GPO, 1970. 59p. $0.35. LC Card No. 72-610004. (LR 1.6/2:L 45/970)

Provides a basic framework for a better understanding of the National Labor Relations Act and its administration. Includes a special chart that arranges systematically the types of cases in which an employer or a labor organization may be involved under the Act, including both unfair labor practice cases and representation election proceedings.

TREATIES

366. U.S. Department of State. **Treaties in Force: A List of Treaties and Other International Agreements of the United States in Force on January 1, 1970.** Washington, GPO, 1970. 386p. $2.75. LC Card No. 56-61604. (S 9.14:970)

367. U.S. Department of State. **Treaties in Force: A List of Treaties and Other International Agreements of the United States in Force on January 1, 1971.** Washington, GPO, 1971. 394p. $2.75. LC Card No. 56-61604. S/N 4400-1334. (S 9.14:971)

Lists all treaties and other international agreements signed by the President and in force between the United States and foreign countries. Part one lists bilateral treaties and other agreements first by country and then by subjects. Part two lists multilateral treaties and agreements by subject with names of participating countries after each entry. Kept up to date during each year by the weekly issues of the Department of State *Bulletin*.

POLITICAL SCIENCE AND INTERNATIONAL RELATIONS

COMMUNISM

368. U.S. Department of State. **World Strength of the Communist Party Organizations.** Washington, GPO, 1970. 223p. $1.75. (S 1.111:970)

369. U.S. Department of State. **World Strength of the Communist Party Organizations.** Washington, GPO, 1971. 248p. $1.75. LC Card No. 56-60986. S/N 4400-1346. (S 1.111:971)
    Provides statistical and analytical reviews of world communist parties in and out of power. Arrangement is alphabetical within geographical regions, excluding the Communist Party of the United States. Information includes date of last election; vote totals for communists and non-communists; percentage figures of total votes; number and percentage of seats in government; and estimated party membership. A useful checklist provides brief details with page reference to complete reviews.

INTERNATIONAL AFFAIRS

GENERAL WORKS

DIRECTORIES

370. U.S. Department of State. **Biographic Register.** Washington, GPO, 1970. 465p. (Department and Foreign Service Series. Publication 7722) $4.50. LC Card No. 9-22072. (S 1.69:126)

371. U.S. Department of State. **Biographic Register.** Washington, GPO, 1971. 468p. (Department and Foreign Service Series. Publication 7722) $4.50. (S 1.69:126/6)
    The *Biographic Register* provides "information and background on personnel of the Department of State and the Foreign Service, and other Federal Government Agencies that participate in the field of foreign affairs." Includes biographies for ambassadors, ministers, foreign service officers, reserve officers, chiefs of overseas missions, employees of comparable grade in the Agency for International Development, Peace Corps, U.S. Information Agency, and Foreign Agricultural Service of the Department of Agriculture. Civil Service employees of the Department of State in Grade GS-12 and above are included. For each individual the following information is given: place of birth, college, degree, military service, State Department assignments and dates, rank, and the name of a foreign language in which that individual has received a rating of at least S-3 through examinations of the Foreign Service Institute.

372. U.S. Department of State. **Foreign Consular Offices in the United States, 1970.** Washington, GPO, 1970. 90p. $0.45. LC Card No. 32-26478. (S 1.69:128/6)

373. U.S. Department of State. **Foreign Consular Offices in the United States, 1971.** Washington, GPO, 1971. 94p. $0.45. (S 1.69:128/7)

This is the official listing of foreign consular offices in the United States. Under each country consular offices are listed by state and city. Gives name, rank, jurisdiction of chief officer, and date of recognition. Consuls are indicated as provisionally recognized, commissioned, or non-commissioned.

GUIDES

374. U.S. Department of State. **A Pocket Guide to Foreign Policy Information Materials and Services of the Department of State.** Washington, GPO, 1971. 18p. $0.20. (S 1.40/2:F 76/971)

Lists information materials in a bibliographic essay. Also contains a subject listing of "other sources of information," which tells where to write for data on such things as arms control, consular affairs, economics, etc.

375. U.S. Senate. Committee on Foreign Relations. **Legislation on Foreign Relations with Explanatory Notes.** Washington, GPO, 1971. 1112p. $4.50. S/N 5270-1050. (Y 4.F 76/2:L 52/971)

The full texts of laws relating to foreign relations are listed here, together with annotations showing the history of the laws.

MILITARY AFFAIRS

376. U.S. Arms Control and Disarmament Agency. **Arms Control Achievements, 1959-1971.** Washington, GPO, 1971. 14p. $0.25. S/N 0200-0039. (AC 1.2:Ac 4/959-71)

A brief summary of arms control agreements entered into by the United States since 1959.

377. U.S. Arms Control and Disarmament Agency. **World Military Expenditures, 1969.** Washington, GPO, 1970. 26p. $0.60. LC Card No. 76-601635. (AC 1.16:969)

378. U.S. Arms Control and Disarmament Agency. **World Military Expenditures, 1970.** Washington, GPO, 1971. 37p. $0.65. LC Card No. 76-601635. (AC 1.16:970)

Charts and graphs for world military expenditures are provided, plus related data on expenditures for education and health, gross national product, etc.

379. U.S. Department of the Army. **Nuclear Weapons and NATO: An Analytical Survey of the Literature.** Washington, GPO, 1970. 450p. $7.50. LC Card No. 79-607373. (D 101.22:50-1)

This book of bibliographic material on nuclear weapons and the North Atlantic Treaty Organization was compiled by research analysts of the United States Army Library in response to requests for sources of current information on the subject. It updates a similar survey published in 1965 and includes over

900 abstracts. It also contains background notes and maps on each member state of NATO with texts of various treaties, charts and other useful information. A bibliographic supplement covers Communist China's nuclear threat in order to "point up the shrinking nuclear dimensions of the world with implications to both the West and the East." Entries are categorized into: "NATO at the 20 Year Mark," "West European Security and National Aspirations," "East-West Strategic Balance: Influencing Factors," and "Arms Control, Disarmament and Nuclear Proliferation." A list of general references is also included. Not indexed.

PROTOCOL

380. U.S. Department of State. **Diplomatic Social Usage: A Guide for United States Representatives and Their Families Abroad.** Washington, GPO, 1971. 20p. $0.30. S/N 4400-1354. (S 1.40/2:D 62/2)

This publication, a guide for U.S. representatives abroad, introduces basic rules of protocol and some of the needed social usage practices. It discusses the responsibilities of foreign service members and gives complete details on visiting, entertaining, dress, titles, introductions, and accepted courtesies. Examples are provided in most cases.

381. U.S. Office of Naval Operations. **Social Usage and Protocol: A Guide for Personnel of the U.S. Navy.** Washington, GPO, 1970. 69p. $1.00. LC Card No. 72-610055. (D 207.6/2:So 1)

Provides guidance on social usage and protocol matters for U.S. Naval personnel involved in planning, organizing, and conducting official and unofficial social events, and gives current information on formal and informal activities which have a distinctly naval, military and/or diplomatic setting.

RESEARCH

382. U.S. Department of State. **Foreign Affairs Research, Special Papers Available: Near East and South Asia; A List of Papers Accessioned Between 1964-70 in the Foreign Affairs Research Documentation Center.** Washington, Department of State, 1970. 72p. (Office of External Research) Issuing agency. (S 1.126/2:N 27)

383. U.S. Department of State. **Foreign Affairs Research, Special Papers Available: Western Europe, Great Britain, and Canada; A List of Papers Accessioned Between 1964-1970 in the Foreign Affairs Research Documentation Center.** Washington, Department of State, 1970. 72p. (Office of External Research) Issuing agency. (S 1.126/2:W 52)

In both of these bibliographies, general works are listed first by subject followed by a list of materials on specific countries. There are no annotations or index.

384. U.S. Department of State. **Government-Supported Research: International Affairs; Research Completed and in Progress, July 1968—June 1969.**

Prep. by the Office of External Research. Washington, GPO, 1970. 158p. Issuing agency. (S 1.126:In 8)

385. U.S. Department of State. **Government-Supported Research: International Affairs; Research Completed and in Progress, July 1969—June 1970.** Prep. by Allan E. Suchinsky and Janet Nash. Washington, GPO, 1971. 216p. Issuing agency. (S 1.101/9:969-70)

    The catalog describes current research projects in the social and behavioral studies dealing with international affairs, foreign affairs, and U.S. government foreign policy. Lists only those projects conducted by private organizations and individuals under contract with, or grants from, the federal government. Research projects are listed under subjects and are briefly annotated. Includes a geographic index and an index of contractors, researchers and titles.

UNITED STATES GOVERNMENT

ATLASES

386. U.S. Bureau of the Census. **Congressional District Atlas: Districts of the 92d Congress.** Washington, GPO, 1970. $1.75. LC Card No. A 66-7901. S/N 0301-0142. (C 3.62/5:970)

    Official maps for Congressional representatives. Counties of the United States are keyed to maps of their Congressional districts, which are arranged alphabetically by state. In addition, this atlas includes listings of the Congressional district or districts in which counties and specified cities are located, and provides an alphabetical list of the counties in each Congressional district.

BIBLIOGRAPHIES

387. U.S. Senate. Committee on Government Operations. **Bibliography of Federal Grants-in-Aid to State and Local Governments, 1964-1969.** Prep. by the Legislative Reference Service. Washington, GPO, 1970. 456p. $1.75. LC Card No. 76-610490. (Y 4.G 74/6:G 76/6)

    Although not exhaustive, this is a very extensive list of references to federal grants-in-aid programs. The bibliography is divided into 24 subject areas, arranged alphabetically. Cross references at the beginning of each subject refer the user to other chapters in which related information may be found. Entries within each chapter are arranged alphabetically by author or title (if no author is known). One especially useful chapter lists catalogs of federal aid programs. Not indexed.

DIRECTORIES

388. U.S. Congress. **Biographical Directory of the American Congress, 1774-1971.** Rev. ed. Washington, GPO, 1971. 1972p. $15.75 (cloth). LC Card No. 79-616224. S/N 5271-0249. (92-1:S.doc.8)

    This authoritative directory contains more than 10,800 short biographies of senators and representatives elected or appointed to the Continental

Congress (1774-1788) and to the Congress of the United States from the first through the 91st (1789-1971). Also included are lists of the officers of the executive branch of government from the administration of George Washington through that of Richard Nixon; the delegates to the Continental Congress and all members of Congress up to 1971. For the first time, this edition contains biographies of presidents who have never served as members of Congress.

389. U.S. Congress. Joint Committee on Printing. **Congressional Pictorial Directory, 92nd Congress.** Washington, GPO, 1971. 202p. $2.75. LC Card No. 68-61223. S/N 5270-0568. (Y 4.P 93/1:1p/92)

   A pocket directory of members of Congress, containing photographs of the President, Vice-President, and Senate and House members. It also lists members of Congress by state and alphabetically within each house.

390. U.S. Congress. Joint Committee on Printing. **Official Congressional Directory for the Use of the Congress, 91st Congress, 2d Session, Beginning January 19, 1970.** Washington, GPO, 1970. 1037p. $4.00 (cloth); $5.50 (thumb-indexed). LC Card No. 6-35330. (Y 4.P 93/1:1/91-2)

391. U.S. Congress. Joint Committee on Printing. **Official Congressional Directory for the Use of the Congress, 92d Congress, 1st Session, Convened January 21, 1971.** Washington, GPO, 1971. 1064p. $3.00; $5.50 (cloth); $7.00 (thumb-indexed). LC Card No. 6-35330. (Y 4.P 93/1:1/92-1)

   This directory includes 1) biographies by state of senators and representatives; 2) delegations by state with names of senators and representatives; 3) alphabetical lists of senate and house members with home address, Washington address, and page number of biographies; 4) chronological lists of terms in office by year of expiration and by years of continuous service; 5) lists of committees and members; 6) administrative assistants and secretaries; 7) statistical information on sessions of Congress, votes cast in last elections for senators, representatives and governors; 8) officers of the Senate and House; 9) officers in executive departments and independent agencies; 10) biographies of members of the Supreme Court; 11) government of the District of Columbia; 12) list of international organizations and officials; 13) foreign diplomatic representatives and consular offices in the United States; 14) U.S. diplomatic and consular offices; 15) members of the press admitted to House and Senate galleries, newspapers represented, photographers admitted, television and radio newsmen admitted; and 16) maps of Congressional districts. Altogether, there is biographical material on over 1,500 top staff personnel in the legislative branch, all of which is cross-indexed. Also contains a general index of names.

392. U.S. Department of the Army. **United States Army Installations and Major Activities in the Continental United States.** Washington, GPO, 1970. 17p. $0.30. LC Card No. 55-63776. (D 101.22:210-1/25)

   Contains a list of Army bases and major activities (limited to depots, hospitals and industrial activities). One list is alphabetical by name, showing the address of each, the other is an alphabetical listing with each U.S. Army

Area and the Military District of Washington, showing the location of each installation and the activity at it.

393. U.S. National Archives and Records Service. **Directory of U.S. Government Audiovisual Personnel.** Washington, GPO, 1970. 58p. Issuing agency. LC Card No. 79-607199. (GS 4.24:970)

394. U.S. National Archives and Records Service. **Directory of U.S. Government Audiovisual Personnel.** Washington, GPO, 1971. 73p. Issuing agency. LC Card No. 79-607199. (GS 4.24:971)

    Lists names of federal agencies' personnel who are concerned with radio, television, motion pictures, sound recordings, exhibits, and graphic arts.

INDEXES

395. U.S. Senate. **Cumulative Index of Congressional Committee Hearings (Not Confidential in Character): 3d Quadrennial Supplement, 90th Congress (January 2, 1967)—91st Congress (January 2, 1971).** Comp. by Carmen Carpenter and Polly Sargent. Washington, GPO, 1971. 695p. $7.50 (cloth). S/N 5201-0049. (Y 1.3:H 35/2/959/supp.-3)

    This index is of value primarily to those persons seeking information about the actual publication of hearings. Citations are to numbers assigned in the Senate library and are thus not applicable to other libraries. Hearings are indexed by subject, by committee, and by bill number.

MANUALS

396. U.S. House of Representatives. **Constitution, Jefferson's Manual, and Rules of the House of Representatives of the United States 92d Congress.** Washington, GPO, 1971. 797p. $3.25. S/N 5271-0230. (92-1:H.doc. 439)

    Popularly known as the *House Manual*, this publication is issued for each session of Congress. It contains the rules of the House of Representatives, with notes and annotations.

397. U.S. Marine Corps. **Flag Manual.** Washington, GPO, 1971. 101p. $0.70. S/N 0854-0055. (D 214.9/2:F 59)

    This manual sets forth designs and prescribes the use and display of flags, guidons, streamers, and automobile and aircraft plates used within the Marine Corps. It contains a history and background of the national flag, and color illustrations depicting prominent flags of our early history, the Marine Corps, the United Nations, and the President and other government officials.

398. U.S. Office of the Federal Register. **United States Government Organization Manual, 1970-71.** Washington, GPO, 1970. 820p. $3.00. LC Card No. 35-26025. (GS 4.109:970)

399. U.S. Office of the Federal Register. **United States Government Organization Manual, 1971/72.** Washington, GPO, 1971. 809p. $3.00. LC Card No. 35-26025. S/N 2203-0887. (GS 4.109:971)

This official organization handbook of the federal government describes the creation and authority, organization, and functions of the agencies in the legislative, judicial, and executive brances; provides supplemental information including brief descriptions of quasi-official agencies and selected international organizations. Included in most agency statements are new "Sources of Information" listings which tell the public what offices to contact for information on such matters as consumer activities, environmental programs, government contracts, services to small businesses, employment, and the availability of speakers and films for educational and civic groups. Also included are approximately 45 charts showing the organization of the government, the Senate, the House of Representatives, the departments, and the major independent agencies; a literal print of the Constitution of the United States, its signers, and amendments to date; an alphabetical listing of names mentioned in the manual; and a comprehensive index.

400. U.S. Senate. **Senate Manual.** Washington, GPO, 1971. 924p. $3.75. S/N 5271-0241. (92-1:S.doc. 1)

This biennial publication contains a wealth of information, including the general rules regarding the conduct of the Senate; *Jefferson's Manual*, lists of presidents pro tempore of the Senate from the first Senate on; lists of Senators; numbers of electoral votes in presidential elections; justices of the Supreme Court, etc.

RECREATION AND TRAVEL

GENERAL WORKS

401. U.S. Federal Power Commission. **Recreation Opportunities at Hydroelectric Projects Licensed by the Federal Power Commission.** Washington, GPO, 1971. 78p. $2.00. S/N 1500-0011. (FP 1.2:R 24/970)

This guide for outdoor recreation contains a summary of the 515 reservoir-lakes and more than 6,200 recreational facilities maintained for the use of the entire American public at hydroelectric power projects licensed by the Federal Power Commission. Map-keyed pages list the recreational facilities available at each licensed project.

402. U.S. Travel Service. **Festival U.S.A., 1972.** Washington, GPO, 1971. 39p. $0.45. S/N 0312-0013. (C 47.2:F 42/972)

Lists more than 500 events occurring in the United States in 1972, including major sporting events in the fields of horseracing, auto racing, tennis, golf, boating, surfing and skiing. "Fun" festivals such as the National Egg Striking Contest, the Jumping Frog Rodeo, and the National Marbles Tournament are included.

ARTS AND CRAFTS

403. U.S. Department of the Army. **Crafts Techniques in Occupational Therapy.** Washington, GPO, 1971. 508p. (Technical Manual, TM 8-290) $4.50. S/N 0820-0397. (D 101.11:8-290)

Provides a basic knowledge of the major arts and crafts and the most common tools associated with them. It includes chapters on art and design; ceramics; mosaics; plastics; metalwork and jewelry; weaving; cord knotting or macrame; braiding and hooked rugs; huck toweling, rake knitting, and needlework; leather; printing; woodworking; engines; and children's activities.

OUTDOOR RECREATION

ASSISTANCE PROGRAMS

GOVERNMENT ASSISTANCE PROGRAMS

404. U.S. Bureau of Outdoor Recreation. **Federal Assistance in Outdoor Recreation, Available to States, Their Subdivisions, Organizations, Individuals.** Rev. ed. Washington, GPO, 1970. 100p. $0.50. (I 66.11:1/5)

Gives information on programs under which states, their political subdivisions, individuals, groups and associations may qualify for assistance in outdoor recreation programs such as credit, cost-sharing, technical aid, educational services and research. Arranged by departments and their bureaus with full descriptions of the programs.

405. U.S. Bureau of Outdoor Recreation. **Federal Outdoor Recreation Programs and Recreation-Related Environmental Programs.** Washington, GPO, 1970. 226p. $2.75. LC Card No. 70-607632. (I 66.2:P 94/970)

This work was prepared as part of the Bureau of Outdoor Recreation's responsibility to "formulate and maintain a comprehensive nationwide outdoor recreation plan." The first section is arranged by departments of the federal government, subdivided by their agencies and bureaus, which have outdoor recreation responsibilities. The functions of the agencies are summarized in this part with their specific outdoor recreation programs listed and cross-referenced to the detailed descriptions in the second section. Two indexes are provided: Index A is a "cross-reference chart" to programs (arranged alphabetically) showing type of program, supervising agency, and page number of the detailed description in Part B. Index B is an alphabetical listing of the federal agencies and bureaus which have outdoor recreation programs with page references to Part A.

406. U.S. Travel Service. **Inventory of Federal Tourism Programs, Federal Agencies, Commissions, Programs Reviewed for Their Participation in the Development of Recreation, Travel, and Tourism in the United States.** Washington, GPO, 1970. 88p. $0.75. LC Card No. 78-607721. (C 47.2:T 64/3)

Provides information on the extent to which the federal government is a participant in travel, recreation, and tourism development. The programs are reviewed by department and agency and then categorized into the following eight major areas: natural resources, recreation, cities, historic areas, transportation, data, travelers and cultural attractions. Gives program titles, authorizing legislation, person or department to contact for further information and the purpose of the program.

PRIVATE ASSISTANCE PROGRAMS

407. U.S. Bureau of Outdoor Recreation. **Private Assistance in Outdoor Recreation: A Directory of Organizations Providing Aid to Individuals and Public Groups.** Washington, GPO, 1970. 82p. $0.45. LC Card No. 79-608082. (I 66.2:D 62/2/970)

A selective listing of organizations which provide inexpensive "publications and other aids to the planning, development, and operation of outdoor recreation areas." Includes nonprofit professional societies and national organizations. Arranged alphabetically by specific type of recreation (e.g., archery, fishing, picnicking) with the concerned groups and their publications within these subjects. Gives a brief statement of policy for each organization, and a very brief annotation for each publication (including price and frequency).

408. U.S. President's Council on Youth Opportunity. **Camping Opportunities for Disadvantaged Youth: Planning and Coordinating Guide.** Washington, GPO, 1971. 80p. $0.75. (Pr 36.8:Y 8/C 15)

Of particular note are the following appendixes: 1) a directory of source contacts for information on improving camping opportunities for children and youth of low-income areas; 2) contacts within the Office of Surplus Property Utilization; 3) a directory of state education agencies involved with environmental education; 4) state personnel concerned with environmental education; and 5) colleges and universities which offer environmental/conservation education programs.

NATIONAL PARKS AND RECREATION AREAS

409. U.S. Bureau of Outdoor Recreation. **1971 Directory of Federal Recreation Entrance, Admission, and User Fee Areas.** Washington, GPO, 1971. 24p. Issuing agency. (I 66.16:971)
Lists areas which require fees, but does not indicate the cost.

410. U.S. National Park Service. **Camping in the National Park System.** Rev. ed. Washington, GPO, 1970. 12p. $0.25. (I 29.71:970)
Lists camping accommodations in each area, name and address of area, and name of camping site in the National Parks. Also gives pertinent information for campers such as camping season, campground type, number of sites or spaces, fees, water and toilet facilities, stores, swimming, boating, fishing information, and includes a reference map.

411. U.S. National Park Service. **National Park Guide for the Handicapped.** Washington, GPO, 1971. 80p. $0.40. S/N 2405-0286. (I 29.9/2:H 19)
This is a state-by-state guide to 242 national parks, monuments, historic sites, seashores, and recreation areas offering addresses, descriptions, and a resume of facilities and of obstacles.

412. U.S. National Park Service. **National Parks and Landmarks.** Washington, GPO, 1970. 141p. $0.60. (I 29.66:970)
Gives name, address, acreage, and outstanding characteristics for each of the national parks, monuments, battlefields, cemeteries, historic sites, memorials, parkways, seashores, and recreation areas. Arranged alphabetically within each section by name of the area. Indexed.

RESEARCH

413. U.S. Bureau of Outdoor Recreation. **Outdoor Recreation Research: A Reference Catalog, 1969, No. 3.** Prep. in cooperation with the Science Information Exchange of the Smithsonian Institution. Washington, GPO, 1970. 126p. $1.25. LC Card No. 68-61830. (I 66.18:3)

414. U.S. Bureau of Outdoor Recreation. **Outdoor Recreation Research: A Reference Catalog, 1970, No. 4.** Prep. in cooperation with the Science Information Exchange of the Smithsonian Institution. Washington, GPO, 1971. 118p. $1.25. LC Card No. 68-61830. (I 66.18:4)
Based on project outlines submitted by outdoor recreation research workers throughout America, these volumes present brief descriptions of

currently active or recently completed outdoor recreation and related environmental research projects, to promote the coordination and development of effective programs relating to outdoor recreation.

STATISTICS

415. U.S. Bureau of Outdoor Recreation. **Selected Outdoor Recreation Statistics.** Washington, GPO, 1971. 145p. $1.25. S/N 2416-0041. (I 66.2: St 2/2/971)

Consists of data on recreation compiled from many federal agencies. Includes statistics on recreation surveys and planning, selected state programs, expenditures, specific activities (golf, fishing, hunting), and special studies. A detailed index facilitates use of this work.

STAMP COLLECTING

416. U.S. Postal Service. **Postage Stamps of the United States.** Washington, GPO, 1970. 241p. $2.00. LC Card No. 22-27645. (P 4.10:970)

This is a comprehensive catalog of all adhesive stamp series issued since the first in 1847, including commemorative stamps and plates. Lists all designers and engravers with their stamps, date of issue and the number in the first issue. Stamp series are arranged chronologically by denomination with information on subject, colors, and dates. Indexed by subjects depicted on stamps.

TRAVEL GUIDES

417. U.S. Armed Forces Information Service. **A Pocket Guide to Vietnam.** Washington, GPO, 1971. 90p. $0.55. LC Card No. 76-612227. S/N 0801-0011. (D 2.8:V 67/971)

This pocket guide provides a brief history of Vietnam as well as information on the customs and ways of the people.

418. U.S. Office of Information for the Armed Forces. **Pocket Guide to Japan.** Washington, GPO, 1970. 116p. $1.00. (D 2.8:J 27/970)

Contains information on the size, political and economic structure, and history of Japan, and the ethnic background and customs of the Japanese. Includes a glossary of commonly used words and phrases, and a selected bibliography.

419. U.S. Office of Information for the Armed Forces. **Pocket Guide to Korea.** Rev. ed. Washington, GPO, 1970. 106p. $1.00. (D 2.8:K 84/970)

This handy guide is designed to be used by U.S. military personnel stationed in Korea, but it is a useful guide for anyone wanting general information on the country. Ranks and uniforms of Korean military personnel are shown, a map and a brief glossary of useful words and phrases are also provided.

420. U.S. Office of Information for the Armed Forces. **Pocket Guide to the Low Countries (Netherlands, Belgium, and Luxembourg).** Rev. ed. Washington, GPO, 1970. 127p. $1.25. (D 2.8:L 95/970)

In addition to general discussions of each country, this guide includes conversion tables for currencies, distance, weights and measures, etc., language guides for French and Dutch, a bibliography, and a list of Dutch signs frequently seen (and an English translation).

SOCIOLOGY

GENERAL WORKS

421. U.S. Social and Rehabilitation Service. **Publications.** Washington, GPO, 1971. 22p. Issuing agency. (HE 17.17:P 96)
    Lists all available publications under issuing division. Gives publication date and cost but is not annotated or indexed.

422. U.S. Social and Rehabilitation Service. **Research 1970: An Annotated List of Research and Demonstration Grants, 1955-69, Cooperative Research or Demonstration Projects, Demonstration Projects, Rehabilitation Research and Demonstration Projects, Research and Training Centers.** Ed. by Dorothy G. Jackson. Washington, GPO, 1970. 263p. Issuing agency. LC Card No. 70-607751. (HE 17.15:970)
    Projects are listed with detailed annotations under types and subjects. Indexed by project numbers and subjects.

MINORITY GROUP RELATIONS

GENERAL WORKS

423. U.S. Commission on Civil Rights. **Catalog of Publications.** Washington, GPO, 1970. 25p. Issuing agency. (CR 1.9:C 28/970)
    In two sections—In Print and Out of Print Publications. Gives title, annotation, year published, pages, SuDocs number, and (for in-print materials) price.

424. U.S. Department of Justice. **Directory of Organizations Serving Minority Communities.** Washington, GPO, 1971. 88p. $1.00. LC Card No. 78-614515. S/N 2700-0077. (J 1.2:Or 3)
    Lists, by state and city, names and addresses of federal agencies, private organizations, colleges and universities, newspapers, and radio and television broadcasters serving women, Negro, Spanish-surname, American-Indian, and Oriental communities.

425. U.S. Manpower Administration. Bureau of Apprenticeship and Training. **Directory for Reaching Minority Groups.** Washington, GPO, 1970. 255p. $2.00. LC Card No. 79-609666. (L 23.2:M 66)
    This directory lists, alphabetically by state and city, the names, addresses, and telephone numbers of organizations and people who are able to reach minority groups to "tell them about affirmative action programs for job training and job opportunities." Following the body of entries for each state are listings of organizations which have statewide or regionwide contacts with special groups.

AMERICAN INDIANS

426. U.S. Bureau of Indian Affairs. **American Indian Calendar.** Washington, GPO, 1970. 40p. $0.25. (I 20.2:C 12/2/970)

427. U.S. Bureau of Indian Affairs. **American Indian Calendar.** Washington, GPO, 1971. 44p. $0.30. S/N 2402-0023. (I 20.2:C 12/2/971)
    A handy guide for tourists and those interested in Indian ceremonies, dances, feasts, and celebrations. Arranged first by state and then by date.

428. U.S. Economic Development Administration. **Federal and State Indian Reservations: An EDA Handbook.** Washington, GPO, 1971. 416p. $3.75. LC Card No. 72-610682. (C 46.8:In 2/3)
    Presents detailed information on federal and state Indian reservations, giving land status, history, culture, government, population profile, tribal economy, climate, transportation, utilities and recreation.

NEGROES

429. U.S. Bureau of Labor Statistics. **Black Americans: A Chartbook.** Washington, GPO, 1971. 141p. $1.25. S/N 2901-0650. (L 2.3:1699)
    This chartbook presents, in tabular and graphic form, information about the progress and problems of blacks in recent years. The primary areas of concern are migration and population, employment and unemployment, income, poverty, family, vital statistics, health, housing, crime, citizenship, and future projections.

430. U.S. Department of the Air Force. **Black Literature.** Prep. by Norman E. Dakan. Washington, Department of the Air Force, 1970. 69p. (PACAF Basic Bibliographies for Base Libraries) Available from CINCPACAF (DPSR) Director, PACAF Libraries, APO, San Francisco, Calif. 96553. LC Card No. 76-611246. (D 301.62:B 56)

431. U.S. Library of Congress. **The Negro in the United States: A Selected Bibliography.** Comp. by Dorothy B. Porter. Washington, GPO, 1970. 313p. $3.25. LC Card No. 78-606085. (LC 1.12/2:N 31)
    "The mounting interest in Negro history and culture, manifested particularly by the introduction of courses in these subjects in high school, college, and university curricula, has given rise to a demand for lists of books that can be used to support such studies." This bibliography is designed to meet the needs of students, teachers, librarians, research, and the general public. It is a selective bibliography on a wide range of subjects related to Negro history and culture in the United States with emphasis on recent monographs in the Library of Congress collection. Entries are alphabetical by author under broad subject headings and include brief annotations only when the title is not self-explanatory. Indexed by subjects and authors.

SPANISH AMERICANS

432. U.S. Cabinet Committee on Opportunity for the Spanish Speaking. **Directory of Spanish Speaking Organizations in the United States.** Washington, GPO, 1970. 224p. Issuing agency. LC Card No. 77-608446. (Y 3.Sp 2/7:2D 62)

Cover title: *Directory of Spanish Speaking Community Organizations.*

This directory was compiled to meet the demands for information about citizen groups involved in their communities which are making contributions toward the social development of the Spanish-surnamed minority. Groups are in alphabetical order by state, city, and name, with a separate section for national organizations. Because only 207 organizations replied to the 800-plus questionnaires, this directory is not very complete. However, it is the only directory of its kind and is considered a "temporary edition" by the Cabinet Committee until such time as a permanent data storage and retrieval system is fully developed.

433. U.S. Cabinet Committee on Opportunities for the Spanish Speaking. **The Spanish Speaking in the United States: A Guide to Materials.** Washington, GPO, 1971. 192p. Free from the Committee. LC Card No. 75-614612. (Y 3.Sp 2/7:2G 94)

This bibliography contains more than 1,300 citations to books, essays, and other materials on Mexican Americans, Puerto Ricans, and Cuban refugees and their role in the social, political, educational, and institutional development of the United States. The bibliography's chapters include books, periodical articles, government publications, theses, serials (including newspapers and magazines), audiovisual materials, Spanish language radio and television stations, and a subject index. Some bibliographic entries are annotated. The subject index refers only to the chapters for books and periodical articles. A supplement is planned which will index theses, government publications, and unpublished works as well as list additional materials on education and provide an author index.

SOCIAL CONDITIONS

AGING

434. U.S. Administration on Aging. **Home Delivered Meals, A National Directory.** Washington, GPO, 1971. 127p. $1.25. S/N 1762-0039. (HE 17.302:M 46)

This directory describes approximately 350 home-delivered meals programs in the United States, alphabetically by state and city. Information includes program name, sponsor, number of meals per week, number of persons served per week, what meals are served, cost if any, provisions for special diets, maximum and minimum length of enrollment and age distribution of participants.

435. U.S. Administration on Aging. **Senior Centers in the United States: A Directory.** Washington, GPO, 1970. 260p. $2.00. LC Card No. 74-607609. (HE 17.302:Se 5/3)

    The previous edition (1966) was entitled *National Directory of Senior Centers.* This directory lists more than 1,200 senior centers and other organizations working specifically with older persons. Centers are listed by state and city, with pertinent data such as hours of operation, address, and eligibility requirements.

436. U.S. Administration on Aging. **Words on Aging: A Bibliography.** Washington, GPO, 1970. 190. $0.75. LC Card No. 76-610099. (HE 17.311:Ag 4)

    This bibliography of selected, annotated references was compiled to assist practioners, teachers, students, and laymen working in the field of aging. It lists periodical articles published from 1963 through 1967 and books from 1900 through 1967. Updated by the following.

437. U.S. Administration on Aging. **More Words on Aging: A Bibliography of Selected 1968-70 References: Supplement.** Washington, GPO, 1971. 107p. $0.55. S/N 1762-0040. (HE 17.311:Ag 4/supp.)

    Covers books, periodical articles and pamphlets published from 1968 through 1970.

438. U.S. Department of Housing and Urban Development. **The Built Environment for the Elderly and the Handicapped: A Bibliography.** Comp. by the Library and Information Division. Washington, GPO, 1971. 46p. $0.50. LC Card No. 78-616473. S/N 2300-1191. (HH 1.23:El 2/2)

    Arranged by broad subjects with complete bibliographical information and brief annotations. Includes a list of periodicals cited, organizations, publishers, and an author index.

439. U.S. Senate. Special Committee on Aging. **Publications List, 87th to 91st Congresses, 1961-1970.** Washington, the Committee, 1971. 8p. Issuing agency. LC Card No. 76-609589. (Y 4.Ag 4:P 96)

CHILDREN AND YOUTH

440. U.S. Children's Bureau. **Research Relating to Children, April—December 1969.** Washington, GPO, 1970. 131p. (Bulletin 25, Clearinghouse for Research in Child Life) $1.25. LC Card No. 52-60018. (HE 21.112:25)

441. U.S. Children's Bureau. **Research Relating to Children, January—May 1970.** Washington, GPO, 1971. 96p. (Bulletin 26, Clearinghouse for Research in Child Life). $1.25. LC Card No. 52-60018. (HE 21.112:26)

442. U.S. Children's Bureau. **Research Relating to Children, June 1970—February 1971.** Prep. by Sandra Byford Wake, Dorothy O'Connell, and Charlene Brash. Washington, GPO, 1971. 138p. (Bulletin 27, ERIC Clearing-

house on Early Childhood Education) $1.50. S/N 1700-0087. (HE 21. 112:27)

443. U.S. Children's Bureau. **Research Relating to Children, March—August 1971.** Prep. by Sandra Byford Wake, Dorothy O'Connell, and Charlene Brash. Washington, GPO, 1971. 141p. (Bulletin 28, ERIC Clearinghouse on Early Childhood Education) $1.50. S/N 1780-0875. (HE 21.112:28)

    This series reports current and recently completed studies on growth and development, personality and adjustment, educational process, exceptional children, the child in the family, socioeconomic and cultural factors, social services, and health services. Contains detailed indexes in each issue.

444. U.S. Maternal and Child Health Service. **Publications of the Centre International de l'Enfance Coordinated Growth Studies, 1951-68.** Comp. by Frank Falkner. Washington, GPO, 1970. 22p. Issuing agency. LC Card No. 74-606581. (HE 20.2759:En 2/951-68)

    Lists works alphabetically by author. Not annotated or indexed.

445. U.S. Office of Child Development. **Guide and Resources for the Community Coordinated Child Care Program.** Washington, GPO, 1971. 140p. Issuing agency. (HE 21.2:C 43)

    Of particular interest are 1) a directory of persons involved in 4-C committees; 2) selected documents developed by pilot projects; 3) selected reference sources; and 4) the appendix which lists regional offices and 4-C publications.

446. U.S. Office of Child Development. Project Head Start. **Bibliography on Early Childhood.** Washington, GPO, 1970. 35p. Issuing agency. LC Card No. 610516. (HE 21.211:Ea 7)

    Items are listed in two sections: books and pamphlets and reprints. Not annotated or indexed.

447. U.S. President's Council on Youth Opportunity. **Youth Resources Manual for Coordinators.** Washington, GPO, 1971. 233p. $1.75. LC Card No. 74-612177. (Pr 36.8:Y 8/48/971)

    Nearly half of this manual contains reference-type information in appendixes. Most of these are directories such as "State and Local Youth Coordinators," "Public Interest Groups," and "National Forest Camps." In addition, each of the nine chapters contains detailed, annotated bibliographies of related publications and films.

448. U.S. White House Conference on Children. **An Annotated Bibliography on Children.** Washington, GPO, 1970. 75p. $0.70. LC Card No. 71-610411. (Y 3.W 58/3-2:9C 43)

    This bibliography was prepared by the Department of Health, Education and Welfare Library for use by the participants in the White House Conference on Children. Covers many areas such as individuality, learning, health, child service institutions, and parents and families. Also includes research reports, trends and achievements over the last five years.

449. U.S. White House Conference on Children. **World of Children: Films from the 1970 White House Conference on Children.** Comp. by Victor Margolin. Washington, GPO, 1970. 18p. $0.40. (Y 3.W 58/3-2:2W 89)

    The films included in this annotated list are resource materials for parents, teachers, doctors, law enforcement officers, and anyone who works with children. They represent some of the best films available, culled from hundreds, on subjects related to children.

450. U.S. Youth Development and Delinquency Prevention Administration. **Publications and Films.** Washington, GPO, 1970. 15p. Issuing agency. (HE 17.809:P 96/970)

    Lists publications and films produced by the Youth Development and Delinquency Prevention Administration. Brief annotations and number of pages (or time, for films) are provided.

SOCIAL PROBLEMS

BEHAVIOR

451. U.S. National Institute for Mental Health. **Television and Social Behavior: An Annotated Bibliography of Research Focusing on Television's Impact on Children.** Ed. by Charles K. Atkin, John P. Murray, and Oguz B. Nayman. Washington, GPO, 1971. 150p. Issuing agency. LC Card No. 70-612410. (HE 20.2417:T 23)

    This bibliography is the by-product of a research program on television and social behavior. It was compiled to provide researchers with an idea of previously conducted research on television and social behavior. The 285 publications are listed in the first sections, which cover such topics as television content and programming, audience viewing patterns, and the impact of television on children and youth. Very detailed annotations are provided. A supplemental reading list gives bibliographic information on an additional 210 publications. Author index refers to both bibliographies.

CRIMINOLOGY

452. U.S. Bureau of Prisons. **Corrections: A Bibliography.** Washington, GPO, 1971. 14p. Issuing agency. (J 16.10:C 81)

453. U.S. Department of Justice. **LEAA Reference List of Publications.** Washington, GPO, 1971. 19p. $0.20. S/N 2700-0078. (J 1.20/2:L 41)

    This is a selected list of publications on law enforcement, criminal justice, federal grants, crime problems, research and development, police, courts, corrections, rehabilitation, juvenile delinquency, collective violence, organized crime, drugs and drug abuse, commission reports, and committee reports. Lists publications describing the programs and activities and the financial and technical assistance provided by the Law Enforcement Assistance Administration (LEAA) for increasing the effectiveness of law enforcement and criminal justice systems throughout the nation.

454. U.S. Department of Justice. **National Jail Census, 1970.** By Anthony Turner. Washington, GPO, 1971. 19p. $0.35. LC Card No. 74-610148. (J 1.37/2:1)

Presents the results of a National Jail Census conducted in the Spring of 1970. Discusses the state of the nation's jails and their inmates; the number of jails; the number and type of inmates; the number of jail employees; operating costs, and other pertinent data. Includes a glossary of terms used.

455. U.S. Department of Transportation. **Hijacking: A Selected List of References.** Springfield, Va., NTIS, 1971. 53p. (Bibliographic List, No. 5) $3.00. LC Card No. 73-614747. (TD 1.15:5)

456. U.S. Federal Bureau of Investigation. **Uniform Crime Reports for the United States, 1969.** Washington, GPO, 1970. 185p. $1.50. LC Card No. 30-27005. (J 1.14/7:969)

457. U.S. Federal Bureau of Investigation. **Crime in the United States: Uniform Crime Reports, 1970.** Washington, GPO, 1971. 208p. $1.75. LC Card No. 30-27005. (J 1.14/7:970)

Provides a nationwide view of crime based on police statistics made possible by the voluntary cooperation of local law enforcement agencies. The first section is for those interested in the general crime picture for the United States. The volume trend and rate of crime related to current populations are discussed in context with the Crime Index offenses. In subsequent sections technical data of interest primarily to police, social scientists and other students are presented. Included are 58 statistical tabulations based on the distribution of crime for the United States as a whole, the regions, geographic divisions, states, and standard metro statistical areas.

DRUG ABUSE

BIBLIOGRAPHIES

458. U.S. National Clearinghouse for Drug Abuse Information. **Drug Dependence and Abuse: A Selected Bibliography.** Washington, GPO, 1971. 51p. $0.60. LC Card No. 73-611414. (PrEx 13.10:D 84/971)

This bibliography is designed to provide an introduction to the scientific as well as the more substantive popular drug abuse literature. Includes works written by "recognizable and authoritative writers," most of them published in 1969 or 1970 (although some "classic" works are listed). Works are listed under broad subjects with no annotations. The introduction states that an updated, annotated edition is planned. Not indexed.

459. U.S. National Clearinghouse for Drug Abuse Information. **Selected Bibliography on the Use of Drugs by Young People.** Washington, GPO, 1971. 4p. (Selected Reference Series 1, No. 1) Issuing agency. (PrEx 13.10/2:1/1)

The books and articles listed were selected on the basis of currency, significance in the field, and availability in bookstores and research libraries.

Works are simply listed without annotation, and the bibliography is not indexed.

460. U.S. National Institute of Mental Health. **Government Publications on Drug Abuse.** Washington, GPO, 1970. 16p. Issuing agency. LC Card No. 73-606747. (HE 20.2417:D 84)

Publication titles are listed under issuing agency and then by intended audience. Gives only titles and annotations.

461. U.S. National Institute of Mental Health. **Selected Bibliography on Drugs of Abuse.** Washington, GPO, 1970. 25p. Issuing agency. LC Card No. 71-606583. (HE 20.2417:D 84/2)

Publications are listed under the following headings: "General Drug Abuse Information," "Hallucinogens (Includes Marihuana)," "Amphetamines and Barbiturates," and "Opiates." Includes books, journal articles and government documents. Not annotated or indexed.

DICTIONARIES

462. U.S. Bureau of Narcotics and Dangerous Drugs. **Glossary of Terms in Drug Culture.** Washington, GPO, 1971. 15p. Issuing agency. LC Card No. 70-611665. (J 24.2:D 84/4)

This glossary of "street" terms for drugs and drug-related activities was prepared by forensic scientists and law enforcement officers.

DIRECTORIES

463. U.S. Bureau of Narcotics and Dangerous Drugs. **Drugs of Abuse.** Washington, GPO, 1970. 16p. $0.40. LC Card No. 74-607877. (J 24.2:D 84)

This booklet presents an identification of the most commonly abused drugs, and includes information on narcotics, marihuana, stimulants, depressants and hallucinogens, a description of the drug, how it is taken (through injection, inhalation, etc.) and its effects; also, the many forms it may take, such as capsule, powder, or tablet. A page of illustrations shows these various forms, and characteristics of each drug. The booklet also presents a detailed chart listing the many slang terms used for each drug, symptoms of abuse, symptoms of withdrawal, dangers of abuse, and manner in which each drug is taken.

464. U.S. Bureau of Narcotics and Dangerous Drugs. **Guidelines for Drug Abuse Prevention Education.** Washington, GPO, 1971. 77p. $0.75. S/N 2704-0016. (J 24.8:D 84/4)

This booklet shows educational approaches to drug abuse prevention and offers sample courses of study from kindergarten to grade 12. It is intended as a guide for programs to be incorporated into the regular school curriculum in such courses as science, health, physical education, biology, and social sciences. The appendix lists many supplementary references and visual aids.

465. U.S. National Clearinghouse for Drug Abuse Information. **Drug Abuse Prevention Materials for Schools.** Washington, GPO, 1971. 48p. $0.50. S/N 1724-0177. (PrEx 13.2:D 84)

This guide provides facts and resources for the teacher on the latest education techniques of drug abuse prevention; how one becomes aware of his own and others' emotional reactions to drug abuse; various proven approaches used in drug prevention and education activities throughout communities in the United States; and beginning approaches or alternatives to drug abuse. Describes the materials to begin effective education about all aspects of drug abuse, particularly relative to elementary, junior, and senior high school students. Order forms are included for obtaining materials from the National Clearinghouse for Drug Abuse Information.

466. U.S. National Institute of Mental Health. **Directory of Narcotic Addiction Treatment Centers in the United States, 1968-69.** By Deena Watson and S. B. Sells. Washington, GPO, 1970. 162p. $1.25. LC Card No. 75-608162. (HE 20.2402:N 16/3/968-69)

This directory is limited to programs focused specifically on the treatment of narcotic addiction. It is a report of a study that has examined treatment in depth and contains information on approximately 150 treatment programs.

467. U.S. National Institute of Mental Health. **Drug Abuse Education Programs Supported by State Education Agencies.** Washington, GPO, 1970. 25p. Issuing agency. LC Card No. 79-606585. (HE 20.2402:D 84/3)

Gives a state-by-state summary of programs including details of selected local programs.

468. U.S. National Institute of Mental Health. **Drug Abuse Information, Education, and Rehabilitation Programs Supported by State Health Agencies and Voluntary Organizations.** Washington, GPO, 1970. 41p. Issuing agency. LC Card No. 78-606582. (HE 20.2402:D 84/4)

Lists states alphabetically with names and addresses of state health commissioners and agencies responsible for drug abuse programs. Gives a summary of each program.

469. U.S. National Institute of Mental Health. **Drug Abuse Information Programs Supported by National Organizations.** Washington, GPO, 1970. 10p. Issuing agency. (HE 20.2402:D 84/5)

Gives a brief summary of the activities of certain national organizations such as the Jaycees. Is not a directory as such, because no addresses or other details are provided.

470. U.S. National Institute of Mental Health. **A Guide to Drug Abuse Education and Information Materials.** Washington, GPO, 1971. 23p. $0.20. LC Card No. 70-611606. S/N 1724-0129. (HE 20.2408:D 84)

This guide describes materials produced by the NIMH on drug abuse education, and gives suggestions for communicating drug information by print, visual, and mass media.

FILMOGRAPHIES

471. U.S. National Clearinghouse for Drug Abuse Information. **Selected Drug Abuse Education Films.** Washington, GPO, 1970. 15p. $0.10. (PrEx 13.8:F 48)

472. U.S. National Clearinghouse for Drug Abuse Information. **Selected Drug Abuse Education Films.** Washington, GPO, 1971. 16p. $0.10. S/N 4110-0012. (PrEx 13.8:F 48/971)

   These publications list films which are considered useful in drug abuse information and education programs. Gives title, producer, distributor, date, description, purchase or rental price, target audience and synopsis of each film.

473. U.S. National Institute of Mental Health. **Films on Drug Abuse.** Washington, GPO, 1970. 21p. Issuing agency. LC Card No. 72-606728. (HE 20.2402:D 84/6)

   This is an annotated listing of films on drug abuse. Gives the following information for each: title and date, length, black and white or color, subjects covered, target audience, producer or distributor, purchase and rental fees, summary of contents.

FAMILY PLANNING

474. U.S. Maternal and Child Health Service. **Selected References for Social Workers on Family Planning: An Annotated List.** Comp. by Mary E. Watts. Washington, GPO, 1971. 38p. $0.50. LC Card No. 78-611907. (HE 20.2759:So 1)

   The purpose of this bibliography is to provide social workers with references to information in articles, pamphlets and books from the past six years. Arranged by broad areas such as "family planning for teenagers." Not indexed.

POVERTY

475. U.S. Social Security Administration. **Poverty Studies in the Sixties: An Annotated Bibliography.** Comp. by James S. Parker. Washington, GPO, 1970. 126p. (SS Publication No. 70-27) $0.60. LC Card No. 78-605471. (HE 3.38: P 86)

   This bibliography includes references to works with a "broad view of the general field of poverty and its related problems" such as housing, unemployment and education. Studies of some antipoverty programs and proposals such as the guaranteed annual income and negative income tax are also included. It covers literature from 1960 through 1969, including selected administrative and research reports prepared by or for federal agencies, with detailed annotations. Indexed by authors.

STATISTICS AND DEMOGRAPHY

BIBLIOGRAPHIES

476. U.S. Bureau of the Census. **Census Bureau Methodological Research, 1969: An Annotated List of Papers and Reports.** Prep. by Deane Harris. Washington, GPO, 1970. 17p. $0.35. LC Card No. 75-602088. (C 3.163/4: M 56/969)

477. U.S. Bureau of the Census. **Census Bureau Methodological Research, 1970: An Annotated List of Papers and Reports.** Prep. by Deane Harris. Washington, GPO, 1971. 15p. $0.30. (C 3.163/4:M 56/970)
   Listing of staff papers and publications about Census Bureau methodological research. The series was initiated to inform the Census staff of research being done, and to "provide access to documents from other relevant research and encourage wider dissemination of reports on research developments." Arranged by type of research, with an author index.

478. U.S. National Archives and Records Service. **Federal Population Censuses, 1790-1890: Catalog of Microfilm Copies of the Schedules.** Washington, National Archives, 1971. 90p. Issuing agency. LC Card No. 72-610891. (GS 4.2:P 81/2/790-890-5)
   Arranged chronologically by census year, followed by name of state or territory (alphabetical) and county. For each microfilm publication, it gives photocopy number, total number of rolls, price, price of the microfilm for each state or territory. Also includes a complete list of microfilm showing for each roll its number, contents, and price.

479. U.S. Public Health Service. National Center for Health Statistics. **Annotated Bibliography on Vital and Health Statistics.** Washington, GPO, 1970. 143p. (Public Health Service Bibliography Series, No. 82) $1.25. LC Card No. 76-608017. (HE 20.11:82)
   This bibliography is intended for researchers, faculty, students, and others in the field of vital and health statistics and is designed to "acquaint the reader with the existence of relevant literature through brief descriptions of the selected citations." It is divided into five major subjects (morbidity, mortality, maternal and infant studies, methodology, and miscellaneous). The 1,001 entries are numbered and the author index refers to entry numbers. Detailed annotations are given.

COMPENDIA

480. U.S. Bureau of the Census. **1970 Census Users' Guide.** Prep. by the User Communication Staff. Washington, GPO, 1970. 2 pts. $1.25 (pt. 1); $2.75 (pt. 2). LC Card No. 71-610123. (C 3.6/2:C 33/2/970-2/pts.)
   The *1970 Census Users' Guide* has been designed to serve data users as the principal resource for information about the 1970 Census of Population

and Housing. Furnishes the information which data users need in order to deal effectively with terminology often uniquely associated with census programs or tabulations. The guide is organized into two separately bound sections. Part I includes text and three appendixes, dictionary, comparison of printed reports and summary tapes, and glossary. Part II includes seven appendixes, technical conventions character set, first through fourth count technical documentation, and address coding guide technical documentation.

481. U.S. Bureau of the Census. **Pocket Data Book USA, 1971.** 3rd ed. Washington, GPO, 1971. $1.75. S/N 0301-1731. (C 3.134/3:971)

This pocket-sized quick statistical reference source is in its third biennial edition. Part one, Summary, contains 31 charts and easy-to-read graphs which summarize the data in part two. Part two, Tables, includes 29 tables on population, vital statistics, labor, welfare, finance, etc., covering the same areas as the *Statistical Abstract*. Both tables and graphs are simplified, and some are in color; they are easy to read and to use. The data are condensed from the *Statistical Abstract*, and general source of information is cited.

482. U.S. Bureau of the Census. **Statistical Abstract of the United States, 1970: National Data Book and Guide to Sources.** 91st ed. Prep. under the direction of William Lerner. Washington, GPO, 1970. 1018p. $5.75 (cloth). LC Card No. 4-18089. (C 3.134:970)

483. U.S. Bureau of the Census. **Statistical Abstract of the United States, 1971: National Data Book and Guide to Sources.** 92nd ed. Prep. under the direction of William Lerner. Washington, GPO, 1971. 1008p. (5.50 (cloth). LC Card No. 4-18089. (C 3.134:971)

From 1878 through 1902 the *Statistical Abstract* was prepared by the Bureau of Statistics of the Treasury Department; 1903 through 1911, the Bureau of Statistics, Department of Commerce and Labor; 1912 through 1937 by the Bureau of Foreign and Domestic Commerce.

This handy guide is an indispensable source for summary statistics on the social, political, and economic organization of the United States. It also serves as a guide to other statistical publications and sources. Summarizes data from governmental and private agencies. Emphasis is on national data, but international as well as regional and state tables are included. Each annual edition represents a review and updating of all the tables and charts, and well as text notes, presenting data for the most recent year or period available. Each edition is divided into major subjects, and statistics are preceded by brief summaries which explain terms, sources of the statistics, or other pertinent data. Statistics in the tables cover a time range of 15 to 20 years with some dating back to 1789. A very comprehensive index is included.

DIRECTORIES

484. U.S. Bureau of the Census. **Directory of Non-Federal Statistics for Local Areas: A Guide to Sources, 1969.** Prep. by Francine E. Schacter and others. Washington, GPO, 1970. 678p. $6.75. LC Card No. 76-605082. (C 3.6/2:St 2/4)

This is the first directory published by the Census Bureau of non-federal statistics sources for local areas. Included with the 50 U.S. states are the District of Columbia, Guam, Puerto Rico, and the Virgin Islands and some of their component parts. It is intended to "direct the user to published sources of non-federal statistics on social, political and economic aspects."

485. U.S. Health Services and Mental Health Administration. **Where to Write for Birth and Death Records, United States and Outlying Areas.** Rev. ed. Washington, GPO, 1970. 11p. (Public Health Service Publication 630A-1) $0.15. (HE 20.2002:B 53/970)

Gives addresses of offices which maintain files of birth and death records, cost of copies of these records, as well as special remarks about such things as gaps in the records. Arrangement is alphabetical by state and territory.

486. U.S. Health Services and Mental Health Administration. **Where to Write for Marriage Records.** Washington, GPO, 1971. 6p. $0.15. S/N 1701-0301. (HE 20.2002: M 34/970)

Provides addresses of vital statistics offices where marriage records can be obtained. The booklet also includes information on the cost of the records, data on how far back the records go in the offices, and other general facts helpful in obtaining these records.

487. U.S. Office of the Budget and Management. **Federal Statistical Directory.** 22nd ed. Washington, GPO, 1970. 314p. $1.50. LC Card No. 49-51647. (PrEx 2.10:970)

This directory was published annually from 1946 until 1967, when the 21st edition was published. Designed to facilitate communication between governmental agencies, it lists key persons engaged in statistical programs, whether or not they are classified as statisticians. Responsibility for coordinating all U.S. statistical activities is given to the Bureau of the Budget by the Budget and Accounting Procedure Act of 1950. Arranged by department with detailed subdivisions. Indexed by names.

HANDBOOKS

488. U.S. Office of Management and Budget. **Household Survey Manual 1969.** Washington, GPO, 1970. 237p. $2.00. (PrEx 2.6/2:H 81/968)

Designed to aid the many groups throughout the country that are attempting to conduct surveys using concepts more or less in line with the current practices of the federal statistical agencies. It describes the concepts currently in use and the appropriate questions for measuring the important basic characteristics of the population and the kind and quality of their homes. It also furnishes some advice on survey operation, including the criteria for obtaining reliable samples, that should be useful to those who are making surveys but who are not professional survey operators.

INDEXES

489. U.S. National Bureau of Standards. **Author and Permuted Title Index to Selected Statistical Journals.** By Brian L. Joiner and others. Washington, GPO, 1970. 506p. $5.75 (cloth). LC Card No. 75-604267. (C 13.10:321)

Indexes over 5,000 articles from seven journals up to 1969. The articles indexed correspond to those appearing since the most recent cumulative subject index was published for six of the seven journals. The index consists of three sections: an author index; a permuted title index which lists each article under every important word in its title; and a bibliographic listing.

URBANOLOGY

GENERAL WORKS

BIBLIOGRAPHIES

490. U.S. Department of Housing and Urban Development. **Catalog of Federally Financed Housing and Building Research and Technology.** Prep. by the Science Information Exchange, Smithsonian Institution. Washington, GPO, 1970. 135p. $1.25. LC Card No. 74-608910. (HH 1.2:H 81/40)
   Lists studies reported by 19 federal agencies in two major sections. Part one is the subject index, referring to ID numbers used in the second part. In part two, each study is listed by number with title, objective, agency number, project monitor, principal investigator and organization, estimated completion date, and reports issued.

491. U.S. Department of Housing and Urban Development. **Citizen and Business Participation in Urban Affairs: A Bibliography.** Washington, GPO, 1970. 84p. $0.75. LC Card No. 72-607157. (HH 1.23:C 49/2)
   Contains 650 citations to the literature from 1960 to 1970, under broad subject headings. Not annotated. Indexed by geographic areas and authors. Includes a directory of publishers.

492. U.S. Department of Housing and Urban Development. **Environment and the Community: An Annotated Bibliography.** Comp. by the HUD Library. Washington, GPO, 1971. 66p. $0.65. LC Card No. 71-611967. (HH 1.23:En 8)
   This bibliography lists books, reports and journal articles about the deteriorating quality of life in U.S. cities. Entries, arranged alphabetically within major subject headings, include complete bibliographical data and brief annotations.

493. U.S. Department of Housing and Urban Development. **Landlord-Tenant Relationships: A Selected Bibliography.** Comp. by the HUD Library. Washington, GPO, 1971. 53p. $0.60. LC Card No. 73-613707. S/N 2300-0180. (HH 1.23:L 23)

DICTIONARIES

494. U.S. Department of Housing and Urban Development. **Urban Vocabulary.** Washington, GPO, 1971. 81p. Issuing agency. (HH 1.2:V 85)
   This is a revision of *Subject Headings Used in the Catalog of the HHFA Library*, which was published in 1962 by the Housing and Home Finance Agency Library. This, therefore, is actually the subject authority list for cataloging materials in the HUD Library. Scope notes are provided where necessary to clarify terminology or to indicate the range of subject matter. Classification numbers are given with the subject headings. Includes see and see also references. The second part of this work is the HUD classification numbers in order with the subject.

DIRECTORIES

495. U.S. Renewal Assistance Administration. **Urban Renewal Directory, December 31, 1969.** Washington, GPO, 1970. 139p. Issuing agency. LC Card No. 68-61152. (HH 7.8/2:969/2)

496. U.S. Renewal Assistance Administration. **Urban Renewal Directory, June 30, 1970.** Washington, GPO, 1971. 147p. Issuing agency. LC Card No. 68-61152. (HH 7.8/2:970)

497. U.S. Renewal Assistance Administration. **Urban Renewal Directory, Decmeber 31, 1970.** Washington, GPO, 1971. 148p. Issuing agency. (HH 7.8/2:970/2)

    This directory, issued every six months, covers local urban renewal programs approved for federal assistance under Title I of the Housing Act of 1949. These include Urban Renewal Projects, Neighborhood Development Programs, General Neighborhood Renewal Plans, Feasibility Surveys, Code Enforcement Projects, Demolition Projects, Community Renewal Programs, and Demonstration Programs. Consists of two parts: Part A—Summary tables by program; Part B—listing of programs by region, state, locality. In tabular form, shows location, type, ID number, approval dates, and grant status.

LAWS

498. U.S. Department of Housing and Urban Development. **State Laws Enacted in 1969 of Interest to the Department of Housing and Urban Development: As Reported by the Commerce Clearing House and Other Unofficial Sources.** Washington, GPO, 1970. 181p. Issuing agency. (HH 1.5:St 2/2/969)

    The compendium is arranged by states with brief summaries of the laws and date of enactment. Indexed by subjects.

STATISTICS

499. U.S. Department of Housing and Urban Development. **1968 HUD Statistical Yearbook.** Washington, GPO, 1970. 392p. $3.25. LC Card No. 68-62733. (HH 1.38:968)

500. U.S. Department of Housing and Urban Development. **1969 HUD Statistical Yearbook.** Washington, GPO, 1970. 401p. $3.25. LC Card No. 68-62733. (HH 1.38:969)

501. U.S. Department of Housing and Urban Development. **1970 HUD Statistical Yearbook.** Prep. by the Office of Data Systems and Statistics. Washington, GPO, 1971. 334p. (HUD-288-UD) $2.50. S/N 2300-1193. (HH 1.38:970)

    Contains "comprehensive and detailed data on program and financial operations of the Department and related statistical information on housing and urban development activity." One section, "General Statistics," contains information published by other government departments and private sources. The other sections contain HUD data. At the beginning of each section is an index listing each table and its page location. This is a major source of statistical information on housing and urban affairs.

HOUSING AND PLANNING

502. U.S. Department of Housing and Urban Development. **Housing and Planning References: Cumulative Author Index, January/February 1968– July/August 1969, Numbers 16-24.** Washington, GPO, 1970. 54p. $0.60. (HH 1.23/3:16-24/ind.)

    Since July/August 1969 (issue no. 25), author indexes are in each issue of *Housing and Planning References.* This is a cumulative index for the year and a half preceding that.

503. U.S. Department of Housing and Urban Development. **New Communities: A Bibliography.** Washington, GPO, 1970. 84p. $0.75. LC Card No. 75-606174. (HH 1.23:C 73/969)

    This bibliography includes books, chapters of books, articles, conference proceedings, and reports published in the English language throughout the world. "Its major purpose is to contribute to the understanding and improvement of new community building by providing reference sources on the current status of knowledge and experience on the subject." Entries were selected with emphasis on those which directly treat new community topics and are relevant to today's problems. Because of a "scarcity of significant works on new communities," this bibliography includes items of "lesser importance and shorter length." Most entries are annotated, and the bibliography is arranged under "U.S. and Canada" and "Foreign Countries (other than Canada)." Indexed by authors, states and countries, and places.

504. U.S. Department of Housing and Urban Development. **Operation Breakthrough: Mass Produced and Industrialized Housing, A Bibliography.** Washington, GPO, 1970. 72p. $0.70. LC Card No. 78-607713. (HH 1.23: B 74)

    The selected references in this bibliography are aids in the construction aspects of the Operation Breakthrough Program, a program designed to apply modern industrial technology to housing, construction, and marketing. The purpose of the bibliography is to "provide sources of information for the increasing number of people who are becoming aware of the potential of industrialized housing." Citations to the literature (from 1965 to 1970) are arranged under broad subjects. Indexed by authors and geographic areas. Includes a list of suggested periodicals and addresses of publishers.

URBAN TRANSPORTATION

505. U.S. Department of Transportation. **Urban Mass Transportation: A Bibliography.** Comp. by Dawn E. Willis. Springfield, Va., NTIS, 1971. 140p. (Bibliographic List, No. 6) $3.00. (AD-733773) (TD 1.15:6)

506. U.S. Urban Mass Transportation Administration. **Directory of Research, Development and Demonstration Projects.** Washington, GPO, 1971. 342p. $2.50. LC Card No. 75-604441. S/N 5014-0001. (TD 7.9:970)

This directory contains summaries of projects funded under the Urban Mass Transportation Act of 1964, as amended, and some projects funded under earlier programs. Summaries are grouped under four main categories: bus program, rail program, new systems program, and technical planning and evaluation.

507. U.S. Urban Mass Transportation Administration. **Urban Transportation Bibliography.** Springfield, Va., NTIS, 1971. 110p. $3.00. (PB 199 031) (TD 7.10:Ur 1)

This is the first in a planned series of technical and scientific publications concerned with urban mass transportation. It includes abstracts of reports, studies, articles, monographs, etc.

PART TWO

SCIENCE AND TECHNOLOGY

GENERAL WORKS

BIBLIOGRAPHIES

508. U.S. Atomic Energy Commission. **Science and Society: A Bibliography.** Comp. by Hugh E. Voress. Washington, GPO, 1971. 21p. (AEC Research and Development Reports) $0.35. S/N 5210-0272. (Y 3.At 7:22/WASH-1182)

    Contains 410 references to literature published from 1968 through March 1971. Arranged alphabetically by senior author with an author index. Not annotated.

509. U.S. Civil Service Commission Library. **Scientists and Engineers in the Federal Government.** Washington, GPO, 1970. 93p. $1.00. LC Card No. 74-607712. (CS 1.61/3:970)

    This bibliography updates one issued in 1965 and covers materials received in the Civil Service Commission Library from 1965 through 1969. It includes sections on supply and demand for technical personnel; personnel management for scientists and engineers in the federal government and in private industry; evaluating the performance of scientists and engineers; selection and development of personnel for management responsibilities; identifying scientific creativity; factors affecting performance; and personality and professional characteristics of scientists and engineers.

510. U.S. National Aeronautics and Space Administration. **Technology Transfer: A Selected Bibliography.** By Terry Sovel Heller, John S. Gilmore, and Theodore D. Browne. Rev. ed. Springfield, Va., NTIS, 1971. 175p. (NASA Contractor Report CR Series) $3.00. LC Card No. 76-611471. (NAS 1.26:CR-1724)

511. U.S. National Bureau of Standards. **National Bureau of Standards Films.** Washington, GPO, 1971. 32p. Issuing agency. (C 13.2:F 48/970)

    Lists films available for free loan to scientific and professional organizations, colleges, universities, high schools, and other groups. In three sections: science, weights and measures, and dental research and techniques. Provides title, date, size, time, and a synopsis for each film.

512. U.S. National Bureau of Standards. **Time and Frequency: A Bibliography of NBS Literature Published July 1955—December 1970.** By B. E. Blair. Washington, GPO, 1971. 50p. (NBS Spec. Pub. 350) $0.55. LC Card No. 73-611327. S/N 0303-0871. (C 13.10:350)

    This bibliography lists NBS papers and reports in the field of time and frequency, which were published from July 1955 through December 1970. The 232 entries are arranged chronologically within the following five categories: 1) time and frequency standards; 2) time scales, time; 3) distribution and reception of time and frequency signals; 4) statistics of time and frequency analyses, frequency stability; and 5) general, summary, and status reports.

Primarily cites publications of the NBS Time and Frequency Division, but some work of other NBS groups is included. A separate section lists articles about NBS work written in the private sector. An author index is provided.

513. U.S. National Bureau of Standards. **Publications of the National Bureau of Standards, 1968-1969: A Compilation of Abstracts and Key Word and Author Indexes.** By Betty L. Oberholtzer. Washington, GPO, 1970. 497p. $4.50. LC Card No. 48-47112. (C 13.10:305/supp. 1)

This bibliographical series lists both NBS publications and publications of NBS staff members by commercial publishers. Key-word indexes and descriptive annotations are useful features. The second supplement is entitled *Publications of the National Bureau of Standards, 1968-69 (A Compilation of Abstracts and Key Word and Author Indexes): Supplement 2* (364p.; $4.50; LC Card No. 48-47112; S/N 0303-0707; C 13.10:305/supp. 2).

514. U.S. National Science Foundation. **Publications of the National Science Foundation.** Washington, GPO, 1971. 10p. Issuing agency. (NS 1.13:P 96/971)

Lists publications available from either GPO or the National Science Foundation. Not annotated or indexed.

515. U.S. National Science Foundation. **Science Facilities Bibliography, 1970 Supplement.** Washington, GPO, 1970. 11p. (NSF 70-30) $0.10. LC Card No. 79-602480. (NS 1.13:F 11/969/supp.)

See *Government Reference Books 68/69*, entry number 384, for main volume. This supplement contains more current references to literature relating to the design of science facilities.

516. U.S. House of Representatives. Committee on Science and Astronautics. **Publications of the Committee on Science and Astronautics from February 1959–August 1969.** Washington, House, 1970. 12p. Issuing agency. LC Card No. 74-607597. (Y 4.Sci 2:P 96/959-69-2)

517. U.S. House of Representatives. Committee on Science and Astronautics. **Publications of the Committee on Science and Astronautics from February 1959–December 1970.** Washington, the Committee, 1970. 15p. Issuing agency. LC Card No. 75-611314. (Y 4.Sci 2:P 96/959-70)

Publications listed by Congress and date with title and publication number. Not indexed.

518. U.S. Senate. Committee on Government Operations. **Inventory of Congressional Concern with Research and Development, 91st Congress, 1969-70: Part 5, A Bibliography.** Washington, GPO, 1971. pp. 251-315. Issuing agency. (Y 4.G 74/6:R 31/2/pt. 5)

Includes publications which show congressional interest in science and technology. In five sections: public laws (in numerical order); conference committee reports; Senate publications; joint committee publications; and House publications. Indexed by subject.

DIRECTORIES

519. U.S. Federal Council for Science and Technology. **Directory of Federally Supported Information Analysis Centers.** Springfield, Va., CFSTI, 1970. 71p. $3.00. LC Card No. 73-606266. PB 189300. (Y 3.F 31/16: 2 In 3/2)
   This directory of 119 federally supported information analysis centers is descriptive, containing informatiion on the purpose, scope, and services provided by the centers. Included are indexes of subjects and of center directors, and a list of organizations.

520. U.S. Library of Congress. **Directory of Information Resources in the United States: Physical Sciences and Engineering.** Washington, GPO, 1971. 803p. $6.50. LC Card No. 78-611209. S/N 3000-0040. (LC 1.31:D 62/6)
   This directory lists 2,891 organizations and institutions in the United States which provide resources for physical sciences and engineering information. The areas of interest, holdings, publications, and information services are given for each information resource. A subject index is also included.

521. U.S. National Agricultural Library. **Directory of Information Resources in Agriculture and Biology.** Washington, GPO, 1971. 523p. $4.50. LC Card No. 79-614159. S/N 0102-0074. (A 17.2:D 62)
   The Agricultural Science Information Network compiled this directory in cooperation with many land-grant colleges. It includes federal organizations, departments of land-grant colleges and universities, and their campus-affiliated organiztions, arranged alphabetically by state.

522. U.S. National Bureau of Standards. **Calibration and Test Services of the National Bureau of Standards.** Washington, GPO, 1971. 228p. $2.00. LC Card No. 63-60099. S/N 0303-0151. (C 13.10:250/4)
   This directory supersedes the edition published in 1968. It contains "a descriptive listing, item by item, of most of the test and calibration work done at the National Bureau of Standards with the respective fees." A detailed index allows easy access to the data.

523. U.S. National Bureau of Standards. **Directory of Standards Laboratories.** Washington, NBS, 1971. 42p. (C 13.2:St 2/2/971)
   "Designed to fulfill three principal functions: To serve as a 'classified index' of standards laboratories in this country, providing those seeking information on calibration services with a list of available services; to provide information useful to those offering calibration services; to provide information concerning activities in the standards and calibration field essential to the planning and operation of the National Conference of Standards Laboratories."

524. U.S. National Science Foundation. **Directory of Federal R & D Installations.** Washington, GPO, 1970. 1044p. (Office of Economic and Manpower Studies; NSF 70-23) $6.75. LC Card No. 74-607546. (NS 1.2:R 31/18)

It is arranged by department or agency with detailed information on the programs of each research center. Contains an alphabetical list of centers, a list of centers by state, and a subject index based on COSATI Subject Category List.

525. U.S. National Science Foundation. **Guide to Programs, National Science Foundation, Fiscal Year 1971.** Washington, GPO, 1970. 79p. $0.75. (NS 1.20:P 94/971)

526. U.S. National Science Foundation. **Guide to Programs, National Science Foundation, Fiscal Year 1972.** Washington, GPO, 1971. 80p. $0.75. S/N 3800-0107. (NS 1.20:P 94/972)

Provides summary information about support programs of the National Science Foundation, and can be used as a source of general guidance for institutions and individuals interested in participating in these programs. Program listings describe the principal characteristics and basic purpose of each activity, eligibility requirements, closing dates, and the address from which more detailed information, brochures, or application forms may be obtained.

527. U.S. National Science Foundation. **Resources for Scientific Activities at Universities and Colleges.** Washington, GPO, 1970. 152p. $1.25. (NS 1.22:C 68/3/969)

Summarizes the results of the National Science Foundation's 1969 survey of the scientific activities of institutions of higher education.

GUIDES

528. U.S. Department of the Navy. Navy Personnel Bureau. **Tools and Their Uses.** Washington, GPO, 1971. 179p. $1.50. S/N 0847-0145. (D 208.11:T 61/2/971)

Provides descriptions, general uses, correct operation, and approved maintenance procedures for those handtools and power tools commonly used in the Navy. Stresses the importance of good workmanship and emphasizes good safety practices.

INDEXES

529. U.S. National Bureau of Standards. **A World Index of Plastics Standards.** Ed. by Leslie H. Breden. Washington, GPO, 1971. 445p. $5.50 (cloth). S/N 0303-0891. (C 13.10:352)

The National Bureau of Standards conducted a survey of the standards, specifications, test methods and recommended practices of over 100 organizations, both foreign and domestic. The result is this index of over 9,000 national and international plastics and related materials standards. The index, a KWIC or permuted title index, was designed to help engineers, purchasing agents, manufacturers, and others quickly locate plastics standards. Entries include date of publication (or most recent revision) and an acronym designating the issuing agency. A glossary of acronyms gives the agency names and addresses.

530. U.S. Patent Office. **Index of Patents Issued from the United States Patent Office, 1969.** Washington, GPO, 1971. 2 pts. $14.25 (cloth), part 1; $4.50 (cloth), part 2. S/N 0304-0484 (pt. 1); 0304-0490 (pt. 2). (C 21.5/2:969/pts.)

531. U.S. Patent Office. **Index of Patents Issued from the United States Patent Office, 1970.** Washington, GPO, 1971. 2 pts. $14.00 (cloth), part 1; $4.50 (cloth), part 2. S/N 0304-0485 (pt. 1); 0304-0494 (pt. 2). (C 21.5/2:970/pts.)

Part 1, List of Patentees. Contains lists of Reissue Patentees, Design Patentees, Plant Patentees, Defensive Publications (Applicants to Whom Issued), and Disclaimers and Dedications. Decisions published in the Official Gazette in 1970 are also included.

Part 2, Index to Subjects of Inventions. The subject of invention of each patent issued is identified by the class and subclass numbers of the official U.S. Patent Office classification in which the patent was classified at the time of issue. Also listed in the Index are 64,708 patent and reissue patent numbers. A similar listing appears for design patents, plant patents and defensive publications which are shown separately under their respective classifications.

STATISTICS

532. U.S. Bureau of Labor Statistics. **Scientific and Technical Personnel in Industry, 1969.** Washington, GPO, 1971. 35p. $0.45. S/N 2901-0721. (L 2.3:1723)

Contains the results of a 1969 survey of scientific and technical personnel in industry conducted by the Bureau of Labor Statistics. Included are a brief summary of findings; survey methods; questionnaire; reporting instructions and definitions used to collect data; and tables.

AGRICULTURAL SCIENCES

AGRICULTURE

GENERAL WORKS

BIBLIOGRAPHIES

533. U.S. Consumer and Marketing Service. **Available Publications of the USDA's Consumer and Marketing Service.** Washington, the Service, 1970. 16p. (C & MS Series, No. 53) Issuing agency. LC Card No. 72-601799. (A 88.40/2:53)

534. U.S. Department of Agriculture. **Color Filmstrips and Slide Sets of the United States Department of Agriculture.** Rev. Washington, GPO, 1970. 13p. $0.20. (A 1.38:1107)
   Lists filmstrips and slide sets available for loan to interested groups from the USDA.

535. U.S. Department of Agriculture. **Financial Management Research in Farming in the United States: An Annotated Bibliography of Recent Publications and Current Work.** By Virden L. Harrison. Washington, GPO, 1971. 78p. Issuing agency. LC Card No. 79-616240. (A 1.38:1222)
   This annotated bibliography describes the contents of 300 recent publications and 50 current research projects relating to financial management of agricultural firms. A topic index groups the publications and current projects into subject matter areas within financial management. Also included are lists of teachers of graduate level courses in farm management and agricultural finance in state universities.

536. U.S. Department of Agriculture. Information Office. **List of Available Publications of the Department of Agriculture.** Comp. by Mattie W. Johnson. Washington, GPO, 1971. 87p. $0.45. LC Card No. Agr 29-1725. S/N 9103-0002. (A 21.9/8:11/8)
   Lists publications of the U.S. Department of Agriculture currently available as of July 1971. Intended primarily for farmers, consumers, homemakers, suburbanites, research workers, teachers, and others who are interested in agriculture or related subjects.

537. U.S. Farmer Cooperative Service. **List of Publications.** Comp. by Marjorie B. Christie. Washington, GPO, 1971. 58p. (Information Series, No. 4) Issuing agency. (A 89.15:4/8)

DIRECTORIES

538. U.S. Consumer and Marketing Service. **Official Grain Standards of the United States.** Washington, GPO, 1970. 66p. $0.50. LC Card No. 56-1189. (A 88.6/2:G 761/970)

Presents the official United States standards for wheat, corn, barley, oats, rye, grain sorghums, flaxseed, soybeans, and mixed grain.

539. U.S. Department of Agriculture. **Fact Book of U.S. Agriculture.** Rev. ed. Washington, GPO, 1970. 82p. $0.45. LC Card No. 63-61826. (A 1.38: 1063)

This is a convenient guide to agricultural programs in the United States. It contains a narrative summary "designed as a reference for anyone who writes or talks about agriculture." Information is clearly presented and a detailed index facilitates access to the facts.

540. U.S. Department of Agriculture. **Professional Workers in State Agricultural Experiment Stations and Other Cooperating State Institutions, 1969-70.** Washington, GPO, 1970. 289p. $1.50. LC Card No. 66-60940. (A 1.76: 305)

Provides a listing of professional workers in state agricultural experiment stations and other cooperating state institutions.

541. U.S. Department of Agriculture. **USDA Standards for Food and Farm Products.** Washington, GPO, 1971. 15p. $0.15. S/N 0100-0731. (A 1.76: 341/971)

This pamphlet lists all of the federal standards which the U.S. Department of Agriculture has in effect as of January 1, 1971.

LAWS

542. U.S. Department of Agriculture. **Compilation of Statutes Relating to Soil Conservation, Acreage Diversion, Marketing Quotas and Allotments, Wheat Certificates, Commodity Credit Corporation, Price Support, Export and Surplus Removal, Public Law 480, Crop Insurance, Sugar Payments and Quotas, Marketing Agreements and Orders, School Lunch, Child Nutrition, Food Stamp, and Related Statutes, as of February 1, 1971.** Washington, GPO, 1971. 420p. (Agriculture Handbooks, No. 408) $1.75. LC Card No. 72-612226. (A 1.76:408)

This is a compilation of legislation administered by the Agricultural Stabilization and Conservation Service and related laws. Contains a detailed subject index.

543. U.S. Department of Agriculture. **Compilation of Statutes Relating to the Consumer and Marketing Service and Closely Related Activities.** Washington, GPO, 1971. 338p. (Agriculture Handbook, No. 407) $1.50. (A 1.76: 407)

This is a compilation of legislation administered by the Consumer and Marketing Service and related laws. Includes a detailed subject index.

STATISTICS

544. U.S. Department of Agriculture. **Agriculture Statistics 1970.** Washington, GPO, 1970. 627p. $2.75. LC Card No. Agr 36-465. S/N 0100-1150. (A 1.47:970)

545. U.S. Department of Agriculture. **Agriculture Statistics 1971.** Washington, GPO, 1971. 639p. $2.75. LC Card No. Agr 36-465. S/N 0100-1540. (A 1.47:971)

Published annually, *Agricultural Statistics* brings together each year the more important series of statistics concerning agriculture and closely related subjects. Covering many areas of interest that concern the agriculture business community, this handbook is filled with tables and other information on agricultural production, prices, supplies, costs, income, and related subjects. Agricultural data for Alaska and Hawaii are included in the appropriate tables, where available.

546. U.S. Department of Agriculture. **Handbook of Agricultural Charts, 1970.** Washington, GPO, 1970. 145p. (Agriculture Handbooks) $0.65. LC Card No. 64-62697. (A 1.76:397)

547. U.S. Department of Agriculture. **Handbook of Agricultural Charts, 1971.** Washington, GPO, 1971. 146p. (Agriculture Handbooks) $0.65. (A 1.76:423)

Contains many charts and graphs which are available from the Department of Agriculture as photographic prints or slides. The charts cover such topics as the domestic agricultural situation, foreign production and trade, population and rural development, and commodity trends. A handy reference source for general agricultural information.

548. U.S. Department of Agriculture. **Major Statistical Series of the Department of Agriculture: How They Are Constructed and Used.** Washington, GPO. LC Card No. 77-607020. (A 1.76:365/vols.)

The following volumes were published in 1970 and 1971.
Volume 1. Agricultural Prices and Parity. 1970. 44p. $0.50.
Volume 2. Agricultural Production and Efficiency. 1970. 40p. $0.50.
Volume 4. Agricultural Marketing Costs and Charges. 1970. 37p. $0.50.
Volume 6. Land Values and Farm Finance. 1971. 35p. $0.45.
Volume 8. Crop and Livestock Estimates. 1971. 30p. $0.40.
Volume 9. Farmer Cooperatives. 1970. 9p. $0.25.

This series is designed as ready reference, describing each of the major statistical series of the USDA, discussing its uses and comparing it with related series.

549. U.S. Farmer Cooperative Service. **Statistics of Farmer Cooperatives, 1968-1969.** By Richard M. Ackley. Washington, the Service, 1970. 30p. Issuing agency. LC Card No. 79-600829. (A 89.19:16)

550. U.S. House of Representatives. Committee on Agriculture. **Food Costs, Farm Prices: A Compilation of Information Relating to Agriculture.** Washington, the Committee, 1971. 118p. Issuing agency. LC Card No. 70-616180. (Y 4.Ag 8/1:F 73/22/971)

Contains statistics on a wide variety of subjects relating to food costs, farm prices, and government programs.

YEARBOOKS

551. U.S. Department of Agriculture. **Contours of Change: Yearbook of Agriculture 1970.** Ed. by Jack Hayes. Washington, GPO, 1970. 336p. $3.50 (cloth). LC Card No. 79-609702. (A 1.10:970)

552. U.S. Department of Agriculture. **Good Life for More People: Yearbook of Agriculture 1971.** Ed. by Jack Hayes. Washington, GPO, 1971. 391p. $3.50 (cloth). LC Card No. 76-616348. S/N 0100-1459. (A 1.10:971)

Since 1936, each issue of the USDA *Yearbook of Agriculture* has covered one broad subject of popular interest. Although not intended to be definitive, they are comprehensive in treatment. Many issues contain bibliographies for further research.

FARM PRODUCTS

553. U.S. Agricultural Research Service. **Bibliography of Research on the Utilization of Rice in the Western Marketing and Nutrition Research Division, 1947-70.** By D. F. Houston. Washington, GPO, 1971. 29p. (ARS Series, No. 74-58) Issuing agency. (A 77.15:74-58)

554. U.S. Department of Agriculture. **Bibliography of Potato Diseases through 1945, with Common and Scientific Names.** Comp. by Muriel J. O'Brien and E. L. LeClerg. Washington, GPO, 1970. 243p. $1.25. LC Card No. 76-608932. (A 1.38:1162)

A handy guide to all pertinent material published on potato diseases through 1945. This bibliography is in four parts, plus an appendix. Part 1 is the subject index; part 2 is the literature citations arranged alphabetically by author; part 3, a list of general references, and part 4, the author index.

555. U.S. Department of Agriculture. **Wool Statistics and Related Data, 1930-69.** Comp. by Mildred V. Jones. Washington, GPO, 1970. 294p. (Statistical Bulletins, No. 455) $2.25. LC Card No. 70-608952. (A 1.34:455)

SOIL MANAGEMENT

556. U.S. Department of Defense. **Herbicide Manual for Noncropland Weeds.** Washington, GPO, 1971. 219p. $1.75. LC Card No. 75-612346. S/N 0850-0077. (D 1.6/2:H 41)

This manual contains practical instructions for the classification, use, and application of herbicides; detailed information regarding specific weed species and site situations; and unique characteristics and properties of specific herbicides suggested for noncropland use.

557. U.S. Department of the Interior. Library. **Sprinkler Irrigation: A Bibliography Selected from Foreign Literature, 1964-1969.** Comp. by Ludmilla Floss. Springfield, Va., CFSTI, 1970. 54p. (Bibliography Series No. 15) $3.00. LC Card No. 74-608866. (I 22.9/2:15)

558. U.S. Soil Conservation Service. **National Handbook of Conservation Practices.** Washington, GPO, 1970. 241p. Issuing agency. (A 57.6/2:C 76/2)

559. U.S. Soil Conservation Service. **SCS National Engineering Handbook: Section 4, Hydrology.** Rev. ed. Washington, GPO, 1971. 665p. $5.75 (looseleaf). S/N 0107-0259. (A 57.6/2:En 3/sec. 4/rev.)
   Contains methods and examples for studying the hydrology of watersheds, and for solving special hydrologic problems in planning watershed-protection and flood-prevention projects.

FORESTRY

ATLASES

560. U.S. Forest Service. **Forest Atlas of the South.** Washington, Forest Service, 1970. 27p. Issuing agency. LC Card No. 77-653801. (A 13.40/2:At 6)

BIBLIOGRAPHIES

561. U.S. Forest Service. **Forest Service Films Available on Loan for Educational Purposes to Schools, Civic Groups, Churches, Television.** Washington, Forest Service, 1970. 32p. Issuing agency. LC Card No. Agr 52-366. (A 13.55:970)

562. U.S. Forest Service. **Forest Service Films Available on Loan for Educational Purposes to Schools, Civic Groups, Churches, Television.** Washington, GPO, 1971. 34p. Issuing agency. LC Card No. Agr 52-366. (A 13.55:971)
   Lists and describes films available from the Forest Service for loan, and some for sale. Indexed by title.

563. U.S. Forest Service. **List of Publications by Subject.** Washington, GPO, 1970. 85p. Issuing agency. LC Card No. 79-608188. (A 13.11/2:P 96/970)
   This is a computer-produced list of Forest Service publications. Its subject arrangement makes it a handy index to the annotated list of publications which is arranged by author, title, and series.

DIRECTORIES

564. U.S. Forest Service. **Forest Service Organizational Directory.** Washington, GPO, 1971. 143p. $0.65. S/N 0101-0069. (A 13.36/2:Or 3/2/971)

Shows the organization of the Forest Service, with the addresses and telephone numbers of the main field offices. Key personnel are listed.

565. U.S. Forest Service. **Forestry Schools in the United States.** Rev. ed. Washington, GPO, 1970. 24p. $0.15. LC Card No. 52-60486. (A 13.2:F 76/70/970)

Forestry schools are listed alphabetically by state with complete address and official name of the academic department. A brief statement for each school gives such information as the degrees granted, major areas of concentration, special requirements, and accreditation by the Society of American Foresters.

GUIDES

566. U.S. Forest Service. **Forest Service Health and Safety Code: Your Guide to Safe Practices.** Washington, GPO, 1970. 420p. $3.00. LC Card No. 74-610428. S/N 0101-0042. (A 13.36/2:H 34/970)

Prepared primarily for the instruction and guidance of Forest Service personnel, this code presents rules, regulations, and guides for safety which should also be of interest and use to persons in other occupations. It discusses accident prevention and safety as related to travel, fire, public safety, project work, construction and maintenance, equipment, and buildings and grounds. Also includes a chapter on disease control and sanitation.

567. U.S. Forest Service. **Tables of Compound-Discount Interest Rate Multipliers for Evaluating Forestry Investments.** Washington, GPO, 1971. 142p. $1.25. S/N 0101-0077. (A 13.78:NC-51)

Provides a single source for interest-rate tables for evaluating forestry investments, including even the most commonly used in financial analyses. Each table is briefly explained and an example of its use is given.

HOME ECONOMICS

568. U.S. Department of Agriculture. **Family Food Budgeting for Good Meals and Good Nutrition.** Rev. ed. Washington, GPO, 1971. 16p. $0.35. S/N 0100-1377. (A 1.77:94/4)

This is a very handy guide for food budgeting at different income levels.

569. U.S. Department of Agriculture. **Homemaking Handbook for Village Workers in Many Countries.** Washington, GPO, 1971. 237p. $1.75. LC Card No. 72-612112. S/N 4401-0030. (A 1.68:953)

This guide was prepared jointly by the Department of Agriculture and the Agency for International Development. It is designed for use in home economics extension, community development, classroom teaching, health education, and other programs involving home and family life.

570. U.S. National Institute of Arthritis and Metabolic Diseases. **A Guide to Nutrition Terminology for Indexing and Retrieval.** By E. Neige Todhunter. Washington, GPO, 1970. 270p. $2.50. LC Card No. 79-609690. (HE 20. 3308:N 95)

This guide has been prepared as a resource for those who are responsible for indexing, storage and retrieval of information in the broad field of nutrition. The major emphasis is on human nutrition, but the guide has been structured to permit systematic expansion by users in other fields, such as animal nutrition or food technology.

WILDLIFE MANAGEMENT

571. U.S. Bureau of Commercial Fisheries. **Fishery Statistics of the United States, 1967.** By Charles H. Lyles. Washington, GPO, 1970. 490p. $4.25. LC Card No. 72-606807. (I 49.32:61)

572. U.S. National Marine Fisheries Service. **Fishery Statistics of the United States, 1968.** Prep. by Thelma I. Bell. Washington, GPO, 1971. 578p. $5.00. S/N 0320-0028. (C 55.316:62)

These statistical compendia also contain bibliographies of statistical publications issued during the year.

573. U.S. Bureau of Commercial Fisheries. **List of Fishery Cooperatives in the United States, 1969-70.** Washington, Commercial Fisheries Bureau, 1970. 13p. Issuing agency. (I 49.28:627)

574. U.S. Bureau of Sport Fisheries and Wildlife. **Directory of National Wildlife Refuges.** Rev. ed. Washington, GPO, 1971. 16p. (Refuge Leaflet, No. 411) Issuing agency. (I 49.44:411/3)

Arranged by state and refuge name with date of establishment, number of acres, and primary species.

575. U.S. Bureau of Sport Fisheries and Wildlife. **List of National Fish Hatcheries.** Rev. ed. Washington, Bureau of Sport Fisheries and Wildlife, 1970. 11p. Issuing agency. (I 49.28:147/12)

This directory lists fish hatcheries operated by the federal government.

576. U.S. Bureau of Sport Fisheries and Wildlife. **Selected List of Federal Laws and Treaties Relating to Sport Fish and Wildlife.** Washington, GPO, 1970. 4p. (Wildlife Leaflet, No. 489) $0.10. (I 49.13:489)

ASTRONOMY

GENERAL WORKS

ATLASES

578. U.S. National Aeronautics and Space Administration. **Atlas and Gazetteer of the Near Side of the Moon.** Washington, GPO, 1971. 538p. (NASA SP Series, No. 241) $15.00 (cloth). S/N 3300-0320. (NAS 1.21:241)

This atlas and gazetteer is a photographic and tabular compilation of named lunar features appearing on the near side of the Moon. To provide an easy method of locating lunar features in the atlas, the names have been annotated on the photographs, which are accompanied by locational data regarding the named features. Five indexes comprising the gazetteer are provided for appropriate cross-referencing of the high-resolution Orbiter IV photography and the medium-resolution photography obtained from the other Orbiter missions.

579. U.S. National Aeronautics and Space Administration. **Lunar Orbiter Photographic Atlas of the Moon.** By David E. Bowker and J. Kentrick Hughes. Washington, GPO, 1971. 675p. (NASA SP Series, No. 206) $19.25 (cloth). LC Card No. 70-607341. S/N 3300-0314. (NAS 1.21:206)

Presents a selection of photographs which provide essentially complete coverage of the near side and far side of the Moon. Five spacecraft were placed in lunar orbit from 1966 to 1967, and photographs covering landing sites and specific areas of high scientific interest were sent back to Earth. The last flight completed the photographic survey of the entire surface. A selection of these photographs, covering all the lunar surface, both front and back, is collected in this atlas and shows greater surface detail. This store of information is presented as a base for planning future exploration of Earth's nearest neighbor and also to stimulate interest in further scientific study of the Moon.

EPHEMERIDES

580. U.S. Bureau of Land Management. **Ephemeris of the Sun, Polaris and Other Selected Stars with Companion Data and Tables for the Year 1971.** Prep. by the Nautical Almanac Office, U.S. Naval Observatory. Washington, GPO, 1970. 30p. $0.35. LC Card No. 10-35913. (I 53.8:971)

581. U.S. Bureau of Land Management. **Ephemeris of the Sun, Polaris, and Other Selected Stars with Companion Data and Tables for the Year 1972.** Prep. by the Nautical Almanac Office, U.S. Naval Observatory. Washington, GPO, 1971. 30p. $0.35. LC Card No. 10-35913. (I 53.8:972)

The arrangement of astronomical data in these two works conforms to the methods and examples for the determination of time, latitude, and azimuth practiced by engineers at the Bureau of Land Management.

582. U.S. Naval Observatory. **The American Ephemeris and Nautical Almanac 1972.** Washington, GPO, 1970. 568p. $6.00 (cloth). LC Card No. 7-35435. S/N 0854-0029. (D 213.8:972)

Contains the ephemeris of Universal and Sidereal Times, the ephemerides of the Sun, Moon, Mercury, Venus, Mars, Jupiter, Saturn, Uranus, and Neptune, the geocentric ephemerides of Ceres, Pallas, Juno, Vesta and Pluto, the nutation in longitude and obliquity, the Day Numbers, and the Phenomena. This volume also contains data on mean places of stars; eclipses of the Sun and Moon; ephemerides for physical observations of the Sun, Moon, and planets; ephemerides of the satellites of Mars, Saturn, Uranus, and Neptune, and of Satellites V, VI, VII of Jupiter and of the rings of Saturn; and local mean times of moonrise and moonset for the year 1972.

NAVIGATION

583. U.S. Naval Observatory. **Nautical Almanac for the Year 1971.** Washington, GPO, 1970. 276p. $4.00 (cloth). LC Card No. 7-35404. (D 213.11:971)

584. U.S. Naval Observatory. **Nautical Almanac for the Year 1972.** Washington, GPO, 1971. 276p. $4.00 (cloth). LC Card No. 7-35404. S/N 0854-0038. (D 213.11:972)

This publication contains data necessary for the practice of astronomical navigation at sea. An "Index to Selected Stars 1972" is included in the 1972 volume.

585. U.S. Naval Oceanographic Office. **Tables of Computed Altitude and Azimuth.** Washington, GPO, 1970 (repr.) 7 vols. $6.00 (cloth)/vol. (D 203.22:214/v.)

These tables, first published in 1952, consist of tabulated solutions of the navigational triangle, so arranged as to yield computed altitude and azimuth angle by inspection. They are applicable equally to observations of the sun, moon, planets, and navigational stars, whether observed in north or south latitude.

BIOLOGICAL SCIENCES

BOTANY

586. U.S. Department of Agriculture. **Atlas of United States Trees: Volume 1, Conifers and Important Hardwoods.** By Elbert L. Little, Jr. Washington, GPO, 1971. 310p. $16.75 (cloth). LC Card No. 79-653298. S/N 0100-1026. (A 1.38:1146)

This volume contains approximately 300 maps which show the natural distribution or range of 200 native tree species of the continental United States (including Alaska). All native conifers or softwoods and 106 species of important hardwoods are mapped separately on maps of the United States with county boundaries. The scale is 1:10,000,000. Nine transparent overlays are provided to show the correlation of trees with other environmental features such as rivers and lakes, length of growing season, precipitation, and climates.

587. U.S. Department of Agriculture. **Diseases of Forest and Shade Trees of the United States.** Washington, GPO, 1971. 658p. (Agriculture Handbook No. 386) $4.00 (cloth). S/N 0100-1135. (A 1.76:386)

The purpose of this volume is to bring together the information available on the pathology of the more important forest and shade trees of the United States. While it deals largely with the multitude of tree species indigenous to this country, it also annotates the diseases of many introduced species grown widely for shade and ornament. It includes diseases occurring in continental United States, exclusive of Alaska, and in adjacent parts of Canada. The material is arranged first by the tree host species or genus, and within species according to part of the tree mainly attacked—for example, foliage, stem, root, or trunk.

588. U.S. Department of Agriculture. **Guide to the Medicinal Plants of Appalachia.** By Arnold Krochmal, Russell S. Walters, and Richard M. Doughty. Washington, GPO, 1971. 291p. (Agriculture Handbook, No. 400) $1.75. LC Card No. 72-611663. (A 1.76:400)

Provides the following information on 126 medicinal plants: scientific name, common names, physical description, flowering period, habitat, harvest, uses. Sketches or photographs accompany each description. Includes a bibliography and a glossary of botanical and pharmacological terms, and an index of common plant names.

589. U.S. Department of Agriculture. **100 Native Forage Grasses in 11 Southern States.** By Horace L. Leithead, Lewis L. Yarlett, and Thomas N. Shiflet. Washington, GPO, 1971. 216p. $1.00. LC Card No. 70-611239. S/N 0100-1138. (A 1.76:389)

This handbook, designed to give a better understanding of the values and uses of native grasses, describes 100 species which were selected on the basis of their importance in 11 southern states.

590. U.S. Department of Agriculture. **Selected Bibliography of Natural Plant Communities in 11 Midwestern States.** Prep. by Arnold J. Heerwagen. Washington, GPO, 1971. 30p. $0.30. S/N 0100-1436. (A 1.38:1205)

 Contains a list of about 750 entries concerning past and present natural plant communities in 11 midwestern states.

591. U.S. Forest Service. **Selected and Annotated Bibliography of Pitch Pine (Pinus regida Mill).** By Silas Little, Jack McCormick, and John W. Andresen. Upper Darby, Pa., Northeastern Forest Experiment Station, 1970. 103p. (Research Paper NE Series, No. NE-164) Issuing agency. LC Card No. 73-610851. (A 13.78:NE-164)

592. U.S. Forest Service. **Sitka Spruce: A Bibliography with Abstracts.** Comp. by A. S. Harris and Robert H. Ruth. Portland, Ore., Pacific Northwest Forest and Range Experiment Station, 1970. 251p. (Research Paper, PNW Series, No. PNW-105) Issuing agency. LC Card No. 75-610613. (A 13.78:PNW-105)

ZOOLOGY

593. U.S. Agricultural Research Service. **General Catalogue of Homoptera: Index to Genera and Species with Addenda and Corrigenda to Parts 1-17, Fascicle 6, Cicadelloidea.** Comp. by Virginia Wade Burnside. Washington, GPO, 1971. 269p. $1.25. (A 77.20:6/ind.)

 Contains the names of all genera, species, subspecies, and varieties that are listed in Parts 1 through 17, Fascicle VI, Cicadelloidea.

594. U.S. Bureau of Commercial Fisheries. **Bibliography of Lobsters, Genus Homarus.** By R. D. Lewis. Washington, Commercial Fisheries Bureau, 1970. 47p. Issuing agency. (I 49.15/2:591)

595. U.S. Department of Defense. **Poisonous and Venomous Marine Animals of the World, Volume 3.** By Bruce W. Halstead. Sections on Chemistry by Donovan A. Courville. Sponsored by the Departments of Army, Air Force, and Navy. Washington, GPO, 1970. 1006p. $50.00 (cloth). LC Card No. 65-60000. (D 1.2:M 33/v.)

 This guide was compiled "to provide a systematic organized source of technical data on marine biotoxicology covering the total world literature from antiquity to modern times" (Preface). Volume one covers invertebrates and volumes two and three, vertebrates. Volume one was published in 1965, volume two in 1967.

 This enormous work is very comprehensive. It represents an "effort to include references to all published work which has appeared since antiquity." Volume three deals specifically with venomous and ichthyotoxicrine fishes, venomous sea snakes, poisonous turtles, and poisonous mammals inhabiting the marine environment. Includes a general index, personal name index, and a detailed glossary of biotoxicological terms with literature citations.

596. U.S. National Oceanic and Atmospheric Administration. **Annotated Bibliography of Attempts to Rear Larvae of Marine Fishes in the Laboratory.** By Robert C. May. Washington, GPO, 1971. 24p. $0.35. (C 55.13:NMFS-SSRF-632)

This is a bibliography of papers which describe attempts to rear the larvae of marine fishes in the laboratory from 1878 to 1969. Annotations summarize each paper and appendixes list the species of fish studied and the types of food used in attempts to rear them.

597. U.S. National Oceanic and Atmospheric Administration. **Annotated Bibliography of Zooplankton Sampling Devices.** By Jack W. Jossi. Washington, GPO, 1970. 90p. (National Marine Fisheries Special Scientific Report—Fisheries Series) Issuing agency. (C 55.13:NMFS-SSRF-609)

598. U.S. National Oceanic and Atmospheric Administration. **Annotated Bibliography on the Fishing Industry and Biology of the Blue Crab, Callinectes sapidus.** By Marlin E. Tagatz and Ann Bowman Hall. Washington, GPO, 1971. 94p. (National Marine Fisheries Special Scientific Report—Fishery Series) $1.00. LC Card No. 70-614841. (C 55.13:NMFS-SSRF-640)

Provides scientific and industrial investigators with an updated and comprehensive list of references to the literature on the blue crab, Callinectes sapidus.

CHEMISTRY

599. U.S. Bureau of Mines. **Helium: Bibliography of Technical and Scientific Literature, 1963; Including Papers on Alpha Particles.** By Philip C. Tully, Billy Joe King, and Emily Dowdy. Washington, GPO, 1970. 831p. $7.00. LC Card No. 70-601446. (I 28.27:8467)

600. U.S. Bureau of Mines. **Helium: Bibliography of Technical and Scientific Literature, 1964; Including Papers on Alpha Particles.** By Philip C. Tully, Emily Dowdy, and Betty G. Noe. Washington, GPO, 1970. 946p. $7.50. LC Card No. 70-601446. (I 28.27:8489)

601. U.S. Bureau of Mines. **Helium: Bibliography of Technical and Scientific Literature, 1965; Including Papers on Alpha Particles.** By Philip C. Tully, Emily Dowdy, and Betty G. Noe. Washington, GPO, 1971. 760p. $6.25. S/N 2404-0968. (I 28.27:8523)

These three bibliographies contain citations to technical and scientific literature and alpha particles which were abstracted by 12 abstract services. They are in classified arrangement and are indexed by authors and subjects.

602. U.S. Consumer and Marketing Service. **List of Chemical Compounds Authorized for Use Under the USDA Poultry, Meat, Rabbit, and Egg Inspection Programs.** Washington, GPO, 1970. 180p. $1.50. (A 88.6:C 42/970-2)

Lists chemical compounds authorized by the Laboratory Services Division of the Consumer and Marketing Service. Arranged alphabetically by name of chemical manufacturers.

603. U.S. Department of the Interior. **Bibliography of Desalting Literature, 1969.** By the Columbia Software, Inc. Washington, GPO, 1970. 465p. $3.25. (I 1.88:552)

Section one of this work cites 4,925 works under eight major subject headings. Entries are bibliographically complete but are not annotated. Section two is an author index and section three is the subject index.

604. U.S. Geological Survey. **Selected Annotated Bibliography on the Geochemistry of Gold.** By Margaret Cooper. Washington, GPO, 1971. 63p. (U.S. Geological Survey Bulletin No. 1337) $0.35. LC Card No. 77-611048. (I 19.3:1337)

"This bibliography of about 200 references furnishes information on source materials dealing with the genesis and geochemistry of gold and geochemical prospecting for gold deposits." The citations are accompanied by either a very brief annotation or a more detailed abstract. Author and subject indexes.

605. U.S. National Bureau of Standards. **Activation Analysis: A Bibliography.** Ed. by G. J. Lutz and others. Washington, GPO, 1971. 2 vols. (Technical Notes No. TN 467) $5.25. LC Card No. 78-613605. S/N 0303-0852. (C 13.46:467)

This is a computer printout of references to activation analysis in the open literature. Indexed by author, element determined, matrix analyzed, and technique used.

606. U.S. National Bureau of Standards. **Equilibrium Critical Phenomena in Fluids and Mixtures: A Comprehensive Bibliography with Descriptors.** By S. Michaels, M. S. Green, and S. Y. Larsen. Washington, GPO, 1970. 231p. (NBS Special Publication No. 327) $4.00 (cloth). (C 13.10:327)

This bibliography of 1,088 citations comprehensively covers relevant research conducted throughout the world between January 1, 1950, and December 31, 1967. Each entry is characterized by specific key word descriptors, of which there are approximately 1,500, and is indexed by subject and author.

607. U.S. National Bureau of Standards. **JANAF Thermochemical Tables.** 2nd ed. Washington, GPO, 1971. 1139p. (National Standard Reference Data Series) $9.75 (cloth). S/N 0303-0872. (C 13.48:37)

Contains thermodynamic properties for some 1,099 chemical species.

608. U.S. National Institute of Allergy and Infectious Diseases. **Catalog of Research Reagents.** Ed. by Sylvia Cunningham and Robert M. Pennington. Washington, GPO, 1970. 848p. Issuing agency. LC Card No. 79-610054. (HE 20.3252: R 22/970)

This is a catalog of reagents currently available to researchers. Indexed by name and catalog number.

DATA PROCESSING

ABSTRACTS

609. U.S. National Aeronautics and Space Administration. **Computer Program Abstracts: Cumulative Issue, July 15, 1969—July 15, 1971.** Washington, GPO, 1971. 253p. $2.00. S/N 3300-0401. (NAS 1.44/2:969-71)

　　This cumulative issue, not to be considered as a regular quarterly issue of the journal, is an indexed abstract journal listing documented computer programs developed by or for the National Aeronautics and Space Administration, and the Department of Defense.

DICTIONARIES

610. U.S. Department of the Navy. **ADP Glossary.** Washington, GPO, 1971. 106p. $1.25. S/N 0840-0051. (D 201.2:Au 8)

　　This glossary was published as an aid to defining and describing words and terms used in the field of automatic data processing within the Navy, but it also has relevance to those in the same field outside the Navy. Its purpose is to provide a convenient source for arriving at a common terminology. It will be useful to those familiar with computers, their applications, and their related products and operations.

611. U.S. National Bureau of Standards. **Vocabulary for Information Processing.** By J. L. Walkowicz. Washington, GPO, 1970. 4p. (Federal Information Processing Standards) $0.15. (C 13.52:11)

　　Provides an alphabetical listing of approximately 1,200 entries, each consisting of a term and its definition, for use in information processing activities such as the description, representation, communication, interpretation, and processing of data by human or automatic means.

EQUIPMENT

612. U.S. Federal Supply Service. **Inventory of Automatic Data Processing Equipment in the United States Government, Fiscal Year 1970.** Washington, GPO, 1970. 394p. $2.75. LC Card No. 70-600875. (GS 2.15:970)

613. U.S. Federal Supply Service. **Inventory of Automatic Data Processing Equipment in the United States Government, Fiscal Year 1971.** Washington, GPO, 1971. 442p. $3.25. S/N 2201-0029. (GS 2.15:971)

　　Published "to provide information on the number of electronic computers in use throughout the U.S. Government, including owned and leased, average monthly hours in service, operating and capital costs, and number of man-years devoted to ADP functions." Inventories computers by agencies which use them in one section, lists them by manufacturer and by location in two other sections.

614. U.S. General Services Administration. **Source Data Automation Equipment Guide.** Washington, GPO, 1970. 122p. Issuing agency. (GS 1.6/6:So 8)

This guide was prepared by managers and analysts as an aid in selecting equipment suitable for the mechanization of paperwork in the government and for those applications where all or part of the data become input to computer systems. Contains one section describing SDA equipment widely used in the federal government, one on less widely used equipment, and a list of manufacturers and their addresses.

HANDBOOKS AND GUIDES

615. U.S. Library of Congress. **Data Preparation Manual for the Conversion of Map Cataloging Records to Machine-Readable Form.** Washington, GPO, 1970. 317p. $2.75. S/N 3000-0050. (LC 1.6/4:M 32)

Outlines the steps in the data collection process required to prepare map cataloging data for conversion to machine-readable form. Each step in the data collection process is illustrated with appropriate map cataloging examples.

616. U.S. National Bureau of Standards. **Automatic Indexing: A State-of-the-Art Report.** Washington, GPO, 1970. 290p. $2.25. (C 13.44:91/rep.)

This report covers a state-of-the-art survey of current progress in linguistic data processing as related to the possibilities of automatic mechanized indexing. Originally published in 1965, it is now reissued with corrections and additions added as appendices.

EARTH SCIENCES

GEOLOGY

BIBLIOGRAPHIES

617. U.S. Geological Survey. **Bibliography of North American Geology, 1966.** By James W. Clarke and others. Washington, GPO, 1970. 1069p. (Bulletin No. 1266) $4.75. LC Card No. GS 9-427. (I 19.3:1266)

618. U.S. Geological Survey. **Bibliography of North American Geology, 1967.** Washington, GPO, 1970. 1029p. (Bulletin No. 1267) $4.25. LC Card No. GS 9-427. (I 19.3:1267)

619. U.S. Geological Survey. **Bibliography of North American Geology, 1968.** By James W. Clarke and others. Washington, GPO, 1971. 1301p. (Bulletin No. 1268) $5.25. (I 19.3:1268)

    This standard bibliography in the field of North American geology cites journal articles, books, professional papers, and entries from *Dissertation Abstracts.* Alphabetical author lists with detailed subject and geographical indexes. Included along with continental North America are Hawaii, Guam, Greenland, the West Indies, and Panama.

620. U.S. Geological Survey. **Bibliography on the Geology and Resources of Vanadium to 1968.** By R. P. Fischer and Jane P. Ohl. Washington, GPO, 1970. 168p. (U.S. Geological Survey Bulletin No. 1316) $1.00. LC Card No. 73-606274. (I 19.3:1316)

    "This bibliography, which contains nearly 1,400 bibliographic references, was compiled to aid studies on the geology and resources of vanadium." Citations are arranged alphabetically by author and include title of article, publication source, year, and, in most cases, a very brief annotation. Indexed by subjects and geographic location.

621. U.S. Geological Survey. **Popular Publications of the Geological Survey.** Washington, GPO, 1971. 15p. Free from the Geological Survey. (I 19.14/2: P 96/971)

    Lists all nontechnical publications of the Geological Survey which are currently available.

622. U.S. Geological Survey. **Publications of the Geological Survey, 1969.** Washington, GPO, 1970. 54p. Issuing agency. LC Card No. GS 11-221. (I 19.14:969)

    This bibliography, arranged by types of publications—e.g., bulletins, maps—contains subject, geographic area, geological survey research, and author indexes.

623. U.S. Geological Survey. **Selected Annotated Bibliography of the Minor-Element Content of Marine Black Shales and Related Sedimentary Rocks, 1930-1965.** By Elizabeth B. Tourtelot. Washington, GPO, 1970. 118p. (U.S. Geological Survey Bulletin, No. 1239) $0.60. LC Card No. 75-604512. (I 19.3:1293)

Includes abstracts of about 375 selected articles published during 1930-1965, pertaining to worldwide occurrences of black shale.

CATALOGS

624. U.S. Smithsonian Institution. **Catalog of Chemical Analyses of Rocks from the Intersection of the African Gulf, Gulf of Aden, and Red Sea Rift Systems.** By Paul A. Mohr. Washington, GPO, 1970. 271p. (Smithsonian Contributions to Earth Sciences, No. 2) $2.75. LC Card No. 78-610295. (SI 1.26:2)

This is a compilation of "all published chemical analyses of rocks from the Red Sea, Gulf of Aden, and Ethiopian rift junction area. The chemical analyses are accompanied by further computations, in particular weight-norm and Niggli values, and by brief mineralogical descriptions." Includes a list of references and indexes to place names and rock types.

GEOLOGIC NAMES

625. U.S. Geological Survey. **Lexicon of Geologic Names of the United States for 1961-1967.** Washington, GPO, 1970. 848p. (U.S. Geological Survey Bulletin, No. 1350) $3.50. S/N 2401-0984. (I 19.3:1350)

Contains a compilation of the new geologic names introduced into the literature from 1961-1967, in the United States, its possessions, the Trust Territory of the Pacific Islands, and the Panama Canal Zone.

HYDROLOGY

BIBLIOGRAPHIES

626. U.S. Bureau of Reclamation. **List of Bureau of Reclamation Bibliographies.** Comp. by Janet B. Talbot. Denver, Library Branch, Office of Engineering Reference, 1970. 39p. $0.80 (from issuing agency). LC Card No. 75-609350. (I 27.10/5:246)

627. U.S. Department of the Interior. **Water Resources Research Catalog, Volume 5.** Prep. by the Science Information Exchange, Smithsonian Institution. Washington, GPO, 1970. 1515p. (Office of Water Resources Research. Water Resources Scientific Information Center) $9.50. LC Card No. 65-61526. (I 1.94:5)

628. U.S. Department of the Interior. **Water Resources Research Catalog, Volume 6.** Prep. by the Science Information Exchange, Smithsonian Institution. Washington, GPO, 1971. 2 vols. (Office of Water Resources Research,

Water Resources Scientific Information Center)
This series presents "summary descriptions of current research on water resources problems," and makes available information on what is being done, by whom, and where. Volumes describe active research projects and list investigators and organizations. Both federally and privately supported projects are included. Indexed in each volume by subjects, investigators, contractors, and supporting agencies.

629. U.S. Geological Survey. **Bibliography of Tritium Studies Related to Hydrology through 1966.** By Edward C. Rhodehamel, Veronica B. Kron, and Verda M. Dougherty. Washington, GPO, 1971. 174p. (Water Supply Papers, No. 1900) $0.75. LC Card No. 76-608171. (I 19.13:1900)

630. U.S. Tennessee Valley Authority. **Indexed Bibliography of the Tennessee Valley Authority, Cumulative Supplement: January—December 1967.** Knoxville, Tenn., TVA, 1968 [1970]. 39p. (Technical Library) Issuing agency. LC Card No. 36-26628. (Y 3.T 25:31 T 25/2/967)

631. U.S. Tennessee Valley Authority. **Indexed Bibliography of the Tennessee Valley Authority, Cumulative Supplement: January—December 1968.** Knoxville, Tenn., TVA, 1970. 39p. (Technical Library) Issuing agency. LC Card No. 36-26628. (Y 3.T 25:31 T 25/2/968)
Lists journal articles about the TVA program in numerical order. Entries are not annotated. Complete author and subject indexes.

632. U.S. Water Resources Council. **Annotated Bibliography on Hydrology and Sedimentation, 1966-1968: United States and Canada.** Prep. under the auspices of the Hydrology and Sedimentation Committees, Water Resources Council. Washington, GPO, 1970. 613p. $5.25. (Y 3.W 29:9/10)
A guide to the literature of hydrology and sedimentation published in the United States and Canada from 1966 through 1968. Arranged alphabetically by author with full bibliographic information and brief annotation. Detailed subject index.

DICTIONARIES

633. U.S. Bureau of Reclamation. **Thesaurus of Water Resources Terms: A Collection of Water Resources and Related Terms for Use in Indexing Technical Information.** Washington, GPO, 1971. 339p. $3.25. S/N 2403-0070. (I 27.2:T 34)
Contains 6,585 terms arranged according to lead terms and providing broader and narrower hierarchical relationships as well as related terms.

634. U.S. Geological Survey. **Definitions of Selected Ground-Water Terms, Revisions and Conceptual Refinements.** By S. W. Lohman and others. Washington, Geological Survey, 1970. 54p. Issuing agency. (I 19.2:G 91)

DIRECTORIES

635. U.S. Missouri Basin Inter-Agency Committee. **Directory of Federal and State Officials Engaged in Water Resources Development.** Washington, the Committee, 1970. 52p. Issuing agency. LC Card No. 61-62228. (Y 3. M 69:2D 62/971)

636. U.S. Water Resources Council. **Coordination Directory for Planning Studies and Reports.** Washington, GPO, 1971. 204p. Issuing agency. (Y 3. W 29:2C 78)
   This directory is issued "for the use of agencies represented on the Water Resources Council and all other federal, state, local and private interests concerned with the investigation and development of water and related land resources." It provides a description of various agencies' areas of interest and responsibility as well as lists of names and addresses.

INDEXES

637. U.S. Geological Survey. **Index of Surface-Water Records to September 30, 1970.** Washington, GPO, 1971. 16 pts. (circulars) Issuing agency.
   Part 1. North Atlantic Slope Basin. 89p. (I 19.4/2:651)
   Part 2. South Atlantic Slope and Eastern Gulf of Mexico Basins. 88p. (I 19.4/2:652)
   Part 3. Ohio River Basin. 71p. (I 19.4/2:653)
   Part 4. St. Lawrence River Basin. 43p. (I 19.4/2:654)
   Part 5. Hudson Bay and Upper Mississippi River Basins. 65p. (I 19.4/2:655)
   Part 6. Missouri River Basin. 91p. (I 19.4/2:656)
   Part 7. Lower Mississippi River Basin. 67p. (I 19.4/2:657)
   Part 8. Western Gulf of the Mexico Basins. 53p. (I 19.4/2:658)
   Part 9. Colorado River Basin. 55p. (I 19.4/2:659)
   Part 10. The Great Basin. 39p. (I 19.4/2:660)
   Part 11. Pacific Slope Basins in California. 53p. (I 19.4/2:661)
   Part 12. Pacific Slope Basins in Washington and Upper Columbian River Basin. 40p. (I 19.4/2:662)
   Part 13. Snake River Basin. 29p. (I 19.4/2:663)
   Part 14. Pacific Slope Basins in Oregon and Lower Columbia River Basin. 31p. (I 19.4/2:664)
   Part 15. Alaska. 21p. (I 19.4/2:665)
   Part 16. Hawaii and Other Pacific Areas. 27p. (I 19.4/2:666)
   Lists surface-water records which have been or are to be published in reports of the Geological Survey through September 1970. Stations are listed in downstream order with an alphabetical list of streams, lakes, and reservoirs at the end of each volume.

638. U.S. Geological Survey. **Catalog of Information on Water Data: Index to Areal Investigations and Miscellaneous Water Data Activities.** 2nd ed. Washington, Geological Survey, 1971. 178p. Issuing agency. (I 19.2:W 29/20/970)

The *Catalog of Information on Water Data* is a file of information about water-data-acquisition activities which does not contain the actual data. The actual data are obtained by various federal, state, municipal agencies, and private organizations and reported to the Office of Water Data Coordination which compiled this catalog and the three listed below.

This section of the *Catalog of Information on Water Data* is concerned with specific projects or shorter term data activities that involve field or laboratory measurements or observations not included in other sections of the catalog. It contains 1) title of each investigation; 2) geographic area covered; 3) inclusive dates; 4) description of the investigation; 5) plans for report publication; and 6) reporting agency.

639. U.S. Geological Survey. **Catalog of Information on Water Data: Index to Ground Water Stations.** Comp. by J. R. Rapp, W. W. Doyel, and E. B. Chase. Washington, Geological Survey, 1970. 657p. Issuing agency. LC Card No. 72-606499. (I 19.2:W 29/21/968)

This index groups ground water stations by states, by counties within states, and by agencies within counties.

640. U.S. Geological Survey. **Catalog of Information on Water Data: Index to the Surface Water Section.** 4th ed. Washington, Geological Survey, 1970. 677p. Issuing agency. (I 19.2:W 29/12/970)

This section contains 1) identification and location of stations, 2) major types of data collected, 3) frequency of data collection, 4) in what form the data are stored, and 5) agencies storing the data. Stations are grouped by geographic units and listed sequentially by map numbers.

641. U.S. Geological Survey. **Catalog of Information on Water Data: Index to the Water Quality Section.** Washington, Geological Survey, 1970. 443p. Issuing agency. LC Card 73-606877. (I 19.2:W 29/13/970)

In this section stations are grouped by geographic units. The following information is given: 1) identification and location of stations, 2) major types of data collected, 3) frequency of data collection, 4) in what form the data are stored, and 5) agencies reporting activities.

METEOROLOGY

GENERAL WORKS

642. U.S. Environmental Science Services Administration. **The Environmental Data Service: Services and Publications.** Washington, GPO, 1970. 18p. $0.30. (C 52.2:En 8/5)

The Environmental Science Services Administration uses data gathered from the earth, sea, sun, and atmosphere to describe and predict the state of man's physical environment. This booklet describes the products and services of ESSA's centers, the National Climatic Center, Seismological Data Center, Geodetic Data Center, Geomagnetic Data Center, and the Aeronomy and Space Data Center.

643. U.S. Environmental Science Services Administration. **Guide to Soviet Literature Accessions in the Atmospheric Sciences Library and the Geophysical Sciences Library, July—August 1969.** Trans. by Irene A. Donehoo. Springfield, Va., CFSTI, 1969. 68p. (WB/TA Series) $3.00. (C 52.21/2:23)

644. U.S. Environmental Science Services Administration. **Guide to Soviet Literature Accessions in the Atmospheric Sciences Library and the Geophysical Sciences Library, January—February 1970.** Trans. by Irene A. Donehoo. Washington, ESSA, 1970. 92p. (Environmental Data Service, WB/TA Series No. 24) LC Card No. 72-607236. (C 51.21/2:24)

645. U.S. Naval Oceanographic Office. **Bibliography on Meteorology, Climatology, and Physical/Chemical Oceanography.** Prep. by the American Meteorological Society. Washington, Naval Oceanographic Office, 1970. 1 vol. (in 2), 614p. $13.00 (from issuing agency). LC Card No. 72-609667. (D 203.24/3:M 56/v. 1 and ind.)

CLIMATOLOGY

646. U.S. National Air Pollution Control Administration. **The Climate of Cities: A Survey of Recent Literature.** By James T. Peterson. Washington, GPO, 1970. 48p. $0.55. LC Card No. 70-60448. (HE 20.1309:59)

 A survey of the literature on city climatology with emphasis on that written since 1962. The meteorological aspects of urban climate which are most fully covered are temperature, humidity, visibility, radiation, wind and precipitation.

647. U.S. National Oceanic and Atmospheric Administration. **Drought Bibliography.** By Wayne C. Palmer and Lyle M. Denny. Springfield, Va., NTIS, 1971. 236p. (NOAA Technical Memorandum, Environmental Data Service Publication No. 20) $3.00. LC Card No. 73-614160. (C 53.13/2:EDS-20)

648. U.S. National Oceanic and Atmospheric Administration. **Spotter's Guide for Identifying and Reporting Severe Local Storms.** Washington, GPO, 1970. 16p. $0.30. (C 55.108:St 7)

 Provides photographs and narrative descriptions for aid in spotting severe local storms.

MINERALOGY

649. U.S. Bureau of Mines. **List of Bureau of Mines Publications and Articles, January 1, 1965—December 31, 1969.** Comp. by Rita D. Sylvester. Washington, GPO, 1970. 437p. $3.75. (I 28.5:965-69)

650. U.S. Bureau of Mines. **List of Bureau of Mines Publications and Articles, January 1—December 31, 1970.** Comp. by Rita D. Sylvester. Washington, GPO, 1971. 130p. $1.50. S/N 2404-0966. (I 28.5:970)

These two bibliographies list reports and articles published by the Bureau of Mines. Indexed by authors and subjects.

651. U.S. Bureau of Mines. **Mineral Facts and Problems.** 1970 ed. Washington, GPO, 1971. 1291p. (Bureau of Mines Bulletin No. 650) $10.75. LC Card No. 79-612225. (I 28.3:650)

    A one-volume encyclopedia of current information on metals, minerals, and fuels. Easy to read and nontechnical enough for student reference use. Each of the 93 separate commodity chapters is organized into four parts: background (industry pattern, reserves, etc.); outlook (predicts uses to year 2000); problems; references. Each chapter is available separately at 10 cents to 25 cents. A set of unbound chapters is available at $15.80.

652. U.S. Bureau of Mines. **Minerals Yearbook, 1968, Volumes I-II.** Washington, GPO, 1970. 1208p. $6.25 (cloth). LC Card No. 33-26551. (I 28.37:968/v. 1, 2)

653. U.S. Bureau of Mines. **Minerals Yearbook, 1969, Volumes I-II.** Washington, GPO, 1971. 1194p. $6.00 (cloth). LC Card No. 33-26551. S/N 2404-0772. (I 28.37:969/v. 1, 2)

654. U.S. Bureau of Mines. **Minerals Yearbook, 1968, Volume III.** Washington, GPO, 1970. 838p. $5.00 (cloth). LC Card No. 33-26551. (I 28.37:968/v. 3)

655. U.S. Bureau of Mines. **Minerals Yearbook, 1969, Volume III.** Washington, GPO, 1971. 848p. $4.75 (cloth). LC Card No. 33-26551. S/N 2404-0961. (I 28.37:969/v. 3)

656. U.S. Bureau of Mines. **Minerals Yearbook, 1968, Volume IV.** Washington, GPO, 1970. 979p. $5.50 (cloth). LC Card No. 33-26551. (I 28.37:968/v. 4)

657. U.S. Bureau of Mines. **Minerals Yearbook, 1969, Volume IV.** Washington, GPO, 1971. 942p. $5.00 (cloth). LC Card No. 33-26551. S/N 2404-0957. (I 28.37:969/v. 4)

    This standard work is a comprehensive review of U.S. and foreign mineralogical and metallurgical developments, techniques, production, and trade. It is published annually in four volumes. Volumes one and two, "Metals, Minerals and Fuels," contain reviews of the mineral industries, statistical tables, world production and foreign trade reviews. In addition, there are chapters which each deal with a specific mineral, metal, or mineral fuel. Volume three, "Area Reports: Domestic," includes chapters on each state, the U.S. island possessions in the Pacific and Caribbean, Puerto Rico and the Canal Zone. General statistical summaries are also provided. Volume four, "Area Reports: International," contains introductory materials on minerals in the world economy. Other chapters give the latest available mineral data for more than 130 foreign countries and areas, relating these data to the nations' economies.

OCEANOGRAPHY

GENERAL WORKS

ATLASES, MAPS, AND CHARTS

658. U.S. National Science Foundation. **Oceanographic Atlas of the International Indian Ocean Expedition.** Ed. by Klaus Wyrtki. Washington, GPO, 1971. 544p. illus. maps (part col.). $30.00 (cloth). LC Card No. 73-654319. S/N 3800-0104. (NS 1.2:In 2/4)

The International Indian Ocean Expedition was an intensive study of the 28 million-square-mile Indian Ocean by scientists of 28 cooperating nations working from shore stations and an extensive fleet of research vessels. Major areas of interest were biological factors, including possible fishery resources; the formation of the ocean basin and the forces that have shaped and are continuing to shape it; the chemical and physical description of the waters of the Indian Ocean, and the study of their motions; and the interaction between the ocean and the atmosphere particularly with respect to the monsoon winds. This atlas contains 449 colored maps and diagrams. It provides information on water temperature, depth, density, temperature gradient, and transport, as well as the salt, oxygen, phosphate, nitrate, and silicate content of the water. To provide users of this atlas with the greatest amount of information about the relatively unknown Indian Ocean, and to help provide a picture of the Ocean as an entity, the volume includes almost all data collected in the Indian Ocean from the mid-1920s to 1966.

659. U.S. Naval Oceanographic Office. **Catalog of Nautical Charts: Special Purpose Navigational Charts and Publications.** Washington, GPO, 1971. 33p. Issuing agency. (D 203.22:1-N-A)

This catalog contains a list of navigational publications, maps showing regions and areas covered by the various lists and other special purpose oceanographic charts.

BIBLIOGRAPHIES

660. U.S. Coast and Geodetic Survey. **Summary of Coast and Geodetic Survey Technical Publications and Charts.** Washington, GPO, 1970. 45p. Issuing agency. (C 4.12/4:P 96)

661. U.S. Environmental Data Service. **World Data Center A: Oceanography; Catalogue of Accessioned Soviet Publications, 1957-68.** Washington, GPO, 1971. 380p. Issuing agency. (C 55.220/2:957-68)

This is a special supplement to the *Catalogue of Accessioned Publications, 1957-67.*

662. U.S. National Bureau of Standards. **Oceanography: A Bibliography of Selected Activation Analysis Literature.** Ed. by G. J. Lutz. Washington, GPO, 1970. 43p. $0.50. LC Card No. 78-608118. (C 13.46:534)

The literature of oceanography in activation analysis is reindexed in detail with respect to element determined, matrix analyzed, and technique used for precise literature searching. An author index is included.

663. U.S. Naval Oceanographic Office. **Catalog of Publications 1971.** Washington, GPO, 1971. 73p. $0.75. S/N 0842-0054. (D 203.22:1-P/971)

This is a listing of publications of interest to the scientific, oceanographic and maritime communities arranged by subject, with a brief description of the content of each.

DIRECTORIES

664. U.S. Office of the Oceanographer of the Navy. **University Curricula in the Marine Sciences and Related Fields, Academic Years 1971-72 and 1972-73.** Washington, GPO, 1971. 214p. $1.75. S/N 0842-0053. (D 218.9:43)

This directory lists colleges and universities with programs in the marine sciences and provides details of each.

MANUALS

665. U.S. Naval Ship Systems Command. **U.S. Navy Diving Manual.** Washington, GPO, 1970. 710p. $7.25 (cloth). LC Card No. 77-606713. (D 211.6/2:D 64/970)

This manual "reflects all new developments and current procedures in the diving field." Beginning with a brief description of the history of diving, it presents information on the general principles and covers such subjects as underwater physics and physiology, basic diving procedure; diving tables; diving hazards (contains a general description of the causes, symptoms, and signs where hazardous marine life is likely to be found); general safety precautions; and reports (e.g., diving record system and its components, diving log book). It includes timely information on surface-supplied diving and self-contained diving and the precautions, procedures and equipment for each.

OCEANOGRAPHIC SHIPS

666. U.S. Department of the Navy. Office of the Oceanographer of the Navy. **Oceanographic Ships, Fore and Aft.** By Stewart B. Nelson. Washington, GPO, 1971. 240p. $4.50 (cloth). LC 71-614043. S/N 0842-0050. (D 218.2:Sh 6)

This interesting history of oceanographic ships was written primarily for the general public and those interested in careers as marine scientists, naval architects, marine engineers, etc. It contains historical data and illustrations of over 218 ships from the 1800s through 1967. Also included are lists of current oceanographic ships and of pertinent abbreviations and symbols.

667. U.S. National Oceanic and Atmospheric Administration. **Research Vessels of the National Marine Fisheries Service.** Washington, GPO, 1971. 46p. $0.50. S/N 0320-0011. (C 55.13:NMFS Circ-362)

The research fleet of the National Marine Fisheries Service of the

National Oceanic and Atmospheric Administration, U.S. Department of Commerce, is described in detail by individual ship. The descriptions are accompanied by photographs. A brief text covering fleet activities precedes the vessel descriptions.

TIDES

668. U.S. Coast and Geodetic Survey. **Tide Tables, High and Low Water Predictions: Central and Western Pacific Ocean and Indian Ocean, 1971.** Washington, GPO, 1970. 386p. $2.00 (from Issuing agency). LC Card No. 7-36369. (C 4.15/6:971)

669. U.S. National Ocean Survey. **Tide Tables, High and Low Water Predictions: Central and Western Pacific Ocean and Indian Ocean, 1972.** Washington, GPO, 1971. 386p. $2.00 (from Issuing agency). (C 55.421/4:972)

670. U.S. Coast and Geodetic Survey. **Tide Tables, High and Low Water Predictions, 1971: East Coast of North and South America, Including Greenland.** Washington, GPO, 1970. 290p. $2.00 (from Issuing agency). LC Card No. 48-46486. (C 4.15/4:971)

671. U.S. National Ocean Survey. **Tide Tables, High and Low Water Predictions, 1972: East Coast of North and South America, Including Greenland.** Washington, GPO, 1971. 290p. $2.00 (from Issuing agency). (C 55.421/2:972)

672. U.S. Coast and Geodetic Survey. **Tide Tables, High and Low Water Predictions, 1971: Europe and the West Coast of Africa Including the Mediterranean Sea.** Washington, GPO, 1970. 209p. $2.00 (from Issuing agency). LC Card No. 50-60825. (C 4.15/7:971)

673. U.S. National Ocean Survey. **Tide Tables, High and Low Water Predictions, 1972: Europe and the West Coast of Africa, Including the Mediterranean Sea.** Washington, GPO, 1972. 209p. $2.00 (from Issuing agency). (C 55.421/3:972)

674. U.S. Coast and Geodetic Survey. **Tide Tables, High and Low Water Predictions, 1971: West Coast of North America Including the Hawaiian Islands.** Washington, GPO, 1970. 226p. $2.00 (from Issuing agency). LC Card No. 48-47037. (C 4.15/5:971)

675. U.S. National Ocean Survey. **Tide Tables, High and Low Water Predictions: West Coast of North America Including the Hawaiian Islands.** Washington, GPO, 1971. 226p. $2.00 (from Issuing agency). (C 55.421:972)

These works include, in addition to the tables, a bibliography of publications relating to tides and currents and an index map of the tide table coverage.

PALEONTOLOGY

676. U.S. Geological Survey. **Index of Generic Names of Fossil Plants, 1820-1965.** By Henry N. Andrews, Jr. Washington, GPO, 1970. 354p. (U.S. Geological Survey Bulletin No. 1300) $1.75. LC Card No. 75-604645. (I 19.3:1300)

  This index revises and updates Bulletin Number 1013, which covered the years 1820 to 1950. It is based on the Geological Survey's *Compendium Index of Paleobotany* and its accompanying bibliography.

  For each genus a type species or one that is representative is cited. Also, a brief notation is given concerning the age, geographic origin and taxonomic status of most of the fossils. For some plants this information is supplemented with other notations to aid the reader. Complete references are given for all citations. This index is intended to be an "informational source concerning the origin of the respective generic concepts" rather than a critical study and no "organized authority stands behind the proposed types." It is an "attempt to compile a complete list of generic names of fossil plants and to provide information concerning the origin of the generic names." Over 100 pages of bibliography follow the index.

677. U.S. Smithsonian Institution. **Catalog of Illustrated Paleozoic Plants in the National Museum of Natural History.** By Arthur D. Watt. Washington, GPO, 1970. 53p. (Smithsonian Contributions to Paleobiology) $0.60. LC Card No. 77-608935. (SI 1.30:5)

  This catalog of the illustrated Paleozoic fossils in the National Museum of Natural History is up to date as of 1964 and is intended to supplement National Museum Bulletin 53, Part 2, entitled *Catalogue of the Type and Figured Specimens of Fossils, Minerals, Rocks, and Ores in the Department of Geology, United States National Museum: Part 2, Fossil Vertebrates; Fossil Plants; Minerals, Rocks and Ores.* Genera are listed alphabetically as are species under each genus. Indexed by species.

678. U.S. Smithsonian Institution. **Catalog of Type Specimens of Invertebrate Fossils: Conodonta.** Comp. by Frederick J. Collier. Washington, GPO, 1971. 256p. (Smithsonian Contributions to Paleobiology, No. 9) $2.50. LC Card No. 75-614489. S/N 4700-0147. (SI 1.30:9)

  Type specimens of the conodonts in the national collection are listed alphabetically by generic and specific names. Geographic, stratigraphic, bibliographic and other pertinent information concerning each specimen is included in the initial record entry. Additional entries for each specimen list references and binomen changes. Name changes are also cross-indexed in the initial record list. Two appendixes list occurrence of species by stratigraphy and by geographical location.

SEISMOLOGY

679. U.S. Coast and Geodetic Survey. **List of Seismological Publications.** Washington, the Survey, 1970. 12p. Issuing agency. (C 4.50:Se 4/970)

680. U.S. National Ocean Survey. **List of Seismological Publications.** Washington, GPO, 1971. 12p. Issuing agency. (C 55.413:Se 4)

681. U.S. Coast and Geodetic Survey. **United States Earthquakes 1968.** By Jerry L. Coffman and William K. Cloud. Issued by the National Earthquake Information Center. Washington, GPO, 1970. 111p. $1.50. LC Card No. 30-27161. (C 4.25/2:968)

682. U.S. National Ocean Survey. **United States Earthquakes 1969.** By Carl A. von Hake and William K. Cloud. Issued by the National Earthquake Information Center. Washington, GPO, 1971. 80p. $1.00. (C 55.417/2:969)
 Contains detailed technical information for each earthquake registered in the United States, the Panama Canal Zone, Puerto Rico, and the Virgin Islands, and a brief list of major earthquakes of the world. Includes samples of seismograph and tilt-graph readings.

ENGINEERING

GENERAL WORKS

683. U.S. National Bureau of Standards. **Index of U.S. Voluntary Engineering Standards Covering Those Standards, Specifications, Test Methods, and Recommended Practices Issued by National Standardization Organizations in the United States.** Ed. by William J. Slattery. Washington, GPO, 1971. 984p. (NBS Special Publications, No. 329) $9.00 (cloth). LC Card No. 77-607150. (C 13.10:329)

    This computer-produced index contains the permuted titles of more than 19,000 voluntary engineering and related standards, specifications, test methods, and recommended practices in effect as of December 31, 1969, published by 360 U.S. technical societies, professional organizations, and trade associations. The date of publication or last revision, the standard number, and an acronym designating the standards-issuing organization are included in each entry. A list of the acronyms and the names and addresses of the organizations which they represent is found at the beginning of the index.

684. U.S. Naval Ordnance Systems Command. **Maintainability Engineering Handbook.** Washington, GPO, 1970. 464p. $3.75. (D 215.6/2:M 28)

    Presents maintainability engineering principles and procedures applicable to all phases of material acquisitions. This book has been developed for the guidance of project managers, systems engineers, and equipment designers in adapting design techniques and fleet maintenance concepts to available human resources.

AERONAUTICAL AND SPACE ENGINEERING

BIBLIOGRAPHIES

685. U.S. Department of the Air Force. **Aeronautics.** Prep. by Mary Kay Briggs. San Francisco, Pacific Air Force, 1971. 76p. (PACAF Basic Bibliographies for Base Libraries) Available from CINCPACAF (DPSR)/Director, PACAF Libraries, APO, San Francisco, Calif. 96553. LC Card No. 58-61784. (D 301.62:Ae 8/971)

686. U.S. Department of the Air Force. **Air Force Scientific Research Bibliography, Volume VII.** Washington, GPO, 1970. 734p. $7.25 (cloth). LC Card No. 61-60038. (D 301.45/19-2:700/v. 7)

    This volume covers works published from 1963 through 1964. It contains abstracts of all technical notes, technical reports, journal articles, books, symposium proceedings and monographs produced and published by scientists supported in whole or in part by the Air Force Office of Scientific Research.

687. U.S. National Aeronautics and Space Administration. **Aerospace Bibliography.** 5th ed. Comp. by the National Aerospace Education Council.

Washington, GPO, 1970. 102p. $1.00. LC Card No. 66-61596. (NAS 1.19: 48/2)

A selective bibliography for the use of laymen, specifically "elementary and secondary school teachers, their pupils, and . . . the general adult reader." This is an "annotated and graded list of books, reference works, periodicals, and teaching aids dealing with space flight subjects." Reading level of each item is designated by code letters; a separate section lists teaching aids by subject with addresses needed to obtain them. This edition is the first to contain a detailed subject index.

688. U.S. National Aeronautics and Space Administration. **Aerospace Engineering: A Special Bibliography with Indexes.** Springfield, Va., NTIS, 1970. 1145p. $10.00. (NAS 1.21:SP-7037)

This bibliography contains a selection of annotated references to unclassified reports and journal articles which were introduced into the NASA scientific and technical information system. It is indexed by subject, personal author and contract number. This issue was the first in a new series. Monthly issues with annual cumulative indexes are now being published.

689. U.S. National Aeronautics and Space Administration. **Cumulative Index to NASA Tech Briefs, 1963-69.** Springfield, Va., NTIS, 1970. 227 + 877p. [NASA Contractor Report, CR Series No. 5021 (10)] $10.00. [NAS 1.26: CR-5021 (10)]

690. U.S. National Aeronautics and Space Administration. **Scientific and Technical Aerospace Reports: Annual Indexes, Volume 8, Numbers 1-24, January-December 1970.** Washington, GPO, 1971. 4v. $13.25. LC Card No. 64-39060. (NAS 1.9/5:8/1-24/sec. 1-4)

Subject index is in volumes 1 and 2, personal author index in volume 3, corporate source, contract number, report/accession, and accession/report indexes are in volume 4.

691. U.S. National Aeronautics and Space Administration. **Scientific and Technical Aerospace Reports: Semiannual Indexes, Volume 9, Numbers 1-12, January-June 1971.** Washington, GPO, 1971. 2 vols. $5.25. LC Card No. 64-39060. (NAS 1.9/5:9/1-12/sec. 1, 2)

Subject index is in volume 1; volume 2 contains personal author, corporate source, contract number, report/accession, and accession/report indexes.

692. U.S. National Aeronautics and Space Administration. **Space Photography, 1971 Index.** Washington, GPO, 1971. 109p. Issuing agency. (NAS 1.43/4:971)

CHRONOLOGIES AND HISTORIES

693. U.S. National Aeronautics and Space Administration. **Astronautics and Aeronautics, 1968: Chronology on Science, Technology and Policy.** Text by the Science and Technology Division, Library of Congress. Washington, GPO, 1970. 429p. Illus. $2.00. LC Card No. 66-60096. (NAS 1.21:4010)

694. U.S. National Aeronautics and Space Administration. **Astronautics and Aeronautics, 1969: Chronology on Science, Technology and Policy.** Text by the Science and Technology Division, Library of Congress. Washington, GPO, 1971. 534p. illus. $2.25. LC Card No. 66-60096. (NAS 1.21:4014)

These volumes are chronological records of major achievements in space and aeronautical engineering, technology, and development.

695. U.S. Naval Air Systems Command. **United States Naval Aviation, 1910-1970.** Washington, GPO, 1971. 440p. illus. $4.00. S/N 0841-0059. (D 202.2: Av 5/2/910-70)

This is a chronological record of significant events in the growth and development of naval aviation from its beginning through 1970.

696. U.S. Senate. **Soviet Space Program, 1966-1970.** Washington, GPO, 1971. 670p. $3.00. LC Card No. 79-616433. S/N 5271-0263. (92-1:S.doc.51)

Includes data on the goals and purposes, organization, resources, facilities and hardware, manned and unmanned flight programs, bioastronautics, civil and military applications, projections of future plans, attitudes toward international cooperation and space law.

CIVIL AND PUBLIC SAFETY ENGINEERING

CIVIL DEFENSE

697. U.S. Office of Civil Defense. **Abbreviations and Definitions of Terms Used in Civil Defense Training.** Washington, GPO, 1971. 24p. Issuing agency. (D 119.11:51/2)

For use primarily in OCD National Training Programs, to "assist in the understanding and standardization of many civil defense terms." Useful for anyone interested in this area. Dictionary section follows abbreviations list.

698. U.S. Office of Civil Defense. **Civil Defense Motion Picture Catalog.** Washington, GPO, 1971. 35p. Issuing agency. LC Card No. 59-62340. (D 119.11:6/5)

Contains a current list of motion pictures of the Office of Civil Defense. It excludes training films. Films are arranged alphabetically by title, with running time, synopsis, date, price, and address for ordering. Indexed by subjects.

699. U.S. Office of Civil Defense. **National Directory of Qualified Fallout Shelter Analysts.** Washington, GPO, 1970. 592p. Issuing agency. (FS series No. F-1.2) LC Card No. 62-61084. (D 119.8/3:F-1.2/4)

700. U.S. Office of Civil Defense. **National Directory of Certified Fallout Shelter Analysts, Supplement 1.** Washington, GPO, 1971. 59p. Issuing agency. (D 119.8/3:F 1.2/4/supp. 1)

Identifies architectural, engineering, and consulting firms which have certified fallout shelter analysts on their staffs.

FIRE SCIENCES

701. U.S. Department of Agriculture. **Fire Weather: A Guide for Application of Meteorological Information to Forest Fire Control.** Washington, GPO, 1970. 229p. (Agriculture Handbooks, No. 360) $3.75. (A 1.76:360)

    This profusely illustrated handbook is considered by the Department of Agriculture's Forest Service and the Department of Commerce's Weather Bureau to be the world's most complete guide to how fire weather behaves under different kinds of atmospheric, topographic, and tree cover conditions. Growing awareness of fire weather, when combined with related experience on fires, can develop into increasingly intuitive, rapid, and accurate applications. Each chapter is preceded with a paragraph on important points to look for in relating weather factors to fire-control planning and action. Written in everyday language, it is a useful reference and working tool for forest land managers, public and private foresters, rural fire departments, weather forecasters, defense officials, park officials, forestry schools and others associated with the protection of forested lands from fire.

702. U.S. Department of the Interior. Library. **Fire in Northern Regions: A Bibliography.** Comp. by Signe M. Larson. Springfield, Va., CFSTI, 1969. 36p. (Bibliography Series No. 14) $3.00. LC Card No. 70-608865. (I 22.9/2:14)

703. U.S. Forest Service. **Fireline Handbook.** Washington, GPO, 1971. 162p. $3.00 (cloth). S/N 0101-0076. (A 13.36/2:FS 1/6)

    This Forest Service Handbook is a ready reference to fire suppression principles, policies, and data. It tells how to size up the job in relation to fuels, weather, and topography; how to plan the men, equipment, and facilities needed; and how to organize and direct the job efficiently.

704. U.S. National Bureau of Standards. **Bibliographies on Fabric Flammability: Part 1, Wearing Apparel; Part 2, Fabrics Used on Beds; Part 3, Carpets and Rugs.** By Sidney H. Greenfeld, Elizabeth R. Warner, and Hilda W. Reinhart. Washington, GPO, 1970. 36p. (NBS Technical Note No. 498) LC Card No. 79-606550. (C 13.46:498)

705. U.S. National Bureau of Standards. **Bibliographies on Fabric Flammability: Part 4, Interior Furnishings.** By Sidney H. Greenfeld, Elizabeth R. Warner, and Hilda W. Reinhart. Washington, GPO, 1970. 18p. (NBS Technical Note No. 498-1) $0.30. LC Card No. 79-606550. (C 13.46:498-1)

706. U.S. National Bureau of Standards. **Bibliographies on Fabric Flammability: Part 5, Testing and Test Methods.** By Sidney H. Greenfeld, Elizabeth R. Warner, and Hilda W. Reinhart. Washington, GPO, 1970. 33p. (NBS Technical Note No. 498-2) $0.45. LC Card No. 79-606550. (C 13.46:498-2)

    As recognition of the urgency of the flammable fabrics problem, the Flammable Fabrics Act of 1953 was amended in 1967 to include all items of wearing apparel and interior furnishings. In order to facilitate research and assist in the development of new standards and test methods in these areas, a series of bibliographies is being prepared by the National Bureau of Standards Office of Flammable Fabrics in cooperation with the NBS Library. Parts 1-3, published in one volume, cover wearing apparel, fabrics used on beds, and carpets and rugs. Part 4 is on interior furnishings. It includes all of the references on bed fabrics and carpets and rugs that appeared in parts two and three, along with those on upholstered furniture, draperies, curtains, and materials that are used in interior furnishings. Part five relates to test methods and testing of fabrics and products made from fabrics and related materials. Unlike the earlier bibliographies, which cited references to flammability of categories of fabric products, this one cuts across product lines and covers all of the products within the ranges defined in the 1967 amendment to the Flammable Fabrics Act. Approximately 300 citations are included.

LAW ENFORCEMENT

707. U.S. Department of Justice. **Police Telecommunication Systems.** Washington, GPO, 1971. 429p. $3.75. S/N 2700-0075. (J 1.36:71-3)

This guide is written primarily for communications, planning, and supervisory personnel of police agencies, municipal and county officials, state planning agency staff and policy board members, frequency coordinators, and communications consultants. Offers information to enable readers to understand the concepts, elements and techniques of police telecommunication systems and to assess their effectiveness. It provides common standards and suggestions to evaluate performance for guidance in choosing equipment and system modifications, designing new systems, and planning for future demands and improvements. Should also benefit suppliers of equipment and groups associated with similar non-police systems.

708. U.S. Internal Revenue Service. **Firearms Identification for Law Enforcement Officers.** Washington, GPO, 1970. 32p. $0.25. (T 22.19/2:F 51/2/970)

This publication is a visual aid in identifying firearms and destructive devices that must be registered with the Director of the Alcohol, Tobacco and Firearms Division, Internal Revenue Service, in order to be lawfully possessed, as stated under Title II of the Gun Control Act of 1968.

TRANSPORTATION

AVIATION

709. U.S. Bureau of Domestic Commerce. **World Survey of Civil Aviation: Canada, 1970.** Washington, GPO, 1970. 48p. $0.30. (C 41.96:C 16/970)

Report includes an evaluation of air transportation in Canada, with particular emphasis on fleet composition, flight operations, and marketing and investment opportunities. It also gives an extensive description of the Canadian aerospace industry.

710. U.S. Civil Aeronautics Board. **List of Publications.** Washington, CAB, 1971. 16p. Issuing agency. (C 31.255:971)

711. U.S. Federal Aviation Administration. **The FAA Catalog 1971.** Oklahoma City, Federal Aviation Administration, 1971. 20p. free (from FAA, P.O. Box 25082, Oklahoma City, Okla. 73125). (TD 4.17:971)

    The revised edition, published in 1971, is an illustrated, annotated listing of some 70 materials: 16mm films, filmstrips, and slides prepared by the FAA. Some titles of general interest are in areas such as history of aviation, careers, flight instruction, and aerodynamics. The catalog includes information on obtaining loan of the films.

712. U.S. Federal Aviation Administration. **FAA Inspection Authorization Directory.** Washington, GPO, 1971. 104p. $1.25. (TD 4.2:In 7)

    Arranged by FAA region and then by last names. Lists all FAA certified mechanics who hold an inspection authorization as of December 1970.

713. U.S. Federal Aviation Administration. **FAA Statistical Handbook of Aviation.** 1969 ed. Washington, GPO, 1970. 278p. $2.75. (TD 4.20:969)

714. U.S. Federal Aviation Administration. **FAA Statistical Handbook of Aviation.** Prep. by Sylvia M. Goring. 1970 ed. Washington, GPO, 1971. 278p. $2.75. S/N 5007-0166. (TD 4.20:970)

    "Designed to serve as a convenient source for historical data, and to assist in evaluating progress, determining trends, and estimating future activity." Contains charts, graphs and narrative descriptions of U.S. aviation activity including airports, aircraft and airmen, aeronautical products and exports, accidents and general aviation. Includes a glossary and a detailed subject index.

715. U.S. Federal Aviation Administration. **United States Civil Aircraft Register.** Washington, GPO, 1970. 2 vols. $14.75. (TD 4.18/2:970)

716. U.S. Federal Aviation Administration. **United States Civil Aircraft Register.** Washington, GPO, 1970. 2 vols. $13.50. (TD 4.18/2:970-2/v.)

717. U.S. Federal Aviation Administration. **United States Civil Aircraft Register.** Washington, GPO, 1971. 1565p. (Aeronautical Center, Flight Standards Technical Division: AC-20-6P) $11.75. (TD 4.18/2:971)

718. U.S. Federal Aviation Administration. **United States Civil Aircraft Register.** Washington, GPO, 1971. 1650p. $10.25. S/N 5007-0167. (TD 4.18/2:971-2)

    Civil aircraft are listed by registration numbers and the following information is provided for each: manufacturer's serial number, make, model, and type; number of engines, their make, model and type; data of aircraft inspection; and type of registrant.

BOATING

719. U.S. Coast Guard. **Boating Statistics, 1969.** Washington, GPO, 1970. 79p. Issuing agency. LC Card No. 68-61293. (TD 5.11:969)

720. U.S. Coast Guard. **Boating Statistics, 1970.** Washington, GPO, 1971. 73p. Issuing agency. LC Card No. 68-61293. (TD 5.11:970)
    Contains statistics on boat registration, boating accidents and related data. Includes a glossary of terms used in boating accident statistical reports.

HIGHWAYS AND TRAFFIC SAFETY

721. U.S. Federal Highway Administration. **Highway Statistics, 1969.** Washington, GPO, 1970. 212p. $1.75. S/N 5002-0082. (TD 2.23:969)

722. U.S. Federal Highway Administration. **Highway Statistics, 1970.** Washington, GPO, 1971. 199p. $1.75. S/N 5001-0025. (TD 2.23:970)
    Presents statistics and analytical tables of general interest on motor fuel; motor vehicles, driver licensing; highway user taxation; state highway finance; highway mileage; federal aid for highways; and highway finance data for municipalities, counties, townships, and other units of government.

723. U.S. Federal Highway Administration. **Manual on Uniform Traffic Control Devices for Streets and Highways.** Rev. ed. Washington, GPO, 1971. 377p. $3.50. LC Card No. 72-614649. S/N 5001-0021. (TD 2.8:T 67)
    This manual explains the basic principles which govern the design and use of traffic control devices. Traffic control devices are defined as "all signs, signals, markings, and devices placed on or adjacent to a street or highway by authority of a public body or official having jurisdiction to regulate, warn or guide traffic." The devices listed here are for all streets and highways regardless of type or class or the governmental agency having jurisdiction. A separate section covers traffic control devices for school areas.

724. U.S. National Bureau of Standards. **Bibliography on Motor Vehicle and Traffic Safety.** Washington, GPO, 1971. 220p. Issuing agency. LC Card No. 78-613735. (C 13.37/4:M 85)
    This bibliography, published by the Office of Vehicle Systems Research, lists all publications acquired by the OVSR since its establishment in 1967. It is arranged by subjects without annotations or index.

725. U.S. National Highway Safety Bureau. **Highway Safety Literature, Annual Cumulation, 1969: Accident Bibliography, Issues 69-1 through 69-50, January-December 1969.** Washington, GPO, 1970. 120p. Issuing agency. (TD 8.10/3:969/ac)

726. U.S. National Highway Safety Bureau. **Highway Safety Literature, Annual Cumulation, 1969: Human Factors Bibliography, Issues 69-1 through 69-50, January-December 1969.** Washington, GPO, 1970. 137p. Issuing agency. (TD 8.10/3:969/hf)

727. U.S. National Highway Safety Bureau. **Highway Safety Literature, Annual Cumulation, 1969: Highway Safety Bibliography, Issues 69-1 through 69-50, January-December, 1969.** Washington, GPO, 1970. 134p. Issuing agency. (TD 8.10/3:969/hs)

728. U.S. National Highway Safety Bureau. **Highway Safety Literature, Annual Cumulation, 1969: Related Areas Bibliography, Issues 69-1 through 69-50, January-December 1969.** Washington, GPO, 1970. 67p. Issuing agency. (TD 8.10/3:969/ra)

729. U.S. National Highway Safety Bureau. **Highway Safety Literature, Annual Cumulation, 1969: Vehicle Safety Bibliography, Issues 69-1 through 69-50, January-December, 1969.** Washington, GPO, 1970. 214p. Issuing agency. (TD 8.10/3:969/vs)

These five bibliographies are subject cumulations of the weekly *Highway Safety Literature.* Entries contain NHSB accession number, title, personal and corporate authors, date, number of pages, and a detailed abstract. Arranged by subject; not indexed.

730. U.S. National Highway Safety Bureau. **Highway Safety Literature: Annual Indexes to Issues 69-1 through 69-50, January-December 1969.** Washington, GPO, 1970. 188p. Issuing agency. LC Card No. 70-604109. (TD 8.10/2:69-1 through 69-50)

Includes personal and corporate author indexes, and subject index to the 1969 weekly issues of *Highway Safety Literature.*

731. U.S. National Highway Safety Bureau. **NHSB Corporate Author Authority List.** Washington, GPO, 1970. 138p. Issuing agency. LC Card No. 70-604109. (TD 2.202:C 81/970)

This supplement to *Highway Safety Literature* is the authority list for indexing and entering corporate authors.

732. U.S. National Highway Safety Bureau. **NHSB Thesaurus of Traffic and Motor Vehicle Safety Terms.** 2nd ed. Washington, GPO, 1970. 129p. Issuing agency. (TD 8.10/4:T 34)

This is a supplement to *Highway Safety Literature.* It will aid researchers using this bibliography to find the correct subject heading and related headings for specific areas of research.

733. U.S. National Highway Traffic Safety Administration. **Annotated Bibliography: The Relationship Between Vehicle Defects and Vehicle Crashes.** Prep. by the Baylor College of Medicine. Springfield, Va., NTIS, 1970. 59p. $3.00. (TD 8.11:007-369)

734. U.S. National Transportation Safety Board. **Publications of the National Transportation Safety Board, 1970.** Washington, GPO, 1970. 11p. Issuing agency. (TD 1.115:970)

735. U.S. National Transportation Safety Board. **Publications of the National Transportation Safety Board, 1971.** Washington, GPO, 1971. 12p. Issuing agency. LC Card No. 76-603270. (TD 1.115:971)

ELECTRICAL AND ELECTRONIC ENGINEERING

736. U.S. Department of the Air Force. **Communications and Electronics.** Prep. by Harry W. McAnallen. San Francisco, Pacific Air Forces, 1970. 111p. (PACAF Basic Bibliographies for Base Libraries) Available from CINCPACAF (DPSR)/Director, PACAF Libraries, APO, San Francisco, Calif. 96553. LC Card No. 58-61785. (D 301.62:C 73/969)

737. U.S. Department of the Air Force. **Communications-Electronics Terminology.** Washington, GPO, 1970. 320p. $2.50. (D 301.7:11-1)
   The purpose of this glossary is to "provide a comprehensive reference source of specialized terminology" in communication-electronics. Contains concise definitions of technical terms and a separate listing of abbreviations. Selected non-C-E terms that are closely related to, or closely associated with, C-E terms are also included for clarity and convenience.

MILITARY ENGINEERING

738. U.S. Department of the Army. **Small Arms Identification and Operation Guide: Eurasian Communist Countries.** By Harold E. Johnson. Washington, GPO, 1970. 218p. Issuing agency. LC Card No. 79-610945. (D 101.6/5:Eu 7)

739. U.S. Joint Chiefs of Staff. **Dictionary of Military and Associated Terms.** Washington, GPO, 1971. 350p. $3.50. (D 5.12:1/8)
   This dictionary supersedes *Dictionary of United States Military Terms for Joint Usage*, published in 1968. It is a dictionary of terms prepared under the direction of the Joint Chiefs of Staff in coordination with the military services for planning and operational usage. Terms and definitions which have been approved for the NATO, SEATO, CENTO, and IADB glossaries are incorporated in this edition with those which have U.S. joint service approval.

NUCLEAR ENGINEERING

ABSTRACTS AND INDEXES

740. U.S. Atomic Energy Commission. **Index to Conferences Relating to Nuclear Science.** Ed. by Willie E. Clark, Doris H. McGinnis, and Carol B. Patterson. Springfield, Va., NTIS, 1971. 369p. (AEC Research and Development Reports, No. TID-4044) $6.00. LC Card No. 77-611971. (Y 3.At 7: 22/TID-4044)
   Indexes are by permuted titles, cities, numbered conferences, report numbers, and titles.

741. U.S. Atomic Energy Commission. **Nuclear Science Abstracts: Cumulative Report Number Index with Public Availability Citations, Volumes 21-24.** Washington, GPO, 1971. 444 + 113p. $4.25. LC Card No. 50-4390. (Y 3.At 7: 16-2/21-24/ind. rp. nos.)

Updates two earlier cumulations for volumes 1-15 (1948-1961) and volumes 16-21 (1962-1967). This covers the years 1968 through 1970.

742. U.S. Atomic Energy Commission. **Nuclear Science Abstracts, Volume 24, 1970: Annual Index.** Washington, GPO, 1971. 3 vols. $22.50. LC Card No. 50-4390. (Y 3.At 7:16-5/24-2/pts. 1-3)

Personal and corporate author indexes are in part one; subject index is in parts two and three.

743. U.S. Department of Interior. **Abstracts of Literature on Distillation of Seawater and on the Use of Nuclear Energy for Desalting.** By K. O. Johnsson. Washington, GPO, 1970. 280p. (Saline Water Research and Development Progress Reports, No. 589) $2.00. LC Card No. 74-610381. (I 1.88: 589)

Contains abstracts of desalination literature generally available to the public. Divided into the following chapters: Energy Sources, Energy Utilization, Seawater Distillation Processes, Other Desalting Processes, Overall Plant Studies, Siting Considerations, Industrial Applications, Water Utilization, and others. Contains the following information in each entry: author, title, corporate author, number of pages, number of figures, number of references, publication date, document number or journal reference, a detailed abstract, and a list of selected keywords. Indexed by personal authors and keywords.

BIBLIOGRAPHIES

744. U.S. Atomic Energy Commission. **Controlled Fusion and Plasma Research: Literature Search.** Comp. by Milton O. Whitston. Springfield, Va., NTIS, 1971. 344 + 129p. [AEC Research and Development Report, No. TID-3557 (1970 supp.)] $6.00. [Y 3.At 7:22/TID-3557 (1970 supp.)]

745. U.S. Atomic Energy Commission. **Natural Environmental Radioactivity: An Annotated Bibliography.** By Alfred W. Klement, Jr. Springfield, Va., CFSTI, 1970. 72p. $3.00. [Y 3.At 7:22/WASH-1061 (supp.)]

Updates the work with the same title published in 1965.

746. U.S. Atomic Energy Commission. **Pulsars, A Bibliography.** By William D. Matheny. Springfield, Va., CFSTI, 1970. 76p. (AEC Research and Development Reports No. TID-3320) $3.00. (Y 3.At 7:22/TID-3320)

747. U.S. Atomic Energy Commission. **Pulsars, A Bibliography.** By William D. Matheny. Springfield, Va., NTIS, 1971. 40 + 24p. [AEC Research and Development Reports No. TID-3320 (supp. 1)] $3.00. [Y 3.At 7:22/TID-3320 (supp. 1)]

748. U.S. Atomic Energy Commission. **Reactor Safety Literature Search.** Comp. by Henry D. Raleigh. Springfield, Va., NTIS, 1971. 21 + 43p. [AEC Research and Development Reports No. TID-3525 (rev. 5, supp. 6)] $3.00. [Y 3.At 7:22/TID-3525 (rev. 5, supp. 6)]

Includes citations to works which appeared in 1970 on safety aspects of nuclear reactor design, siting, materials, engineered safeguards, and operating procedures. Indexed by subjects, authors, corporate authors, and report number availability.

749. U.S. Atomic Energy Commission. **Selected Annotated Bibliography of Civil, Industrial, and Scientific Uses for Nuclear Explosives.** Comp. by Robert G. West and Robert C. Kelly. Springfield, Va., NTIS, 1971. 359p. [AEC Research and Development Report No. TID-3910 (supp. 7)] $3.00. [Y 3.At 7:22/TID-3910 (supp. 7)]

This bibliography contains detailed abstracts of each work cited. Indexed by report number availability and authors.

750. U.S. Atomic Energy Commission. **Selected Bibliography on Radioactive Occurrences in the United States.** By S. Victoria Krusiewski. Washington, GPO, 1970. 136p. $1.25. (Y 3.At 7:22/RME-4110)

Lists only the "longer and more useful publications on radioactive occurrences in the U.S." that have been issued from 1950 through early 1970. Not annotated or indexed.

751. U.S. Atomic Energy Commission. **Serial Titles Cited in Nuclear Science Abstracts.** Springfield, Va., NTIS, 1971. 434p. [AEC Research and Development Report No. TID-4579 (5th ed.)] $6.00. [Y 3.At 7:22/TID-4579 (5th ed.)]

752. U.S. National Bureau of Standards. **Bibliography on Atomic Transition Probabilities, January 1916 through June 1969.** Washington, GPO, 1970. 104p. (NBS Special Publication No. 320) $1.25. (C 13.10:320)

753. U.S. National Bureau of Standards. **Bibliography on Atomic Transition Probabilities, July 1969 through June 1970.** Washington, GPO, 1971. 60p. [NBS Special Publication No. 320 (supp. 1)] $0.65. S/N 0303-0905. (C 13.10:320/supp. 1)

These bibliographies cite references on atomic transition probabilities from 1916 through June 1970.

754. U.S. National Bureau of Standards. **14-MeV Neutron Generators in Activation Analysis: A Bibliography.** Ed. by G. J. Lutz. Washington, GPO, 1970. 98p. (NBS Technical Note No. 533) $1.00. LC Card No. 72-608312. (C 13.46:533)

The literature of 14-MeV neutron generators in activation analysis is indexed in detail with respect to element determined, matrix analyzed, and technique used for precise literature searching. An author index is included.

CLASSIFICATION

755. U.S. Atomic Energy Commission. **Report Number Codes Used by the USAEC Division of Technical Information in Cataloging Reports.** Comp. by Helen W. White and Edna Cockrell. 9th rev. ed. Springfield, Va., NTIS, 1970. 181p. $3.00. [Y 3.At 7:22/TID-85 (9th rev.)]

756. U.S. Atomic Energy Commission. **Subject Headings Used by the USAEC, Division of Technical Information.** Ed. by Sidney F. Lanier. 10th rev. ed. Springfield, Va., NTIS, 1971. 278p. $3.00. [Y 3.At 7:22/TID-5001 (10th rev.)]

"The subject heading authority is an information indexing and retrieval tool used by the Division of Technical Information Extension in preparing subject indexes to the literature abstracted in *Nuclear Science Abstracts* and in searching these indexes either by manual or machine-assisted means." Includes two appendixes: a list of elements and their symbols and a list of acceptable subheadings.

DICTIONARIES

757. U.S. Atomic Energy Commission. **Safeguards Dictionary.** Washington, GPO, 1971. 64p. $0.35. S/N 5201-0271. (Y 3.At 7:22/WASH-1173)

"Since the expanding effort on safeguards will involve many people from different disciplines and backgrounds," the United States Atomic Energy Commission compiled this dictionary. It supersedes the glossary published in 1970 (see the next entry) and includes a glossary of recommended definitions as well as meanings currently being used (although not recommended).

758. U.S. Atomic Energy Commission. **Safeguards Glossary.** Washington, GPO, 1970. 22p. $0.25. (Y 3.At 7:22/WASH-1162)

DIRECTORIES

759. U.S. Atomic Energy Commission. **Directory of Shipping Containers for Radioactive Materials.** Washington, GPO, 1970. 759p. $6.00. (Y 3.At 7:2 Sh 6/2)

760. U.S. Atomic Energy Commission. **Nuclear Reactors Built, Being Built or Planned in the United States as of December 31, 1970.** Springfield, Va., NTIS, 1971. 36p. $3.00. [Y 3.At 7:22/TID-8200 (23d rev.)]

761. U.S. Atomic Energy Commission. **Nuclear Reactors Built, Being Built or Planned in the United States as of June 30, 1971.** Springfield, Va., 1971. 37p. $3.00. [Y 3.At 7:22/TID-8200 (24th rev.)]

"This compilation contains unclassified information about facilities built, being built, or planned in the United States for domestic use or export ... which are capable of sustaining a nuclear chain reaction." Lists owners, locations, principal contractors, types and power statistics for each.

762. U.S. Congress. Joint Committee on Atomic Energy. **Current Membership of the Joint Committee on Atomic Energy: Membership, Publications, and other Pertinent Information through the 91st Congress, 1st Session.** Washington, Joint Committee, 1970. 57p. Issuing agency. LC Card No. 58-60740. (Y 4.At 7/2:M 51/970)

763. U.S. Congress. Joint Committee on Atomic Energy. **Current Membership of the Joint Committee on Atomic Energy: Membership, Publications, and other Pertinent Information through the 91st Congress, 2d Session.** Washington, Joint Committee, 1971. 62p. Issuing agency. LC Card No. 71-611975. (Y 4.At 7/2:M 51/971)

These guides contain "considerable information that can be of material assistance to any citizen desiring access to unclassified atomic energy data," including lists of unclassified publications, references to atomic energy legislation, names and locations of Atomic Energy Commission depository libraries, and lists of members of the Joint Committee and of the AEC.

TABLES

764. U.S. National Bureau of Standards. **Selected Tables of Atomic Spectra: Section 3; Atomic Energy Levels and Multiplet Tables, CI, CII, CIII, CIV, CV, CVI; Data Derived from Analysis of Optical Spectra.** Washington, GPO, 1970. 84p. (National Standard Reference Data Series No. 3) $1.00. S/N 0303-0744. (C 13.48:3/sec. 3)

765. U.S. National Burea of Standards. **Selected Tables of Atomic Spectra: Section 4; Atomic Energy Levels and Multiplet Tables NIV, NV, NVI, NVII; Data Derived from Analysis of Optical Spectra.** Washington, GPO, 1971. 46p. (National Standard Reference Data Series No. 3) $0.55. LC Card No. 64-60074. (C 13.48:3/sec. 4)

This series is prepared in response to the persistent need for a current revision of two sets of tables containing data on atomic energy levels as derived from analyses of optical spectra.

ENVIRONMENTAL SCIENCES

GENERAL WORKS

BIBLIOGRAPHIES

766. U.S. Advisory Commission on Intergovernmental Relations. **Quest for Environmental Quality: Federal and State Action, 1969-70; An Annotated Bibliography.** By Rochelle L. Stanfield, John J. Callahan, and Sandra Osbourn. Washington, GPO, 1971. 63p. $0.35. LC Card No. 70-612086. (Y 3.Ad 9/8: 2 En 8)

Reports on the legislative and administrative actions of federal and state governments during 1969-70 and provides an annotated bibliography on environmental quality. The bibliography is arranged by subject, then author, and contains lengthy annotations.

767. U.S. Department of the Interior. Library. **Mercury Contamination in the Natural Environment: A Cooperative Bibliography.** Washington, the Library, 1970. 32p. Issuing agency. LC Card No. 75-608877. (I 22.9:M 53)

768. U.S. National Bureau of Standards. **Pollution Analysis: Bibliography of Activation Analysis.** Ed. by G. J. Lutz. Washington, GPO, 1970. 33p. (NBS Technical Notes, No. 532) $0.45. (C 13.46:532)

The literature of the use of activation analysis of pollution samples is indexed in detail with respect to element determined, matrix analyzed, and technique used, for precise literature searching. An author index is included.

769. U.S. National Technical Information Service. **Environmental Pollution: A Selective Bibliography—Information for Business and Industry.** Springfield, Va., NTIS, 1970. 32p. Issuing agency. LC Card No. 72-609703. (C 51.11: En 8)

DIRECTORIES

770. U.S. Office of the President. **The President's 1971 Environmental Program.** Washington, GPO, 1971. 306p. $2.25. S/N 4111-0003. (PrEx 14.2: En 8)

This publication lists bills, letters of transmittal to Congress, and other proposals of the President's Message on the Environment. Also includes a brief description of items which do not require legislation or for which legislation is being drafted.

771. U.S. Smithsonian Institution. **National and International Environmental Monitoring Activities: A Directory.** Cambridge, Mass., Smithsonian Institution, 1970. 292p. $10.00 (from Smithsonian Institution for Short-Lived Phenomena, 60 Garden Street, Cambridge, Mass. 02138). LC Card No. 70-609780. (SI 1.2:En 8/2)

GUIDES

772. U.S. Bureau of Land Management. **All Around You: An Environmental Study Guide.** Washington, GPO, 1971. 126p. $1.50. S/N 2411-0035. (I 53.7/2:En 8)

"Given the tools for discovery, students can learn more about and develop greater responsibility toward the world about them." This study guide, prepared by the U.S. Department of the Interior, acts as an introduction to the world of ecology, for students and teachers alike. Divided into three sections, this guide provides lesson plans on awareness, the urban ecosystem, and nature's ecosystem. Special pages have been provided for teachers to enable them to help students find some answers to their questions regarding the environment. It also includes a bibliography for young readers and a bibliography for advanced readers.

773. U.S. Bureau of Outdoor Recreation. **Miniature Environments, An Environmental Education Guidebook.** Washington, GPO, 1971. 20p. $0.25. S/N 2416-0040. (I 66.8:En 8)

This guide presents examples of teaching tools for bringing environmental education into the classroom and into general education curricula.

774. U.S. Forest Service. **Conservation Tools for Educators.** Rev. ed. Washington, Forest Service, 1970. 76p. (Pacific Northwest Region; Putting Conservation to Work Series) Issuing agency. LC Card No. 70-606852. (A 13.2:C 76/15/970)

AIR POLLUTION

BIBLIOGRAPHIES

775. U.S. Air Programs Office. **Air Pollution Aspects of Emission Sources: Cement Manufacturing; A Bibliography with Abstracts.** Washington, GPO, 1971. 44p. $0.50. S/N 5503-0008. (EP 4.9:95)

776. U.S. Air Programs Office. **Air Pollution Aspects of Emission Sources: Electric Power Production; A Bibliography with Abstracts.** Washington, GPO, 1971. 312p. $2.25. LC Card No. 77-613566. S/N 5503-0011. (EP 4.9:96)

777. U.S. Air Programs Office. **Air Pollution Aspects of Emission Sources: Municipal Incineration; A Bibliography with Abstracts.** Washington, GPO, 1971. 95p. $1.00. (EP 4.9:92)

778. U.S. Air Programs Office. **Air Pollution Aspects of Emission Sources: Nitric Acid Manufacturing; A Bibliography with Abstracts.** Washington, GPO, 1971. 31p. $0.45. LC Card No. 73-612229. S/N 5503-0004. (EP 4.9:93)

779. U.S. Air Programs Office. **Air Pollution Aspects of Emission Sources: Sulfuric Acid Manufacturing; A Bibliography with Abstracts.** Washington,

GPO, 1971. 58p. $0.65. S/N 5503-0007. (EP 4.9:94)

These five bibliographies are arranged by subject with complete bibliographical data and very long, detailed abstracts. Each is indexed by subject and author.

780. U.S. Air Programs Office. **Chlorine and Air Pollution: An Annotated Bibliography.** Washington, GPO, 1971. 113p. $0.55. LC Card No. 74-613943. S/N 5503-0018. (EP 4.9:99)

This bibliography contains abstracts of 162 publications. It is in classified arrangement with subject, author, and geographic location indexes.

781. U.S. Air Programs Office. **Hydrochloric Acid and Air Pollution: An Annotated Bibliography.** Washington, GPO, 1971. 107p. $0.55. LC Card No. 76-614071. S/N 5503-0019. (EP 4.9:100)

Contains 164 abstracts of documents and articles. Indexed by authors, titles, subjects, and geographical locations.

782. U.S. Air Programs Office. **Photochemical Oxidants and Air Pollution: An Annotated Bibliography.** Washington, GPO, 1971. 2 vols. $6.25. (EP 4.9:88/pts. 1, 2)

This bibliography is the result of an effort to collect, condense and organize the literature on photochemical oxidants in relation to air pollution. Contains abstracts of approximately 1,900 documents, most published from 1959 to 1970. Indexed by authors, subjects, titles, and geographical locations.

783. U.S. National Air Pollution Control Administration. **Hydrocarbons and Air Pollution: An Annotated Bibliography.** Washington, GPO, 1970. 2 vols. $5.00. LC Card No. 78-610871. S/N 1713-0029. (HE 20.1309:75/v.)

"This bibliography represents an effort to collect, condense and organize the literature on hydrocarbons in relation to air pollution. The approximately 2,300 documents abstracted here . . . are from recent literature, i.e., 1959-1970." In classified arrangement with accession number, authors, title, imprint information, and abstract for each citation. Includes the following indexes: subject, geographic, author, and title.

784. U.S. National Air Pollution Control Administration. **Nitrogen Oxides: An Annotated Bibliography.** Washington, GPO, 1970. 633p. (NAPCAP Publication No. AP-72) $2.75. (HE 20.1309:72)

There are 1,500 documents listed in this bibliography, with very detailed abstracts. Indexed by author, subject and geographical location.

DIRECTORIES

785. U.S. Air Pollution Control Office. **1969 Inventory of Air Pollution Monitoring Equipment Operated by State and Local Agencies.** Springfield, Va., NTIS, 1971. 27p. $3.00. LC Card No. 79-611709. (EP 4.9/2:0588)

Reported by state, city, and organization are the automatic sampler-analyzers, mechanized samplers, and static sample-collection devices operated during the period July 1, 1968, through June 30, 1969. A glossary of abbreviations and terms is included.

786. U.S. Air Programs Office. **Air Pollution Training Courses, July 1971– June 1972 and University Training Programs, Extramural Programs, Institute for Air Pollution Training, Planning and Special Projects.** Washington, GPO, 1971. 107p. Issuing agency. (EP 4.13:971-72)

Gives detailed descriptions of the various programs and courses.

787. U.S. National Air Pollution Control Administration. **Guide to Research in Air Pollution, 1969.** 7th ed. Washington, GPO, 1970. 193p. $1.50. LC Card No. 67-60390. (HE 20.1308:R 31)

This publication covers projects active in the calendar year 1969 and summarizes the status of air pollution research as a whole. It lists individual projects under investigation by state for domestic projects and by country for foreign ones. For each project this directory provides the project number, location and name of the research organization, project title, name and address of investigators, sponsor, and type of support. Projects are also listed by subject and by names of principal investigators.

PESTICIDES

788. U.S. Bureau of Sport Fisheries and Wildlife. **Handbook of Toxicity of Pesticides to Wildlife.** By Richard K. Tucker and D. Glen Crabtree. Washington, GPO, 1970. 131p. $1.00. LC Card No. 77-607737. (I 49.66:84)

This handbook is directed to research, operational and administrative personnel concerned with the use of pesticides. It satisfies the need for a compendium of pesticide toxicity data for wildlife species that compares one pesticide with another. Chemicals are arranged alphabetically by the most frequently used name–i.e., common or trade names. Other names are included in the alphabetical sequence as cross references. Under each name are other common names, the chemical name, the pesticide's primary use and the purity of the samples tested, followed by a summary table of oral toxicity values. Includes a glossary of terms and a list of literature cited.

789. U.S. Department of Agriculture. **Safety Guide for Pesticides.** Washington, GPO, 1970. 6p. $0.15. (A 1.68:943)

Provides helpful information to dealers in pesticides to help prevent accidents that might injure customers and employees. Brief instruction for receiving shipments of pesticides, handling, storing, and displaying pesticides, serving customers, disposing of pesticides and containers, and taking care of accidents.

790. U.S. Department of the Navy. **Herbicide Manual for Noncropland Weeds.** Washington, GPO, 1971. 205p. $1.75. S/N 0850-0077. (D 209.14:H 41)

This manual contains practical instructions for the classification, use, and application of herbicides; detailed information regarding specific weed species and site situations; and unique characteristics and properties of specific herbicides suggested for noncropland use.

791. U.S. Office of the President. Office of Science and Technology. **Ecological Effects of Pesticides on Nontarget Species.** By David Pimentel. Washington, GPO, 1971. 220p. $2.00. LC Card No. 78-612979. S/N 4106-0029. (PrEx 8.2:P 43)

Summarizes the available evidence concerning the impact of pesticides (insecticides, herbicides, and fungicides) on individuals, populations, and communities of species and the magnitude of the reported damage to the diverse processes of living systems. For each named pesticide, such as 2,4-D, pertinent information has been presented about its influence on non-target mammals, birds, fishes, amphibians, molluscs, arthropods, annellids, plants, and microorganisms, as well as its biological concentration in food chains and persistence.

WASTE DISPOSAL

792. U.S. Environmental Protection Agency. **Solid Waste Management: Abstracts from the Literature, 1964.** Prep. by John A. Connolly and Sandra E. Stainback. Washington, GPO, 1971. 280p. $2.00. LC Card No. 53-60514. (EP 3.9:M 31)

Updates the *Refuse Collection and Disposal: Annotated Bibliography, 1941-50* and its supplements A-F covering 1951 through 1963. Arranged in categories corresponding to the various administrative, engineering and operational phases of solid waste management. Indexed by subject, corporate and personal author, and geographical location.

793. U.S. Geological Survey. **Subsurface Waste Disposal by Means of Wells: A Selective Annotated Bibliography.** By Donald R. Rima, Edith B. Chase, and Beverly M. Myers. Washington, GPO, 1971. 305p. (Water-supply Papers, No. 2020) $1.50. LC Card No. 77-179486. S/N 2401-1229. (I 19.13:2020)

"This bibliography was prepared to gather significant references into a single publication that would be a reference source for both scientific and waste-management needs." Contains 692 abstracts compiled from a selective review of the literature through 1959. Includes subject and geographic indexes.

WATER POLLUTION

794. U.S. Federal Water Quality Administration. **1969 Fish Kills Caused by Pollution.** Washington, GPO, 1970. 20p. $0.20. LC Card No. 61-61886. S/N 2417-0089. (I 67.9:969)

Water pollution killed an estimated 41 million fish in 45 states in 1969. This document provides statistical tables for historical summaries and current information. Current data are arranged by state and city, with information such as date when kill started, estimated number of fish killed, severity of the total kill, miles or acres affected, duration, and cause.

795. U.S. Senate. Committee on Public Works. **Oil Pollution of the Marine Environment: A Legal Bibliography.** Prep. by Carl Q. Christol. Washington, the Committee, 1971. 93p. Issuing agency. LC Card No. 77-610749. (Y 4.P 96/10:92-1)

MATHEMATICS

796. U.S. Bureau of Reclamation. **A Guide to Using Interest Factors in Economic Analysis of Water Projects.** By Bruce P. Glenn. Washington, GPO, 1970. 99p. $1.50. (I 27.19/2:W 29/3/970-2)
   This manual was planned to be a handy reference source for engineers and economists. Part one covers basic principles of discounting and scheduling for economic analysis of federal projects; part two contains methods for calculating power and municipal water rates. Computer programs for deriving tables of interest factor, tables of development period factors, and payout tables are also included.

797. U.S. Department of the Army. **Engineering Design Handbook: Tables of Cumulative Binomial Probabilities.** Washington, GPO, 1971. 577p. Issuing agency. LC Card No. 71-611486. (D 101.22/3:706-109)

798. U.S. National Bureau of Standards. **Handbook of Mathematical Functions: With Formulas, Graphs and Tables.** Rev. Washington, GPO, 1971. 1046p. $9.00 (cloth). S/N 0303-0279. (C 13.25:55)
   This NBS handbook includes every special function normally needed by anyone who uses mathematical tables in his work. This revised edition contains an increase in the number of functions covered and more extensive numerical tables. It gives larger collections of mathematical properties of the tabulated functions. Most people who refer to tables of mathematical functions will find this a valuable aid.

799. U.S. Naval Research Laboratory. **Table of All Primitive Roots for Primes Less than 5000.** By Herbert Hauptman, Emanuel Vegh, and Janet Fisher. Washington, GPO, 1970. 590p. $4.25. (D 210.8:7070)
   The Naval Research Laboratory has produced and publishes in this volume a table of all the primitive roots of the primes less than 5000, the most extensive tabulation of its kind now available. Also presented are a description of its construction and a brief historical account of a number of conjectures and several recent results.

MEDICAL SCIENCES

GENERAL MEDICINE

ABSTRACTS AND INDEXES

800. U.S. Bureau of Radiological Health. **Publications Index.** Washington, GPO, 1971. 265p. Issuing agency. LC Card No. 77-614504. (HE 20.4111: 72-1)

    Prepared primarily for the use of the Bureau of Radiological Health staff. In three sections: 1) KWIC Index lists the title of each publication under every keyword; 2) Author Index lists all names which appear in 3) Bibliography Index, which gives the complete title of each publication.

801. U.S. Federal Health Programs Service. **An Index to Clinical Research in the Federal Health Programs Service: A Bibliography of Published Papers, Presentations, and Current Studies.** Washington, GPO, 1970. 79p. $0.45. LC Card No. 76-610458. (HE 20.2710/2:C 61)

802. U.S. Federal Health Programs Service. **An Index to Clinical Research in the Federal Health Programs Service: A Bibliography of Published Papers, Presentations, and Current Studies.** Washington, GPO, 1971. 101p. $0.45. S/N 1730-0016. (HE 20.2710/2:C 61/971)

    This bibliography is in three sections: published clinical research papers, presentations on clinical research, and current clinical research projects. Each section is arranged by primary author and has its own authors and investigators and subject indexes.

803. U.S. National Institute of Arthritis and Metabolic Diseases. **Diabetes Literature Index: 1969 Index Issue.** Ed. by Arnold Lazarow and others. Washington, GPO, 1970. 1290p. $9.50. (HE 20.3310/2:969/ind.)

804. U.S. National Institute of Arthritis and Metabolic Diseases. **Diabetes Literature Index: 1970 Index Issue.** Ed. by Arnold Lazarow and others. Washington, GPO, 1971. 1488p. $10.75. (HE 20.3310/2:970)

    This is a computer-produced bibliography from MEDLARS tapes which is designed to be "a specialized information medium . . . available free to qualified interested investigators and practitioners in the field of diabetes." Indexes all current scientific papers relevant to the field of diabetes from the world medical literature. Author and key word indexes give complete citations under each entry. These annual issues supersede those published monthly.

805. U.S. National Institute of Neurological Diseases and Stroke. **Epilepsy Abstracts, Volume 2, 1969.** Ed. by F. E. Posthumus Meyjes and N. J. Legg. Cumulated edition. Washington, GPO, 1971. 354p. Issuing agency. LC Card No. 72-606350. (HE 20.3509/2:2/1-12)

806. U.S. National Institute of Neurological Diseases and Stroke. **Epilepsy Abstracts, Volume 3, 1970.** Ed. by F. E. Posthumus Meyjes and N. J. Legg. Cumulated edition. Washington, GPO, 1971. 481p. Issuing agency. (HE 20.3509/2:3/1-12)

These bibliographies are concerned primarily with the clinical and therapeutic aspects of epilepsies including research in physiology, biochemistry, and the psychological, sociological, and epidemiological aspects.

807. U.S. National Institutes of Health. **Research Grants Index, Fiscal Year 1970.** Washington, GPO, 1971. 2 vols. $13.00. LC Card No. 61-64708. (HE 20.3013/2:970/v. 1,2)

Volume one provides information about specific aspects of health-allied research and investigation. Projects are listed under one or more of the 6,500 subject headings and by project number after that. In this volume only project numbers and titles are given. Volume two contains the "Grant Number and Bibliography List" which is arranged by project number and gives the following information: 1) scientific advisory groups, 2) the principal investigator, 3) address, 4) project title, 5) list of publications resulting from the project. This volume also contains an alphabetical list of investigators with project numbers.

808. U.S. National Library of Medicine. **Cumulated Abridged Index Medicus, Volume 1, 1970.** Washington, GPO, 1970. 1159p. $10.00 (cloth). LC Card No. 77-610781. (HE 20.3612/2-2:1)

809. U.S. National Library of Medicine. **Cumulated Abridged Index Medicus, Volume 2, 1971.** Washington, GPO, 1971. 1128p. $10.00 (cloth). (HE 20.3612/2-2:2)

This new series is published monthly and cumulated annually. The bibliography is based on articles from 100 English-language journals and is designed to meet the needs of individual practitioners and small hospital and clinic libraries.

ALMANACS AND YEARBOOKS

810. U.S. National Institutes of Health. **National Institutes of Health Almanac.** Washington, GPO, 1970. 151p. Issuing agency. LC Card No. 66-62557. (HE 20.3016:970)

811. U.S. National Institutes of Health. **National Institutes of Health Almanac.** Washington, GPO, 1971. 164p. Issuing agency. LC Card No. 66-62557. (HE 20.3016:971)

Intended to "offer in one volume all important historical data and other reference material" pertinent to the National Institutes of Health. Includes the following information: historical data, with chronologies and biographical sketches; organizational chart and functions of the NIH; appropriations; a statistical coverage of the federal government's role in support of medical research; real estate and facilities of the NIH with pertinent statistics; field units including overseas and domestic offices; and a calendar of the NIH Lecture Series including dates, titles, speakers, and places of lectures.

812. U.S. National Institutes of Health. **Scientific Directory, 1970, and Annual Bibliography, 1969.** Washington, GPO, 1970. 289p. $1.25. LC Card No. 57-62015. (HE 20.3017:970)

813. U.S. National Institutes of Health. **Scientific Directory, 1971, and Annual Bibliography, 1970.** Washington, GPO, 1971. 311p. $1.25. (HE 20.3017:971)

   This standard work is "intended for reference use by research workers in the biomedical sciences." It includes an outline of the structure of the NIH, its professional staff and their scientific and technical publications. The same type of information is given for the NIMH. The work is arranged by institute and division, and both directory and bibiliographical entries are included together at the lower or branch level. Also included are names of scientific staff members, other key individuals and visiting scientists and guest workers with a tenure of a year or more. Chiefs or heads of divisions are noted. Bibliography contains citations to the previous year's publications; directory is for the current year. Indexed by subjects and names.

ATLASES

814. U.S. Regional Medical Programs Service. **Atlas of Oral Cytology.** By Herman Medak and others. Washington, GPO, 1970. 133p. (Public Health Service Publication 1949) $4.75 (cloth). LC Card No. 71-608904. (HE 20.2602:Or 1)

AUDIO-VISUAL GUIDES

815. U.S. National Archives and Records Service. **List of U.S. Government Medical and Dental 8mm Films for Sale by the National Audiovisual Center.** Washington, GPO, 1970. 57p. Issuing Agency. LC Card No. 73-610066. (GS 4.2:M 46)

   This list was compiled for use by doctors, dentists, hospital personnel, medical and dental schools, and those in related fields. Arranged in two major sections (dental and medical) with specific subject chapters. Gives title, order number, running time, cost, and synopses of each film.

816. U.S. National Library of Medicine. **National Medical Audiovisual Center Catalog, 1970.** Washington, GPO, 1970. 114p. $1.25. LC Card No. 70-600805. S/N 1752-0126. (HE 20.3608/4:970)

   The audiovisuals described in this catalog include motion picture films, filmstrips, videotapes, audiotapes, and slide sets. All deal with some aspect of a medical or health-related problem area, and are made available on a short-term loan basis from the National Medical Audiovisual Center to the biomedical professions.

817. U.S. National Library of Medicine. **1970 Film Reference Guide for Medicine and Allied Sciences.** Comp. by the Federal Advisory Council on Medical Training Aids. Washington, GPO, 1971. 317p. $2.75. LC 56-60040. S/N 1752-0058. (HE 20.3608/2:970)

This guide supersedes the 1969 edition and includes a comprehensive list of films available for biomedical education. Films are listed alphabetically by title within approrpiate subject headings. Each entry includes names of producer or sponsor, country of origin, year of release, physical description (i.e., time, sound, color or black and white, etc.), language if other than English, series reference, contents, credits, sales sources, and distributor.

BIBLIOGRAPHIES

GENERAL BIBLIOGRAPHIES

818. U.S. Department of the Air Force. **Health and Hygiene.** Prep. by Ardys M. Asper. San Francisco, Pacific Air Force, 1971. 59p. (PACAF Basic Bibliographies for Base Libraries) Available from CINCPACAF (DPSR) Director, PACAF Libraries, APO, San Francisco, Calif. 96553. (D 301.62: H 34/971)

819. U.S. Health Services and Mental Health Administration. **Emergency Health Services Selected Bibliography.** Rev. ed. Washington, GPO, 1970. 175p. (Emergency Health Series, No. A-1) $1.25. LC Card No. 78-606811. (HE 20.2013:A-1)

Lists books, pamphlets, journal articles, films and slides. Part one lists works on day-to-day health emergencies such as strokes or automobile accidents. Part two covers major emergencies such as natural disasters. Part three lists films and slides which deal with disaster care and medical self-help. Part four provides further sources (e.g., bibliographies). Indexed by subjects.

820. U.S. Health Services and Mental Health Administration. **Ethical Issues in Health Services: A Report and Annotated Bibliography.** By James Carmody. Washington, GPO, 1970. 38p. $3.00 (from NTIS). PB 195 732. (HE 20.2110:70-32)

This selective, annotated bibliography cites medical, legal, and philosophical studies on care of the aged, euthanasia, organ transplant, abortion, uniform health care standards, and allocation of scarce health care services.

821. U.S. Health Services and Mental Health Administration. **Planning for Hospital Discharge: A Bibliography with Abstracts and Research Reviews.** By August Le Rocco. Washington, GPO, 1970. 95p. $3.00 (from NTIS). PB 193 520. (HE 20.2110:70-17)

This bibliography was based on a search of the whole area of hospital-based patient care. It cites only those studies that advance a methodology for planning hospital discharge. Indexed by authors and subjects.

822. U.S. Maternal and Child Health Service. **Annotated Bibliography on Maternal Nutrition.** Washington, GPO, 1970. 199p. $1.50. LC Card No. 70-608164. (HE 20.2759:M 41)

This bibliography is directed to physicians, nutritionists, and others concerned with "applying the research findings reported in the literature on maternal nutrition." It was published to supplement *Maternal Nutrition and the Course of Pregnancy* (NAS-NRC Publication No. 1761) and includes materials published from 1958 through 1968 in English. Materials are arranged under specific topics such as birth weight, iron deficiency anemia, and the role of the placenta in pregnancy. Annotations are informative, not critical. Not indexed.

823. U.S. National Clearinghouse for Smoking and Health. **Bibliography on Smoking and Health with English Language Abstracts of Foreign Items, 1969 Cumulation, pt. 2.** Washington, GPO, 1970. 362p. (Public Health Service Bibliography Series) $3.25. LC Card No. 68-60300. (HE 20.11:45/pt. 2)

824. U.S. National Clearinghouse for Smoking and Health. **Bibliography on Smoking and Health, 1970.** Washington, GPO, 1971. 351p. $3.25. S/N 1727-0024. (HE 20.11:45/2)

These two bibliographies list all publications added to the collection of the Clearinghouse's Technical Information Center during 1969 and 1970. They are arranged alphabetically within 11 categories with an alphanumeric system of accession numbers. Two indexes are necessary for use of this bibliographical series: individual and organization index, and subject index.

825. U.S. National Library of Medicine. **Bibliography of Medical Reviews, 1966-1970.** Washington, GPO, 1971. 576p. $6.75 (cloth). S/N 1752-0133. (HE 20.3610/2:966-70)

This volume contains a cumulation of citations reviewing articles—well-documented surveys of recent biomedical journal literature—indexed in *Index Medicus* from 1966 through 1970. This present cumulation has been compiled from annual productions generated by five different editions of the Medical Subject Heading (MeSH). To help the user of this volume in locating subject headings of interest, a key of past and current headings is included. This key is an alphabetical list of terms under which material was indexed previously, followed by the terms under which material was indexed subsequently.

826. U.S. National Library of Medicine. **Bibliography of the History of Medicine, No. 4, 1968.** Washington, GPO, 1970. 299p. (Public Health Service Publication 1540-4) $2.75. LC Card No. 66-62950. (HE 20.3615:4)

All chronological periods and geographic areas are included. Covers journal articles, monographs, and contains analytic entries for symposia, congresses and similar composite publications, as well as historical chapters in general monographs. This volume covers material indexed but not necessarily published in 1968. The majority of the journal articles are from *Index Medicus*, while monographs are from the *Current Catalog.* Additional citations were gathered and reviewed from other journals, bibliographies and recent publications. Arranged in three main parts: Part I, Biographies, includes works dealing with medical history of famous non-medical persons, or with medical aspects of the work of literary figures, composers, etc., as well as those dealing with lives and contributions of medical people. Part II, Subject Index, lists the citations under subject headings. Part III, Authors, lists, alphabetically by author, citations appearing in Parts I and II.

827. U.S. National Library of Medicine. **List of Journals Indexed in Index Medicus 1971.** Washington, GPO, 1971. 92p. $1.25. S/N 1752-0718. (HE 20.3612/4:971)

This listing of journals indexed in *Index Medicus* is an excellent bibliography of medical periodicals. There are lists by title, by abbreviation used in *Index Medicus*, by subject, and by geographic area.

828. U.S. National Library of Medicine. **National Library of Medicine Current Catalog, 1965-1970.** Washington, GPO, 1971. 8 vols. $71.75 (cloth). S/N 1752-0131. (HE 20.3609/3:965-70)

Cites monographic publications cataloged by the National Library of Medicine. Listed by author, joint author, title, and subject.

829. U.S. Regional Medical Programs Service. **What's New on Smoking in Print and on Film.** Washington, GPO, 1971. 8p. $0.10. S/N 1727-0018. (HE 20.2602:Sm 7/6)

Lists films and filmstrips and educational materials on smoking and health which have been issued by member organizations of the National Interagency Council on Smoking and Health. It covers a wide range of interests, and is directed to many audiences, including young people and adults, smokers, and nonsmokers.

DISEASES AND HANDICAPS

830. U.S. Maternal and Child Health Service. **Galactosemia: Annotated Bibliography.** Comp. by Donough O'Brien. Washington, GPO, 1971. 37p. $0.30. S/N 1791-0158. (HE 20.2759:G 13)

This annotated bibliography was compiled using the MEDLARS search service of the National Library of Medicine. It includes English language references up to 1971. Arranged by subject with author index.

831. U.S. National Cancer Institute. **Partial Bibliography on Human Cancer Involving Viruses, January 1966—December 1969.** Washington, GPO, 1970. 71p. Issuing agency. LC Card No. 71-608072. (HE 20.3165:H 88/966-69)

832. U.S. National Cancer Institute. **Partial Bibliography on Type-B and Type-C Viruses in Relation to Animal Neoplasia, Covering the Period of January 1967—December 1970.** Washington, GPO, 1971. 103p. Issuing agency. (HE 20.3165:V 81/967-70)

833. U.S. National Heart and Lung Institute. **Fibrinolysis, Thrombolysis, and Blood Clotting Bibliography: Annual Compilation, 1969.** Prep. in cooperation with the National Library of Medicine. Washington, GPO, 1970. 2 vols. Issuing agency. (HE 20.3209:969/pt. 1,2)

834. U.S. National Heart and Lung Institute. **Fibrinolysis, Thrombolysis, and Blood Clotting Bibliography: Annual Compilation, 1970.** Prep. in cooperation with the National Library of Medicine. Washington, GPO, 1971. 899p. Issuing agency. LC Card No. 67-62840. (HE 20.3209:970)

    Contains a subject section (with entries arranged under selected subject headings), author section (arranged by first author), subject index, and author index. Citations were processed by MEDLARS.

835. U.S. National Institute of Neurological Diseases and Stroke. **Bibliography, Collaborative Study on Cerebral Palsy, Mental Retardation, and Other Neurological and Sensory Disorders of Infancy and Childhood, No. 3, July 1969–June 1970.** Washington, GPO, 1970. 24p. Issuing agency. LC Card No. 75-610865. (HE 20.3513:C 33/no. 3)

836. U.S. National Institute of Neurological Diseases and Stroke. **Bibliography, Collaborative Study on Cerebral Palsy, Mental Retardation, and Other Neurological and Sensory Disorders of Infancy and Childhood, No. 4, July 1970–June 1971.** Washington, GPO, 1971. 22p. Issuing agency. (HE 20.3513:C 3/no. 4)

    This is a compilation of citations to publications of the Collaborative Perinatal Research Project. Indexed by subject and author.

837. U.S. National Institute of Neurological Diseases and Stroke. **Biblio-Profile on Human Communication and Its Disorders, A Capsule State-of-the-Art Report with Bibliography: Number 2, Otitis Media; Diagnosis, Therapy, and Prevention and Control.** Washington, GPO, 1971. 47p. $0.55. (HE 20.3513/2:2)

    This is a bibliography of 400 works published from 1964 through 1970. It is arranged by subject with an author index.

838. U.S. National Institute of Neurological Diseases and Stroke. **Biblio-Profile of Human Communication and Its Disorders, A Capsule State-of-the-Art Report with Bibliography: Number 3, Surgical Treatment of Deafness.** Washington, GPO, 1971. 71p. Issuing agency. (HE 20.3513/2:3)

    This bibliography lists 579 works published from 1968 through July 1971. It is arranged by subject and indexed by author.

839. U.S. National Institute of Neurological Diseases and Stroke. **Parkinson's Disease and Related Disorders: Cumulative Bibliography, 1800-1970.** Prep. by the Parkinson Information Center, College of Physicians and Surgeons, Columbia University. Washington, GPO, 1971. 3 vols. $13.75. LC Card No. 79-610736. (HE 20.3511/3:800-970/v. 1-3)

    Volume 1 contains citations; volumes 2 and 3 are author and subject indexes, respectively.

HEALTH TESTING

840. U.S. Bureau of Health Manpower and Education. **Equivalency and Testing: A Descriptive Compilation of Existing Testing Programs in Allied Health and Other Health Occupations, with an Annotated Bibliography.** Washington, GPO, 1970. 83p. Issuing agency. LC Card No. 78-609880. (HE 20.3102:T 28)

841. U.S. Federal Health Programs Service. **Automated Multiphasic Health Testing: A Bibliography.** Washington, GPO, 1970. 175p. $1.50. LC Card No. 77-608927. (HE 20.2710:1/1)
   This annotated bibliography has been developed as a research service to others interested in the field of automated multiphasic health testing.

842. U.S. National Center for Health Services Research and Development. **Multiphasic Health Testing Systems: Reviews and Annotations.** By Anna C. Gelman. Washington, GPO, 1971. 155p. Issuing agency. LC Card No. 77-614007. (HE 20.2110:71-1)
   This bibliographic essay covers a wide range of subjects pertaining to multiphasic health testing as well as periodic health examinations. Not indexed.

PUBLIC HEALTH SERVICE AGENCIES' CATALOGS

843. U.S. Health Facilities Planning and Construction Service. **Publications of the Health Facilities Planning and Construction Service, Hill-Burton Program.** Rev. ed. Washington, GPO, 1970. 41p. (Public Health Service Publication No. 930-G-3) $0.30. LC Card No. 67-61255. (HE 20.2511:G-3)
   Lists in-print publications only. Includes materials on the operation of hospitals and medical facilities such as dietary equipment, in-patient care, medical records, etc. It also lists newsletters and audiovisual aids. Not indexed.

844. U.S. Health Services and Mental Health Administration. **Publications of the Health Services and Mental Health Administration.** Washington, GPO, 1971. 158p. Issuing agency. LC Card No. 75-614052. (HE 20.2012/2:P 96)
   This catalog lists all available publications of the Health Services and Mental Health Administration as of December 30, 1970. It excludes periodicals, reprints, training materials and publications issued in limited quantities. Some entries are annotated. Indexed by subject and title.

845. U.S. Maternal and Child Health Service. **Publications of the Maternal and Child Health Service.** Washington, GPO, 1970. 7p. Issuing agency. (HE 20.2759:P 96/970)

846. U.S. Maternal and Child Health Service. **Publications of the Maternal and Child Health Service.** Washington, GPO, 1971. 21p. $0.20. S/N 1730-0012. (HE 20.2759:P 96/971)
   This is an annotated bibliography arranged by subject and indexed by title and subject.

847. U.S. National Institutes of Health. **NIH Publications List, January 1970.** Washington, GPO, 1970. 22p. Issuing agency. (HE 20.3009:970)

848. U.S. National Institutes of Health. **NIH Publications List, July 1970.** Washington, GPO, 1970. 37p. Issuing agency. (HE 20.3009:970-2)

849. U.S. National Institutes of Health. **NIH Publications List, January 1971.** Washington, GPO 1971. 38p. Issuing agency. (HE 20.3009:971)

850. U.S. National Institutes of Health. **NIH Publications List, May 1971.** Washington, GPO, 1971. 38p. Issuing agency. (HE 20.3009:971-2)

851. U.S. National Institutes of Health. **NIH Publications List, November 1971.** Washington, GPO, 1971. 42p. Issuing agency. (HE 20.3009:971-3)
   Arranged by agencies within the NIH. Indexed by subjects.

DICTIONARIES

852. U.S. National Institutes of Health. **Medical and Health Related Sciences Thesaurus.** 4th ed. Washington, GPO, 1971. 559p. LC Card No. 72-614988. (HE 20.3023:971)
   "Compiled and maintained as an indexing authority list for the preparation of the annual Research Grants Index, a subject-matter index of research projects supported by the Public Health Service," this is also useful as an aid for the research analysts, librarians, and information specialists connected with medical information systems.

DIRECTORIES

853. U.S. Aviation Medicine Office. **Directory of Aviation Medical Examiners.** Washington, GPO, 1970. 295p. Issuing agency. LC Card No. 64-1727. (TD 4.211:970)

854. U.S. Aviation Medicine Office. **Directory, Aviation Medical Examiners.** Washington, GPO, 1970. 303p. Issuing agency. LC Card No. 78-607914. (TD 4.211:970-2)

855. U.S. Aviation Medicine Office. **Directory, Aviation Medical Examiners.** Washington, GPO, 1971. 303p. Issuing agency. LC Card No. 64-1727. (TD 4.211:971)

856. U.S. Aviation Medicine Office. **Directory, Aviation Medical Examiners.** Washington, GPO, 1971. 309p. Issuing agency. (TD 4.211:971-2)

857. U.S. Aviation Medicine Office. **Directory, Aviation Medical Examiners.** Washington, GPO, 1971. 300p. (TD 4.211:971-3)
   This directory lists physicians throughout the United States who are licensed to give pilot's examinations and medical student pilot certificates.

858. U.S. Bureau of Health Manpower Education. **Inventory of Federal Programs that Support Health Manpower Training, 1970.** Ed. by Lucy M. Kramer. Washington, GPO, 1971. 92p. $1.00. (HE 20.3114/3:In 8/970)

859. U.S. Bureau of Radiological Health. **Directory of Personnel Responsible for Radiological Health Programs.** Washington, GPO, 1970. 42p. (Bureau of Radiological Health/Office of Regional Operations Series) Issuing agency. LC Card No. 70-608944. (HE 20.1512:70-3)

860. U.S. Bureau of Radiological Health. **University Curriculums and Fellowships in Radiological Health.** Washington, GPO, 1970. 86p. Issuing agency. LC Card No. 71-611025. (HE 20.1515:70-2)

    Arranged by names of universities with full program descriptions.

861. U.S. Library of Congress. Division for the Blind and Physically Handicapped. **Directory of Library Resources for the Blind and Physically Handicapped.** Washington, GPO, 1971. 38p. (Available free from the Division for the Blind and Physically Handicapped) (LC 19.2:L 61/2/970)

    Arranged by states, with the following information given for each library: address, name of librarian, telephone number, hours, staff, number of readers served, book collection statistics, and circulation statistics.

862. U.S. Library of Congress. Division for the Blind and Physically Handicapped. **Volunteers Who Produce Books, Braille, Large Type, Tape.** Washington, GPO, 1971. 69p. (Available free from the Division for the Blind and Physically Handicapped) LC Card No. 79-610882. (LC 19.2:V 88)

    Lists names of individuals and groups who transcribe books and other reading material for the blind and physically handicapped. Arranged alphabetically by state with index of "specialized talents."

863. U.S. National Clearinghouse for Smoking and Health. **1970 Directory of On-Going Research in Smoking and Health.** Comp. by Herner and Company. Washington, GPO, 1970. 294p. $2.25. LC Card No. 67-61689. (HE 20.2612:970)

    This is an international directory of research pertaining to smoking and its relationship to health. This edition contains 438 projects, representing 39 states, the District of Columbia and 28 foreign countries. The scope of the research reported includes activities in the biomedical, behavioral, psychological, and related fields.

864. U.S. National Institute of Neurological Diseases and Stroke. **Parkinson's Disease and Related Disorders: International Directory of Scientists.** Prep. by the staff of the Parkinson Information Center, College of Physicians and Surgeons, Columbia University. Washington, GPO, 1970. 225p. $1.75. LC Card No. 79-610736. S/N 1749-0007. (HE 20.3511/2:970)

    A directory of scientists engaged in research on Parkinson's disease and related neurological movement disorders. It is divided into three sections to enable users to locate individuals by either country, name, or institution. Each scientist has been assigned a sequential entry number in this section. Each item shows the scientist's name, directory entry number, specialty, department, institution, city, and his subject interests.

865. U.S. Regional Medical Programs Service. **Kidney Disease Services, Facilities, and Programs in the United States.** Washington, GPO, 1971. 135p. $0.60. S/N 1727-0025. (HE 20.2602:K 54/4)

    Lists, alphabetically by state, services and facilities concerned with the control of the kidney disease problem.

HEALTH OCCUPATIONS

866. U.S. Bureau of Health Manpower Education. **Directory of Health Occupations Training Programs in Maine, New Hampshire, Rhode Island and Vermont, 1968-69.** Washington, GPO, 1970. 412p. Issuing agency. LC Card No. 70-609775. (HE 20.3102:Oc 1/968-69)

    This directory is in two sections. "Program Profiles" are arranged alphabetically by title and state and list admission requirements, credentials awarded, length of the program, and other relevant data. "List of Training Institutions" lists alphabetically by state, city, and name.

867. U.S. Indian Health Service. **Health Careers for American Indians and Alaskan Natives.** Washington, GPO, 1970. 77p. Issuing agency. LC Card No. 79-610334. (HE 20.2652:H 34)

    Provides an overview of the various educational opportunities in health fields available to American Indians and Alaskan natives.

868. U.S. Training and Employment Service. **Job Descriptions and Organizational Analysis for Hospitals and Related Health Services.** Rev. ed. Washington, GPO, 1971. 732p. $4.25 (cloth). LC Card No. 70-611263. (L 34.8: H 79/971)

LAWS

869. U.S. Department of Health, Education, and Welfare. **Summary of Selected Legislation Relating to the Handicapped.** Washington, GPO, 1971. 12p. $0.20. (HE 1.2:L 52/2/971)

870. U.S. Environmental Health Service. **Occupational Health and Safety Legislation.** Rev. ed. Washington, GPO, 1971. 360p. $1.75. LC Card No. 79-611260. (HE 20.1002:Oc 1/970)

    Contains citations and excerpts or digests of state laws and regulations dealing with occupational health and safety. Arranged by states and their agencies.

STATISTICS

871. U.S. National Center for Health Statistics. **Health Manpower: A County and Metropolitan Data Book.** Washington, GPO, 1971. 164p. $1.75. (HE 20.1500:T 23)

Contains data on the distribution of medical personnel throughout the United States. For pharmacists and registered nurses, the data are for 1966; physicians and dentists, 1967; and podiatrists and veterinarians, 1968. Arranged by state, standard metropolitan statistical area, and county.

872. U.S. National Center for Health Statistics. **Health Resources Statistics, Health Manpower and Health Facilities, 1969.** Washington, GPO, 1970. 286p. (Publication No. 1509) $2.75. LC Card No. 66-62580. (HE 20.2215:969)

This statistical compendium of the health resources of the United States provides information on health manpower and facilities for planners, administrators, researchers, and those who are concerned with development of national, state, and regional health programs. The first section is on health manpower by types of service or occupational training. Part two covers inpatient health facilities. An appendix contains a list of health occupations. Indexed by subject.

873. U.S. National Center for Health Statistics. **Nursing Homes: A County and Metropolitan Area Data Book.** Washington, GPO, 1970. 234p. $2.25. S/N 1722-0171. (HE 20.2202:C 83/sec. 2)

Statistics presented in this publication cover ownership of nursing homes, number of beds, number of personnel in both nursing and personal care homes. The tables are by state, standard metropolitan statistical areas, and county.

DENTISTRY

874. U.S. Health Professions Education and Manpower Training Bureau. **Fluoridation Census 1969.** Washington, GPO, 1970. 72p. (Division of Dental Health) Issuing agency. LC Card No. 65-61456. (HE 20.3112:969)

Provides statistics on many aspects of water fluoridation and lists communities which have fluoridated water.

875. U.S. National Institute of Dental Research. **Dental Science Handbook.** Ed. by Lon W. Morrey and Robert J. Nelsen. Washington, GPO, 1970. 311p. $2.75. LC Card No. 75-603909. (HE 20.3408:D 43)

Presents a manual of information about dental science and dental practice prepared primarily for those in vocations other than dentistry. This manual provides a wide, orderly, and comprehensive panoramic view of the biologic and physical aspects of dental science, the various techniques employed in rendering service, and the methods employed to meet the rapidly growing demands for more comprehensive dental care.

MENTAL HEALTH AND PSYCHIATRY

BIBLIOGRAPHIES

876. U.S. Health Services and Mental Health Administration. **Consultation Research in Mental Health and Related Fields: A Critical Review of the Literature.** By Fortune V. Mannino and Milton F. Shore. Washington, GPO, 1971. 55p. $0.35. LC Card No. 70-610128. (HE 20.2018:79)
   Covers published works and unpublished doctoral dissertations concerning research and evaluation in consultation.

877. U.S. National Institute of Child Health and Human Development. **Selected Bibliography on Death and Dying.** By Joel J. Vernick. Washington, GPO, 1970. 61p. $0.65. LC Card No. 75-607348. (HE 20.3361:D 34)
   References in this bibliography are to books and articles from medical, psychological, and psychiatric journals, religious texts, and literary journals. Covers materials from the past 100 years. Because selections range from serious scientific research studies to advice to parents and friends, this bibliography will be of interest to physicians and educators and to parents and friends of patients with terminal illnesses. Arranged alphabetically by author without annotations. Includes an author-subject index and a list of journals.

878. U.S. National Institute of Mental Health. **Abstracts of the Standard Edition of the Complete Psychological Works of Sigmund Freud.** Ed. by Carrie Lee Rothgeb. Washington, GPO, 1971. 237p. $1.75. LC Card No. 75-613658. S/N 1724-0139. (HE 20.2402:F 86)
   The abstracts in this publication were prepared under contract by the Scientific Literature Corporation of Philadelphia. This is a comprehensive compilation, keyed to all psychoanalytic concepts found in the *Standard Edition of Freud* (ed. by James Strachey, London, 1953-64, 24 vols.). A complete subject index is designed as a guide for both the professional and the layman.

879. U.S. National Institute of Mental Health. **Behavior Modification in Child and School Mental Health: An Annotated Bibliography on Applications with Parents and Teachers.** Washington, GPO, 1971. 41p. $0.30. S/N 1724-0159. (HE 20.2417:C 43)
   An annotated bibliography of references concerned with reports on behavior modification as a treatment in mental health.

880. U.S. National Institute of Mental Health. **Computer Applications in Psychotherapy: Bibliography and Abstracts.** Comp. by Kent Taylor. Washington, GPO, 1970. 92p. (Public Health Service Publication No. 1981). $1.00. LC Card No. 78-607145. (HE 20.2417:C 73)
   The aim of this bibliography is to identify articles of particular interest relating to both the initial sources and collection of data and to the subsequent computer-related application of this knowledge to the scientific study and practice of psychotherapy.

881. U.S. National Institute of Mental Health. **Coping and Adaptation: A Behavioral Sciences Bibliography.** Washington, GPO, 1970. 231p. $1.75. (HE 20.2417:C 79)

    This bibliography cites relevant contributions in the psychological and social sciences concerning stress, coping, and adaptation.

882. U.S. National Institute of Mental Health. **Early Childhood Psychosis: Infantile Autism, Childhood Schizophrenia and Related Disorders; An Annotated Bibliography, 1964-1969.** Prep. by Carolyn Q. Bryson and Joseph N. Hingten. Washington, GPO, 1970. 127p. Issuing agency. LC Card No. 75-614340. (HE 20.2417:P 95/964-69)

    This bibliography contains over 400 citations and abstracts to periodical articles and books appearing from 1964 through 1969. Arranged by subject, with an author index.

883. U.S. National Institute of Mental Health. National Clearinghouse for Mental Health Information. **Bibliography on the Epidemiology of Mental Disorders, 1966-1968.** Comp. by Jack Zusman and others. Washington, GPO, 1970. 114p. $1.25. LC Card No. 70-608452. (HE 20.2417:Ep 4)

    This bibliography was designed for "specialists in mental health epidemiology, for general epidemiologists with interests related to mental health, and for others concerned with mental disorders who wish to integrate epidemiologic approaches and data into their thinking or practice." Mental health epidemiology is defined for this work as the "scientific study of the incidence, course, and patterns of mental illness . . . and mental health in defined populations." The bibliography is alphabetical by author under six main headings. Entries are not annotated. Indexed by authors and subjects.

884. U.S. National Library of Medicine. **Mental Health Film Guide.** Washington, GPO, 1970. 69p. Issuing agency. LC Card No. 79-606794. (HE 20.3608/3:M 52)

    This guide was compiled from the files of the International Index of Film Data.

885. U.S. Veteran's Administration. **Cooperative Studies in Psychiatry: An Annotated Bibliography Summarizing 15 Years of Cooperative Research in Psychiatry, 1956-1970.** Washington, GPO, 1970. 64p. Issuing agency. (VA 1.22:11-3)

DIRECTORIES

886. U.S. National Institute of Mental Health. **Directory of Community Mental Health Centers.** Washington, GPO, 1971. 21p. Issuing agency. (HE 20.2402:C 73/5)

    Names and addresses are listed by states.

887. U.S. National Institute of Mental Health. **Mental Health Directory, 1970.** Washington, GPO, 1970. 445p. (National Clearinghouse for Mental

Health Information. Publication No. 1005) $4.00. LC Card No. 65-60647. (HE 20.2418:970)

888. U.S. National Institute of Mental Health. **Mental Health Directory, 1971.** Washington, GPO, 1971. 480p. (National Clearinghouse for Mental Health Information; Public Health Service Publication No. 1268) $3.75. S/N 1724-0136. (HE 20.2418:971)

    This directory is intended to be used as a reference guide to mental health programs and services throughout the United States by mental health planners, administrators, practitioners, and persons in need of services. New areas of federal, state, and local services are highlighted in this listing of programs of the National Institute of Mental Health, mental health associations, states, and local communities.

MENTAL RETARDATION

BIBLIOGRAPHIES

889. U.S. Children's Bureau. **Selected Reading Suggestions for Parents of Mentally Retarded Children.** Comp. by Kathryn A. Gorham, Eleanor Ernst Timberg and Coralie B. Moore. Washington, GPO, 1970. 58p. $0.60. LC Card No. 78-608378. (HE 21.113:M 52/970)

    Prepared primarily to help parents, families, and nonprofessionals who seek information on mental retardation, these reading suggestions may also be useful to professionals, especially those who are directly involved in helping parents understand and accept their child's handicap.

890. U.S. Department of Health, Education, and Welfare. **Mental Retardation Publications of the Department of Health, Education, and Welfare.** Washington, GPO, 1970. 45p. Issuing agency. LC Card No. HEW 67-35. (HE 1.18:M 52/970)

891. U.S. Department of Health, Education, and Welfare. **Mental Retardation Publications of the Department of Health, Education, and Welfare.** Washington, GPO, 1971. 52p. Issuing agency. LC Card No. 70-613730. (HE 1.18:M 52/971)

    Lists all current publications concerned with mental retardation which are available from the Department of Health, Education, and Welfare. Arranged by broad subjects with brief annotations. Includes subject, author, and abbreviated title indexes.

892. U.S. Maternal and Child Health Service. **Bibliography on Speech, Hearing, and Language in Relation to Mental Retardation, 1900-1968.** By Maryann Peins. Washington, GPO, 1970. 156p. $1.25. LC Card No. 71-606106. (HE 20.2759:Sp 3/900-68)

    This bibliography provides a compilation of references to works written in the English language from 1900 to 1968, with some 1969 references included. It was prepared to serve as a "specialized, yet comprehensive, reference guide for those persons concerned with the communicative processes of the mentally retarded." A preliminary bibliography published in 1962 in the *Journal of the American Speech and Hearing Association* formed the foundation for this work. Entries are classified in seven categories which were considered to be the most practical for users of the work and are not annotated. There is no index.

DIRECTORIES

893. U.S. Department of Health, Education, and Welfare. **Directory of State and Local Resources for the Mentally Retarded.** Comp. by Robert D. Edwards. Washington, GPO, 1970. 124p. Free from HEW. LC Card No. 74-605994. (HE 1.2:M 52/16/970)

  This directory is a checklist of state and local agencies, facilities, and other resources which render specific services to the mentally retarded. Does not include those resources which serve the mentally retarded as a part of their total program. Arranged by states.

894. U.S. Department of Health, Education, and Welfare. **Mental Retardation Construction Program: Research Centers, University Affiliated Facilities, and Community Facilities.** Washington, GPO, 1971. 99p. $1.00. LC Card No. 73-612044. (HE 1.2:M 52/15/971)

  Lists centers recently built or under construction with statistics on cost and descriptions of programs.

895. U.S. Maternal and Child Health Service. **Clinical Programs for Mentally Retarded Children: A Listing.** Comp. by Rudolf P. Hormuth. Washington, GPO, 1970. 37p. Issuing agency. LC Card No. 73-607464. (HE 20.2752: M 52/969)

  Lists names, addresses, areas served, ages accepted and other information by state and city.

896. U.S. President's Committee on Mental Retardation. **In Service to the Mentally Retarded: Directory of National Voluntary Agencies.** Washington, GPO, 1970. 28p. Issuing agency. LC Card No. 70-610552. (Pr 36.8:M 52/Se 6)

  Lists national voluntary agencies which have services or programs for the mentally retarded. Arranged alphabetically by group's name with capsule summaries of programs.

897. U.S. President's Committee on Mental Retardation. **International Directory of Mental Retardation Resources.** Ed. by Rosemary F. Dybwad. Washington, GPO, 1971. 316p. Issuing agency. LC Card No. 72-614168. (Pr 36.8:M 52/R 31/4)

  Part one lists international organizations; part two consists of individual country reports alphabetically by country. Detailed descriptions of each program are included.

NURSING

898. U.S. Bureau of Health Manpower Education. **Division of Nursing Selected Publications.** Washington, GPO, 1971. 8p. Issuing agency. (HE 20.3113:N 93/971)
    Lists only available publications.

899. U.S. Bureau of Health Manpower Education. **Literature Relating to Neurological and Neurosurgical Nursing.** Prep. by Margaret Hulburt. Washington, GPO, 1970. 95p. $0.60. LC Card No. 70-609772. (HE 20.3113: N 39)
    Presents a compendium of references intended primarily for neurological and neurosurgical nurses. These references may also be helpful to physicians, administrators, scientific investigators, and others who care for patients with neurological disorders.

900. U.S. Bureau of Health Manpower Education. **Schools Offering Nurse Traineeships for Full-Time Academic Study, 1971-72, Under the Professional Nurse Traineeship Program.** Washington, GPO, 1971. 20p. Issuing agency. (HE 20.3102:N 93/15/971-72)
    Lists schools alphabetically by state and notes those programs which are either baccalaureate level or above.

901. U.S. Bureau of Health Professions Education and Manpower Training. **Schools Participating in Nursing Student Assistance Programs.** Washington, GPO, 1970. 16p. (Student Loan and Scholarship Branch) Issuing agency. (HE 20.3102:N 93/10)
    A directory which lists schools alphabetically by state with type of degree and city. Symbols denote those schools which participate in the Nursing Student Loan Program only or the Nursing Scholarship Program only.

PHARMACOLOGY

902. U.S. Bureau of Narcotics and Dangerous Drugs. **LSD-25, A Factual Account: Layman's Guide to the Pharmacology, Physiology, Psychology and Sociology of LSD.** Washington, GPO, 1970. 44p. $0.30. (J 24.8:L 99/rep.)
    This first official scientific publication of the new Bureau of Narcotics and Dangerous Drugs brings information on drugs to the attention of the public, and deals specifically with the problems of LSD.

903. U.S. Food and Drug Administration. **National Adverse Drug Reaction Directory.** Washington, GPO, 1970. 292p. Issuing agency. LC Card No. 79-709989. (HE 20.4002:D 63)
    This is a list of coding symbols for a thesaurus of adverse drug reaction terms. It provides a basis for vocabulary control of reports of adverse reactions associated with drugs and is intended to be used in conjunction with *Medical and Pharmacal Coding Guide.*

904. U.S. Food and Drug Administration. **National Drug Code Directory, June 1970.** Prep. by the Science Information Facility. Washington, GPO, 1970. 538p. $3.75. (HE 20.4012:970)

905. U.S. Food and Drug Administration. **National Drug Code Directory, June 1971.** Prep. by the Office of Scientific Coordination, Bureau of Drugs. Washington, GPO, 1971. 622p. $4.25. LC Card No. 73-610799. (HE 20.4012:971)

This is a major work of the FDA. It contains descriptions of approximately 23,000 prescription and over-the-counter drugs. The main section is arranged alphabetically by product name and within product name by an abbreviated form of the manufacturer's name. An index of "established names" refers back to the branded single-ingredient products described in the main section. The National Drug Code Index is a list of codes (alphanumeric designations which denote manufacturers, drug products, and basic trade package sizes) in ascending sequence. An appendix contains a list of manufacturers with their code numbers and addresses.

PUBLIC HEALTH

BIBLIOGRAPHIES

906. U.S. Community Health Service. **Publications Catalog.** 1971-72 ed. Washington, GPO, 1971. 56p. $0.35. S/N 1726-0020. (HE 20.2560:971-72)

Lists currently available publications related to activities and programs of the Community Health Service. Entries are annotated, and there is a title index.

907. U.S. Office of Economic Opportunity. **Bibliography on the Comprehensive Health Service Program.** Washington, GPO, 1970. 31p. $0.45. (PrEx 10.23:6128-8)

Lists 46 articles which appeared in popular magazines and professional journals, and which discuss health problems of the rural and urban poor and possible solutions. Most articles deal with Neighborhood Health Centers, describing them in detail and comparing them.

908. U.S. Regional Medical Programs Service. **Selected Bibliography of Regional Medical Programs.** 2nd rev. ed. Washington, GPO, 1970. 103p. (Public Health Service Publication No. 1861) Issuing agency. LC Card No. 74-607905. (HE 20.2611:970)

Based on materials collected by the Division of Regional Medical Programs from its establishment in Feburary 1966. First lists publications about individual regional programs (alphabetically by region) including those published by the programs themselves, nationally published books and journal articles, and those published by the Division. Second is a list of books and journal articles about regional medical programs in general.

DIRECTORIES

909. U.S. Community Health Service. **Directory of Selected Community Health Services.** Washington, GPO, 1970. 54p. Issuing agency. LC Card No. 74-608535. (HE 20.2552:C 73/2)

910. U.S. Community Health Service. **Directory of Selected Community Health Services.** Washington, GPO, 1971. 73p. Issuing agency. (HE 20.2552: C 73/2/971)

Lists and categorizes a variety of health care services programs supported according to the Public Health Service Act. Includes project titles, locations, telephone numbers, names of directors, and descriptions of programs.

911. U.S. Community Health Service. **Directory of State and Areawide Comprehensive Health Planning Agencies Supported under Sec. 314, Public Health Service Act as of July 1, 1970.** Washington, GPO, 1970. 71p. Issuing agency. LC Card No. 78-606349. (HE 20.2552:H 34/970)

Lists agencies by state with names and addresses, population served, type of organization, type of grant, and dates.

912. U.S. Health Services and Mental Health Administration. **Directory of State, Territorial, and Regional Health Authorities, 1970.** Washington, GPO, 1970. 116p. $0.65. LC Card No. 24-26996. (HE 20.2015/2:970)

This publication provides information useful for persons administering programs of the Health Services and Mental Health Administration and the Crippled Children's Service of the Social and Rehabilitation Service. Health officers are listed by state and by units of health planning agencies. The directory also lists regional medical programs, and state agencies administering Crippled Children's Service programs, hospital and medical facilities construction programs, and mental health programs.

GUIDES

913. U.S. Health Facilities Planning and Construction Service. **Sickness and Poverty, a Handbook for Community Workers.** Washington, GPO, 1971. 89p. $0.45. LC Card No. 77-611502. S/N 1726-0017. (HE 20.2558:Si 1)

Following a general section on the health problems of the poor, this guide discusses the causes, symptoms, treatment and prevention of illness. This will be a useful reference source for community workers.

TOXICOLOGY

914. U.S. Council on Environmental Quality. **Toxic Substances.** Washington, GPO, 1971. 25p. $0.40. LC Card No. 71-611916. S/N 1716-0004. (PrEx 14.2:T 66)

This is a convenient reference source for potentially hazardous materials. It serves as a guide for research needed in setting new occupational health standards. Lists chemical name of the toxic substance, its toxic dose, and effects on man and/or animal, and the literature references.

915. U.S. Food and Drug Administration. **Poison Control Centers Directory.** Rev. ed. Washington, GPO, 1971. 50p. $0.35. LC Card No. 78-614026. S/N 1712-0129. (HE 20.4002:P 75)

Poison control centers are arranged alphabetically by state. Information for each center includes name, address, and director's name. Facilities listed are those which provide for the medical profession, on a 24-hour basis, information concerning the treatment and prevention of accidents involving ingestion of poisonous and potentially poisonous substances.

916. U.S. Maternal and Child Health Service. **Selected Bibliography on Lead Poisoning in Children.** Comp. by Jane S. Lin-Fu. Washington, GPO, 1971. 35p. $0.25. LC Card No. 74-614983. S/N 1730-0014. (HE 20.2759:L 46)

A selected bibliography of papers relating to the problem of childhood lead poisoning. It lists reports on the epidemiology, sources and indexes of exposure, metabolic disturbances and toxicity, prevention, treatment, and other aspects.

VETERINARY MEDICINE

917. U.S. Agricultural Research Service. **Index-Catalogue of Medical and Veterinary Zoology: Supplement 17, Part 7, Parasite-Subject Catalogue, Hosts.** By Dorothy B. Segal and others. Washington, GPO, 1971. 460p. $4.00. (A 77.219/2:17/pt. 7)

918. U.S. National Cancer Institute. **1971 Coding Supplement to Standard Nomenclature of Veterinary Diseases and Operations.** Ed. by William A. Priester. Washington, GPO, 1971. 376p. $3.50. S/N 1742-0033. (HE 20.3152:V 64/Supp.971)

This list of all accepted changes and additional diagnoses proposed since the 1966 edition of the Standard Nomenclature is designed to assign standard and acceptable terminology and a unique code number to each clinically recognizable disease or operation.

PHYSICS

919. U.S. Department of the Navy. **Handbook of Electromagnetic Propagation in Conducting Media.** Washington, GPO, 1970. 123p. $3.00 (cloth). (D 201.6/12:El 2/2)

This handbook, published as an aid to students and researchers, presents in one volume the principal results of investigations in both open literature and reports of government and industry.

920. U.S. National Bureau of Standards. **Bibliography on the High Temperature Chemistry and Physics of Materials.** Washington, GPO, 1968-70. 6 vols. (C 13.10:315-nos.)

A bibliography of references to research involving temperatures above $1000°$ centigrade. In subject arrangement with no indexes.

921. U.S. National Bureau of Standards. **Hydraulic Research in the United States, 1970, Including Contributions from Canadian Laboratories.** Ed. by Gershon Kulin and Pauline H. Gurewitz. Washington, GPO, 1971. 346p. $2.50. LC Card No. 34-3323. S/N 0303-0812. (C 13.10:346)

Current and recently concluded research projects in hydraulics and hydrodynamics for the years 1969-1970 are summarized. Projects from more than 250 university, industrial, state and federal government laboratories in the United States and Canada are reported. Indexed by subjects.

922. U.S. National Bureau of Standards. **Weights and Measures Labeling Handbook.** By David E. Edgerly. Washington, GPO, 1971. 419p. (NBS Handbook, No. 108) $3.25. LC Card No. 74-610444. S/N 0303-0853. (C 13.11:108)

Prepared for use by state weights and measures officials in the enforcement of state laws and regulations pertaining to the packaging and labeling of commodities. Provides a cross-indexed compilation of the requirements of many federal rules, regulations, and requirements.

PART THREE

HUMANITIES

ART AND ARCHITECTURE

923. U.S. Department of the Air Force. **Architecture, Building and Engineering.** Prep. by Deloris Lawrence. San Francisco, Pacific Air Force, 1970. 93p. (PACAF Basic Bibliographies for Base Libraries) Available from CINCPACAF, Attn: DPSR, Command Librarian, APO, San Francisco, Calif. 96553. LC Card No. 58-61780. (D 301.62:Ar 2/970)

924. U.S. Library of Congress. **Catalog of the 22d National Exhibition of Prints Held at the Library of Congress, May 14—September 7, 1971.** Washington, GPO, 1971. 16p. Issuing agency. LC Card No. 43-16468. (LC 25.8:971)

Lists prints by artists residing in the United States and accepted by a panel of judges for showing in the 22d National Exhibition of Prints. Arranged alphabetically by artists with addresses, titles of prints, media and costs. Eight prints from the exhibit are reproduced in the catalog.

925. U.S. Smithsonian Museum. **The Life Portraits of John Quincy Adams.** Washington, GPO, 1970. 106p. $2.50. (SI 11.2:Ad 1)

This catalog of a National Portrait Gallery exhibition includes an essay by Gallery Director Marvin Sadik, a brief biography of John Quincy Adams, and 43 life portraits of Adams. There is also a list of related objects that were on display and biographic essays about the artists, silhouettists, daguerreotypists, and photographers for whom Adams sat.

926. U.S. Smithsonian Institution. **Trade Goods: A Study of Indian Chintz in the Collection of the Cooper-Hewitt Museum of Decorative Arts and Design.** Washington, GPO, 1970. 135p. $3.00. (SI 1.2:T 67/2)

Contains a definition of "chintz," followed by a historical description of English trade with India and the importation to colonial America of trade goods, especially chintz; a complete and technical description of how the chintzes were made; an illustrated catalogue portion describing the chintzes in the collection of the Cooper-Hewitt Museum; a definitive bibliography; and a glossary. This study was undertaken to accompany the great exhibition of Indian Chintz from the collections of the Victoria and Albert Museum in London and the Royal Ontario Museum in Toronto which was held in New York at the Cooper-Hewitt Museum.

LANGUAGES

927. U.S. Department of State. **From Spanish to Portuguese.** Washington, GPO, 1971. 91p. $1.00. (S 1.114/2:P 83/2)

This manual is for those whose native language is English but who also speak Spanish and want to learn Portuguese. There are four major sections: the sounds, the grammar, hints on vocabulary transfer, and supplementary pronunciation exercises.

928. U.S. Department of the Army. **Norwegian Language Guide.** Washington, GPO, 1970. 96p. $0.45. S/N 0820-0342. (D 101.11:30-310/2)

A guide to the spoken Norwegian language, this pocket-sized booklet gives hints on pronunciation, as well as useful words and phrases. Included are important signs and alphabetical word list, and fill-in sentences designed to quiz individuals.

LITERATURE

929. U.S. Department of the Air Force. **Fiction Men Read.** Prep. by Julie M. O'Brien. San Francisco, Pacific Air Force, 1971. 34p. (PACAF Basic Bibliographies for Base Libraries) Available from CINCPACAF (DPSR)/ Director, PACAF Libraries, APO, San Francisco, Calif. 96553. (D 301.62: F 44/2)

930. U.S. National Council on the Arts. **A Partial Directory of American Poets.** Washington, National Council on the Arts, 1971. 155p. mimeographed.

The poets listed in this "partial directory" are those who have expressed their willingness to work with high school age or younger children. The National Endowment for the Arts has been, since 1967, funding programs to put professional writers in the schools. This directory has been compiled in response to the demand from state arts councils and project coordinators for more information on writers. After an alphabetical listing of poets' names only, the main section of the directory is an alphabetical listing by state, including name, address, most recent work, publisher, and teaching preference (coded for elementary through college and beyond). The final section includes anthologies, films, and videotapes, with information for ordering such materials.

MOTION PICTURES AND DRAMA

931. U.S. Copyright Office. **Catalog of Copyright Entries, Cumulative Series: Motion Pictures, 1960-1969.** Washington, GPO, 1971. 744p. $8.00 (cloth). LC Card No. 53-60032. (LC 3-8:M 85/960-69)

For more recent information, consult current issues of *Catalog of Copyright Entries: Parts 12-13, Motion Pictures and Filmstrips.* The *Library of Congress Catalog* and *National Union Catalog* also contain sections which list all films and filmstrips cataloged on Library of Congress printed cards.

932. U.S. Smithsonian Institution. **Portraits of the American Stage, 1771-1971.** Washington, GPO, 1971. 203p. $4.50. S/N 4700-0181. (SI 11.2: St 1/771-971)

The National Portrait Gallery, Smithsonian Institution. Issued to coincide with an exhibition in celebration of the inaugural season of the John F. Kennedy Center for the Performing Arts, this publication portrays 92 personalities of the American stage, with a short biographical sketch of each. It spans two centuries of personalities of the American stage whose primary achievements have been in the drama, dance, opera, musical comedy, and on the concert stage. A photograph, sketch, or bust of each personality is included.

MUSIC

933. U.S. Library of Congress. **The Sousa Band: A Discography.** Comp. by James R. Smart. Washington, GPO, 1970. 123p. $1.50. LC Card No. 70-604228. (LC 12.2:So 8)

The purpose of this work is to "present in one source the recording history of the Sousa Band." It also includes recordings made by the U.S. Marine Band during the last three years of Sousa's leadership (1890-92) and the Philadelphia Rapid Transit Company Band, which recorded two compositions under Sousa's direction. Recordings by the Sousa Band are listed first under one of two headings: cylinder records and disc records, and second alphabetically by title under record manufacturer. Excludes foreign releases of Sousa Band records. The exclusion of a title index makes it necessary for one to peruse the list of recordings of each individual company (as well as lists for the other two bands) in order to locate a specific title. The appendix contains a chronological list of Victor recording sessions. Indexed by soloists, composers, and conductors by companies.

RELIGION

934. U.S. Department of the Air Force. **Basic Religious Books and Chaplains' Services.** Prep. by Mae L. Johnson. San Francisco, Pacific Air Force, 1970. 86p. (PACAF Basic Bibliographies for Base Libraries) Available from CINCPACAF, Attn: DPSR. Command Librarian, APO, San Francisco, Calif. 96553. LC Card No. 70-609306. (D 301.62:R 27/970)

PART FOUR

GENERAL REFERENCE

GENERAL BIBLIOGRAPHIES

935. U.S. Library of Congress. Hispanic Foundation. **Cuban Acquisitions and Bibliography: Proceedings and Working Papers on the International Conference Held at the Library of Congress, April 13-15, 1970.** Comp. and ed. by Earl J. Pariseau. Washington, Library of Congress, 1970. 164p. Issuing agency. LC Card No. 76-609231. (LC 1.12/2:C 89)

This contains a number of bibliographic essays covering all aspects of the acquisition of social, political, historical, cultural, and legal publications relating to Cuba. Separate chapters list resources in the United Kingdom, in Spain, and in Germany for the study of Cuba.

936. U.S. Library of Congress. **Latin America, Spain, and Portugal: An Annotated Bibliography of Paperback Books.** Comp. by Georgette M. Dorn. Washington, GPO, 1971. 180p. (Hispanic Foundation. Bibliographical Series, No. 13) $0.75. LC Card No. 71-37945. S/N 3013-0005. (LC 24.7:13)

This bibliography lists 1,512 in-print paperback books in the humanities and social sciences, including travel guides, dictionaries and grammars, readers and textbooks. Each entry is annotated. A directory of publishers is included for those wishing to order works listed. Indexed by subject.

937. U.S. Library of Congress. **National Union Catalog of Manuscript Collections, 1969, and Index 1967-69.** Washington, Library of Congress, 1970. 1082p. $10.00 (cloth). LC Card No. 62-17486. (LC 9.8:969)

Lists manuscript collections in libraries throughout the United States.

GOVERNMENT PUBLICATIONS

938. U.S. Library of Congress. General Reference and Bibliography Division. Reference Department. **Botswana, Lesotho, and Swaziland: A Guide to Official Publications, 1868-1968.** Comp. by Mildred Grimes Balima. Washington, GPO, 1971. 84p. $1.00. LC Card No. 74-171029. S/N 3001-0043. (LC 2.8:B 65/868-969)

This bibliography contains a list of published official records of Botswana, Lesotho, and Swaziland from 1868 to 1968. Included are citations to documents of the former High Commission Territories during British protection and since independence and a selection of publications issued by the Colony of the Cape of Good Hope, the South African Republic and Transvaal Colony. Also included is a brief history of the three countries.

939. U.S. Library of Congress. **Library of Congress Catalogs in Book Form and Related Publications.** Washington, GPO, 1971. 18p. Issuing agency. LC Card No. 72-612348. (LC 1.12/2:C 28/971)

This is a detailed listing of LC catalogs such as the *National Union Catalog*,

New Serial Titles, and *Library of Congress Classification*. It discusses the contents and frequency of each and lists the parts which constitute full holdings of each.

940. U.S. Library of Congress. **Library of Congress Publications in Print.** Prep. by Edwin R. Turnley. Washington, GPO, 1970. 38p. Issuing agency. LC Card No. 6-35005. (LC 1.12/2:P 96/970)

941. U.S. Library of Congress. **Library of Congress Publications in Print.** Prep. by Judith R. Farley and Judith L. Richelieu. Washington, GPO, 1971. 39p. Issuing agency. LC Card No. 6-35005. (LC 1.12/2:P 96/971)

    This is a complete list of Library of Congress publications. Each issue supersedes the previous one. Publications are listed alphabetically by title. Note is made of works reprinted by private companies, of those available from GPO, and of those available from LC. This work is not annotated but does contain a detailed index.

942. U.S. Library of Congress. **Non-GPO Imprints Received in the Library of Congress, July 1967 Through December 1969.** Washington, GPO, 1970. 73p. (Available from the Card Division, Library of Congress, $1.25). LC Card No. 70-606580. (LC 30.2:Im 7)

943. U.S. Library of Congress. **Non-GPO Imprints Received in the Library of Congress in 1970: A Selective Checklist.** Washington, GPO, 1971. 25p. (Available from the Card Division, Library of Congress, $1.25). LC Card No. 79-611051. (LC 30.2:Im 7/970)

    Includes publications of research value only and lists those non-GPO imprints which were not included in the *Monthly Catalog.* Indexed but not annotated. Updates *United States Government Publications: A Partial List of Non-GPO Imprints*, edited by Jennings Wood (Chicago, ALA, 1964, 84p.).

944. U.S. Library of Congress. **Popular Names of U.S. Government Reports: A Catalog.** Comp. by Bernard A. Bernier, Jr., and Charlotte M. David. Rev. ed. Washington, GPO, 1970. 43p. $0.55. LC Card No. 77-608261. S/N 3005-0004. (LC 6.2:G 74/970)

    Contains a selection of significant reports published as early as 1821 and reports appearing after 1965. Many of the 753 reports of U.S. executive, legislative, and judicial bodies cited here are important documents in U.S. history and are primary sources for research. The reports in the catalog are arranged alphabetically by popular name. In order to provide the fullest descriptive detail, including notes and tracings, the entries comprise photographic reproduction of LC printed catalog cards without further editing for this publication.

945. U.S. National Museum. **Publications of the United States National Museum (1947-1970).** Washington, GPO, 1971. 77p. $0.60. S/N 4701-0106. (SI 3.3:298)

    Updates an earlier cumulative volume entitled *A List and Index of the*

Publications of the United States National Museum (1875-1946). This bibliography lists publications by series—e.g., Annual Reports, Bulletins, etc. The index (for titles, subjects, authors) refers to chapter and entry number.

LIBRARY SCIENCE

946. U.S. Office of Education. **1970 Directory: Coordinators of Children's Services and of Young Adult Services in Public Library Systems Serving at Least 100,000 People.** Washington, GPO, 1970. 35p. Issuing agency. LC Card No. 79-608957. (HE 5.215:15069)
   Lists libraries and librarians by state and city.

947. U.S. Office of Education. **Planning for a Nationwide System of Library Statistics.** Washington, GPO, 1971. 117p. $1.25. S/N 1780-0758. (HE 5.215:15070)
   These guidelines are designed to serve as directions for the development of a nationwide system of library statistics, emphasizing the collection, evaluation, and dissemination of complete and accurate library statistics.

948. U.S. Office of Education. **Study of Resources and Major Subject Holdings Available in U.S. Federal Libraries Maintaining Extensive or Unique Collections of Research Materials.** By Mildred Benton and others. Washington, Office of Education, 1970. 670p. Issuing agency. LC Card No. 79-609579. (HE 5.2:L 61/10)
   "This report, covering 188 selected special libraries, represents an initial attempt to study the resources and major subject holdings available in U.S. Federal libraries maintaining extensive or unique collections of research materials." Provides extensive statistical tables on library holdings, a partial list of federal libraries, and a subject index to the resources reported by libraries followed by Dewey Decimal Classification numbers.

MICROFORMS

949. U.S. Library of Congress. **National Register of Microform Masters, 1969.** Washington, Library of Congress, 1970. 183p. $5.00 (from Card Division, Library of Congress). LC Card No. 65-29419. (LC 30.8/8:969)
   Published "in order to avoid duplication of costly master negatives and to make it known which library materials have been transferred to microforms under the preservation program of American research libraries." Arranged by LC or NUC card numbers and includes a section by main entry for those publications without LC cards. Serials are listed alphabetically by main entry. Includes holdings in libraries and commercial firms.

PERIODICALS AND SERIALS

950. **U.S. Department of Housing and Urban Development. HUD Library Periodicals List.** Comp. by the Library and Information Division. Washington, GPO, 1971. 87p. Issuing agency. (HH 1.23:P 41/971)
    Lists all periodicals in the HUD Library as of March 1971 in three sections—title, subject, and publisher.

951. **U.S. Department of Labor. Daily Newspapers, General Periodicals and Official State (U.S.) Periodicals Received in the Department of Labor Library.** Washington, Department of Labor, 1971. 43p. Issuing agency. (L 1.34:N 47)

952. **U.S. Department of the Air Force. When to Buy What: A Buying Calendar for Annual Publications.** Prep. by Eleanor F. Ballon and Gloria D. Dean. San Francisco, Pacific Air Force, 1971. 141p. (PACAF Basic Bibliographies for Base Libraries) Available from CINCPACAF (DPSR) Director, PACAF Libraries, APO, San Francisco, Calif. 96553. LC Card No. 79-611402. (D 301.62:B 98)

953. **U.S. Library of Congress. Accessions List: India; Annual Supplement Cumulative List of Serials, 1970.** Washington, Library of Congress, 1970. 477p. Issuing agency. LC Card No. 63-24164. (LC 1.30/1-2:970)

954. **U.S. Library of Congress. Accessions List: India, Annual Supplement Cumulative List of Serials, 1971.** Washington, Library of Congress, 1971. 504p. Issuing agency. LC Card No. 63-24164. (LC 1.30/1-2:971)

955. **U.S. Library of Congress. Accessions List: Pakistan, Annual Supplement Cumulative List of Serials, 1970.** Washington, GPO, 1971. 102p. Issuing agency. LC Card No. 63-24162. (LC 1.30/2-2:970)
    These accessions lists are issued as part of the PL 480 project for acquisition of foreign publications by American libraries.

956. **U.S. Library of Congress. New Serial Titles, A Union List of Serials Commencing Publication after December 31, 1949: 1966-1969 Cumulation.** Washington, Library of Congress, 1971. 2 vols. $115.00 (includes monthly and quarterly issues and all cumulations) from LC. LC Card No. 53-60021. (LC 1.23/4:966-69/v. 1-2)
    Arranged alphabetically by title (or issuing body if the title is not distinctive) with place of publication, beginning date and date of cessation (if applicable), recording holdings of more than 700 libraries.

957. **U.S. Library of Congress. Newspapers Currently Received and Permanently Retained in the Library of Congress.** Comp. by the Serial Division, Reference Department. Rev. ed. Washington, GPO, 1970. 20p. $0.35. LC Card No. 68-61877. (LC 6.7:970)
    Lists newspapers by state and city or, if foreign, by country and city.

PART FIVE

PERIODICALS

PERIODICALS

This section lists reference periodical publications—primarily directories and bibliographical works—of government agencies. Works issued more frequently than twice a year are in this section; other serials (semi-annuals, annuals, etc.) are listed under appropriate subject categories in the preceding four sections. All periodicals listed are available from GPO with the exception of those which contain an "order from" note following the bibliographical description. The "order from" note gives complete addresses for ordering non-GPO periodicals.

958. **Abridged Index Medicus.** 1970– . Monthly. $12.00/yr. (HE 20.3612/2:v. and nos.)

This monthly bibliography is based on articles from 100 English-language journals and is designed for use by individual practitioners and in the libraries of small hospitals and clinics. Annual cumulations are published (see entry nos. 808-809 in this volume) but are not included in the subscription price.

959. **Abstracts of North American Geology.** 1966-1971. Monthly. LC Card No. GS 66-78. (I 19.54:date)

This supplement to the annual *Bibliography of North American Geology* (entry nos. 617-619 in this volume) ceased publication with the December 1971 issue.

960. **Accessions List: Ceylon.** 1967– . Quarterly. (Free to libraries.) LC Card No. SA 67-7489. (LC 1.30/7:v. and nos.) Order from: Public Law 480 Project; Library of Congress; American Libraries Book Procurement Center; New Delhi, India.

Annual author index is included in each December issue.

961. **Accessions List: Eastern Africa.** 1968– . Quarterly. (Free to libraries.) (LC 1.30/8:v. and nos.) Order from: National Program for Acquisitions and Cataloging; Library of Congress; Nairobi, Kenya.

An annual serial supplement is included.

962. **Accessions List: India.** 1962– . Monthly. (Free to libraries.) LC Card No. 63-24164. (LC 1.30:v. and nos.) Order from: Public Law 480 Project; Library of Congress; American Libraries Book Procurement Center; New Delhi, India.

Cumulative author index is included annually in the December issue. An annual serial supplement is published separately each year.

963. **Accessions List: Indonesia, Malaysia, Singapore, and Brunei.** 1966– . Monthly. (Free to libraries.) LC Card No. SA 66-444. (LC 1.30/5:v. and nos.) Order from: National Program for Acquisitions and Cataloging; Library of Congress; Djakarta, Indonesia.

Cumulative author index is in the last issue of each volume. A cumulative list of serials (covering the years 1964 through 1968) was published in 1969, and a cumulative list of additions and changes for 1969 was published in 1970. Formerly called *Accessions List: Indonesia.*

964. **Accessions List: Israel.** 1964— . Monthly. (Free to libraries.) LC Card No. HE 66-1615. (LC 1.30/4:v. and nos.) Order from: Public Law 480 Project; Library of Congress; American Libraries Book Procurement Center; Tel-Aviv, Israel.

A cumulative author index is published in the December issue each year. A cumulative list of serials is published separately each year.

965. **Accessions List: Middle East.** 1963— . Monthly. (Free to libraries.) LC Card No. 63-24163. (LC 1.30/3:v. and nos.) Order from: Public Law 480 Project; Library of Congress; American Libraries Book Procurement Center; Cairo, Egypt.

Cumulative author index is published annually.

966. **Accessions List: Nepal.** 1966— . 3 issues/yr. (Free to libraries.) LC Card No. SA 66-4579. (LC 1.30/6:v. and nos.) Order from: Public Law 480 Project; Library of Congress; American Libraries Book Procurement Center; New Delhi, India.

An annual author index is included in each December issue.

967. **Accessions List: Pakistan.** 1962— . Monthly. (Free to libraries.) LC Card No. 63-24162. (LC 1.30/2:v. and nos.) Order from: Public Law 480 Project; Library of Congress; American Libraries Book Procurement Center; Karachi-Dacca.

Annual author index is included in each December issue.

968. **Adult Development and Aging Abstracts of the National Institute of Child Health and Human Development, Scientific Information Centers Branch.** 1968— . Irregular. (HE 20.3359:nos.) Order from: National Institute of Child Health and Human Development; Bethesda, Md. 20014.

Reports on the results of research with abstracts of completed studies in the fields of adult development and aging.

969. **Advanced Abstracts of Scientific and Technical Papers Submitted for Publication and Presentation.** Quarterly. (D 104.23/2:date) Order from: U.S. Army Medical Research and Development Command; Washington, D.C. 20310.

970. **Aeronautical Engineering, Special Bibliography.** 1970— . Monthly. $3.00/issue. LC Card 71-613578. [NAS 1.21:7037 (nos.)] Order from: National Technical Information Service; Springfield, Va. 22151.

Contains a selection of annotated references to unclassified reports and journal articles that were introduced into the NASA scientific and technical information system and announced in *Scientific and Technical Aerospace Reports* and *International Aerospace Abstracts.*

971. **Aerospace Medicine and Biology: A Continuing Bibliography.** 1952– . Monthly. $3.00/issue. LC Card No. 65-62677. [NAS 1.21:7011 (nos.)] Order from: National Technical Information Service; Springfield, Va. 22151.

Concentrates on biological, physiological and environmental effects of real or simulated space flight. Indexed by subjects, personal and corporate authors. Each January issue contains a cumulative index to the previous year's issues. Formerly called *Aviation Medicine* and published quarterly.

972. **Air Pollution Abstracts.** 1971– . Monthly. $22.00/yr. (EP 4.11:v. and nos.)

Published in 1970 as *NAPCA Abstract Bulletin*. Transferred to the Environmental Protection Agency and title changed with volume two, number two (February 1971).

973. **Air University Library Index to Military Periodicals.** 1949– . Quarterly. (Free to libraries only, on exchange basis.) LC Card No. 51-4277. (D 301.26/2:v. and nos.) Order from Air University Library; Maxwell Air Force Base, Alabama.

This is a subject index to periodical articles from English language military and aeronautical periodicals which are not indexed in other standard periodical indexes. The quarterly issues are superseded by annual and triennial cumulations.

974. **Arms Control and Disarmament: A Quarterly Bibliography with Abstracts and Annotations.** 1965– . Quarterly. $2.50/yr. LC Card No. 64-62746. (LC 2.10:v. and nos.)

Contains abstracts and annotations of current literature in English, French, German, Russian, and other languages when an English language translation exists. Each issue is arranged by subjects and indexed by authors and subjects. The final issue (Fall) each year contains cumulative indexes.

975. **Arthritis and Rheumatic Diseases Abstracts.** 1964-1970. Monthly. LC Card No. 66-4061. (HE 20.3312:v. and nos.)

This journal is in classified arrangement with author and subject index. Annual cumulative indexes were also published.

976. **Artificial Kidney Bibliography.** 1967– . Quarterly. $1.00/yr. (HE 20.3311:v. and nos.)

Published in order to provide a "current awareness tool for scientists and to facilitate greater integration of research and developmental efforts" in the areas of renal failure, artificial kidneys, and kidney transplantation.

977. **Bimonthly List of Publications and Motion Pictures.** 1896– . Bimonthly. LC Card No. Agr 9-1414. (A 21.6/5:date) Order from: Information Office; Department of Agriculture; Washington, D.C. 20250.

Each issue is a four-page list arranged by USDA agencies. Recent publications (including motion pictures) are annotated.

978. **Bureau of the Census Catalog.** 1947– . Quarterly (with monthly supplements). $3.00/yr. LC Card No. 47-46253. (C 3.163/3:date; monthly supplements, C 3.163/2:date)

This is an annotated bibliography of publications issued by the Census Bureau. Divided into two parts—publications and unpublished materials. The final issue each year is an annual cumulation.

979. **Business Service Checklist.** 1946– . Weekly. $2.50/yr. LC Card No. 52-35963. (C 1.24:v. and nos.)

This is a weekly announcement of publications of the Department of Commerce and its agencies. Cumulated annually.

980. **Cancer Chemotherapy Abstracts.** 1959– . Bimonthly. $4.00/year. LC Card No. 62-3741. (HE 20.3160/4:v. and nos.)

Contains abstracts, annotations or citations for significant cancer chemotherapy articles appearing in the major biomedical sources of the world. Annual cumulative author and subject indexes (not included in subscriptions) are available for 70 cents.

981. **Carcinogenesis Abstracts.** 1963– . Monthly. LC Card No. 65-53489. (HE 20.3159:v. and nos.) Order from: National Cancer Institute; Bethesda, Md. 20014.

This abstract journal covers articles dealing with cancer-producing agents found in humans and animals. Annual cumulative indexes are included in subscriptions.

982. **Climatological Data: National Summary.** 1948– . Monthly. $2.50. LC Card No. 55-58495. (C 55.214:v. and nos.)

Contains general summaries of weather conditions, condensed climatological data for the states, etc. An annual summary is available for an additional 40 cents.

983. **Commercial Fisheries Abstracts.** 1948– . Monthly. LC Card No. 52-40434. (C 55.310/2:v. and nos.)   Order from: National Marine Fisheries Service Scientific Publications Unit; Bldg. 67, Naval Support Activity; Seattle, Wash. 98115.

Contains references to selected works in various subjects relating to the fishing industry. Arranged by subjects with author and subject indexes.

984. **Computer Program Abstracts.** 1969– . Quarterly. $1.00/yr. LC Card No. 76-604507. (NAS 1.44:v. and nos.)

This is an indexed abstract journal listing documented computer programs developed by or for the National Aeronautics and Space Administration, the Department of Defense, and the Atomic Energy Commission.

985. **Crime and Delinquency Abstracts.** 1966– . Bimonthly. $4.50/yr. (HE 20.2420:v. and nos.)

Contains abstracts of the current published scientific and professional literature and of ongoing research projects. Each issue contains author and subject indexes; annual cumulative indexes are also published.

986. **Cryogenic Data Center Current Awareness Service.** Weekly. (C 13.51: nos.) Order from: Cryogenic Data Center; National Bureau of Standards; Boulder, Colo. 80302.

Lists publications and reports of interest in cryogenics.

987. **Current Literature on Venereal Diseases: Abstracts and Bibliography.** 1966– . Irregular. (HE 20.2311:yr./nos.) Order from: Health Services and Mental Health Administration; Center for Disease Control; State and Community Services Division; Venereal Disease Branch; Atlanta, Ga.

This is a survey of recently published literature on venereal disease, specifically on the diagnosis and management, research and evaluation, and public health methods. Individual issues are not indexed but annual cumulative indexes are published.

988. **Diabetes Literature Index.** 1966– . Monthly. $12.00/yr. (HE 20.3310:v. and nos.)

Indexes all current scientific papers concerning the nature, causes, and therapy for diabetes. Author and key word indexes give complete citations under each entry. Annual cumulative indexes supersede monthly issues and are not part of the subscription.

989. **Diplomatic List.** 1893– . Quarterly. $1.50/yr. LC Card No. 10-16292. (S 1.8:yr./no.)

This directory lists foreign diplomats stationed in the United States in order of rank by country. Information for each person includes Washington address and telephone number, and the names of any other family members living in Washington. National holidays are listed under the name of the country. Also lists ambassadors by order of precedence with their date of presentation of credentials, the Dean of the Diplomatic Corps, and a special list of countries with temporary chancery addresses.

990. **Directory of Meat and Poultry Inspection Program Establishments, Circuits and Officials.** 1954– . Bimonthly. $7.00/yr. (A 88.16/20:yr./nos.)

Until March 1, 1969, this directory was titled *Working Reference of Livestock Regulatory Establishments, Circuits, and Officials.* From then until the end of 1970, it was called *Directory of Consumer Protection Programs, Establishments, Circuits, and Officials.*

991. **EDA Directory of Approved Projects.** 1966– . Quarterly. (C 46.19/2: yr./nos.) Order from: Office of Administration and Program Analysis; Economic Development Administration; Washington, D.C. 20230.

Lists all projects, by states, approved for EDA assistance and Public Law 89-136, passed August 26, 1965.

992. **Electromagnetic Metrology Current Awareness Service.** 1970– .
Monthly. $100.00/yr. (C 13.54:yr. and nos.) Order from: Electromagnetic
Metrology Information Center; Electromagnetics Division; National Bureau
of Standards; Boulder, Colo. 80203.

Contains abstracts of selected articles on measurement techniques and
standards of electromagnetic quantities from D-C to millimeter-wave frequencies.

993. **Endocrinology Index.** 1968– . Bimonthly. $16.00/yr. (HE 20.3309;
v. and nos.)

This bibliography is intended to supply scientists working in the field
of endocrinology with a current awareness tool and to help facilitate greater
integration of research and clinical efforts. Includes sections by subjects,
reviews, methods, and authors, and is indexed by subjects and authors.

994. **Epilepsy Abstracts.** 1968– . Monthly. (HE 20.3509:v. and nos.) Order
from: National Institute of Neurological Diseases and Stroke; Bethesda,
Md. 20014.

Concerned primarily with the clinical and therapeutic aspects of
epilepsies, including research in physiology, biochemistry, and the psychological, sociological and epidemiological aspects. Superseded by annual cumulated editions (see entry nos. 805 and 806 in this volume).

995. **Fast Announcement Service.** Irregular. $5.00/yr. (C 51.7/2:nos.) Order
from: National Technical Information Service; Springfield, Va. 22151.

Highlights selected new government research and development reports
received by NTIS for sale to the public. Available in 57 subject categories
(any or all for the $5.00 subscription price).

996. **Fertilizer Abstracts.** 1968– . Monthly. $25.00/yr. LC Card No. 71-
11106. (Y 3.T 25:36/v. and nos.) Order from: Fertilizer Abstracts Service;
National Fertilizer Development Center; Tennessee Valley Authority; Muscle
Shoals, Ala. 35660.

This abstract journal is compiled from articles in technical journals,
patents, and miscellaneous scientific and technical reports. Some abstracts
are from *Chemical Abstracts*, with permission. An annual index is issued
separately.

997. **Foreign Affairs Research Papers Available.** 1969– . Monthly. (S 1.126:
yr./nos.) Order from: State Department; Office of External Research;
Washington, D.C. 20520.

This is the monthly accessions list of the Foreign Affairs Research Documentation Center. For related bibliographies, see entry numbers 382 and 383
in this volume.

998. **Foreign Service List.** 1929– . 3 issues/yr. $3.50/yr. LC Card No. 10-
16369. (S 1.7:yr.)

Lists embassies, legations, missions, consulates, and U.S. diplomatic
representatives in foreign countries with their titles.

999. **Foreign Statistical Publications.** 1949— . Quarterly. LC Card No. 49-3797. (C 3.199:yr.) Order from: Census Bureau; Suitland, Md. 20233.
Lists the Census Bureau's accessions.

1000. **Gastroenterology Abstracts and Citations.** 1966— . Monthly. $16.00/yr. LC Card No. 67-1468. (HE 20.3313:v. and nos.)
This specialized bibliography is designed to aid in the support of laboratory and clinical research into the nature, causes, and therapy of diseases of the gastrointestinal tract. Annual cumulative author and subject indexes are also published.

1001. **Geophysical Abstracts.** 1929-1971. Monthly. LC Card No. GS 37-206. (I 19.43:nos.)
Discontinued with the December 1971 issue. Contains abstracts of literature pertaining to the physics of the solid earth, physical methods, geological problems, and geophysical exploration. Monthly issues were indexed by author with annual cumulative author and subject indexes.

Government Report Announcements. See entry nos. 1052, 1053, and 1054.

1002. **Health Aspects of Pesticides: Abstract Bulletin.** 1968— . Monthly. $6.50/yr. (EP 5.9:v. and nos.)
Abstracts over 500 foreign and domestic journals. Its purpose is to foster a current awareness of the major literature concerning the effects of pesticides on human health. An annual index is issued separately. Volume one through volume three, number two, were classified HE 20.1211:nos.; the remainder of volume three was classified HE 20.4011:nos.; transferred to the Environmental Protection Agency with volume four.

1003. **Highway Safety Literature: Announcement of Recent Acquisitions.** 1967— . Biweekly. (TD 8.10:yr.-nos.) Order from: National Highway Safety Bureau; Transportation Department; Washington, D.C. 20591.
Lists recent acquisitions of the National Highway Safety Bureau's Documentation Center and includes publications on all phases of highway or traffic safety. Arranged by subject with annual author and subject indexes. Published weekly until 1971.

1004. **Housing and Planning References, New Series.** 1965— . Bimonthly. $4.00/yr. (HH 1.23/3:nos.)
This bimonthly selection of publications and articles on housing and planning lists recent acquisitions of the HUD library. Arranged by subject with geographic and author indexes in each issue. See entry number 502 in this volume for cumulations.

1005. **Index Medicus, New Series.** 1960— . Monthly. $63.00/yr. LC Card No. 61-60337. (HE 20.3612:v. and nos.)
Index Medicus is a bibliographic listing of references to current articles from approximately 2,500 of the world's biomedical journals. Each issue contains a subject listing and a name listing (which includes names of biographees).

In addition, each issue contains a section entitled "Bibliography of Medical Reviews." This is designed to provide quick reference to the latest reviews in periodical literature in the field of biomedicine, and contains an author and name section. This is also published separately each month under the title *Monthly Bibliography of Medical Reviews* (q.v.).

The subscription to *Index Medicus* includes a separate part of each January issue entitled *Medical Subject Headings* (also available separately). Cross references are provided in this list, not in the Index itself. Therefore, a search in *Index Medicus* on a particular topic is facilitated if this list is consulted first.

The January issue also contains a complete list of journals indexed. Subsequent monthly issues list only those added or discontinued. Journals are listed by full title and by abbreviation used in *Index Medicus*.

Annual cumulations were published by the American Medical Association from 1960 to 1964. From 1965 on they have been published by GPO but are not included in subscriptions to the monthly *Index Medicus*. Entitled *Cumulated Index Medicus* (HE 20.3612/3:vol.), these annual indexes are multivolume sets. For example, the 1970 cumulation ($84.00/set) consists of the following eight volumes: 1) Introduction, Medical Subject Headings, List of Journals Indexed, Bibliography of Medical Reviews, Author List A-B; 2) Authors C-L; 3) Authors, M-Z; 4) Subject List, A-Ce; 5) Subjects, Ch-Gl; 6) Subjects, Gn-Me; 7) Subjects, Mi-Q; 8) Subjects, R-Z.

1006. **Library Accessions.** 1962-71. Monthly. (I 27.10/4:yr./nos.)

This list of the Bureau of Reclamation (Denver Federal Center) library accessions ceased with the November 1971 issue and merged with BuRec's current awareness program series entitled RECAP, which began in 1972.

1007. **List of Available Publications.** Quarterly. (A 13.66/14:yr./nos.) Order from: Pacific Northwest Forest and Range Experiment Station; P.O. Box 3141; Portland, Ore. 97208.

1008. **List of Available Publications.** Quarterly. (A 13.62/11-3:yr./nos.) Order from: Pacific Southwest Forest and Range Experiment Station; P.O. Box 245; Berkeley, Calif. 94701.

1009. **List of Library Accessions.** Irregular. (GS 1.14/6:yr.) Order from: Federal Fire Council; General Services Administration; Washington, D.C. 20405.

1010. **List of Publications.** Quarterly. (A 13.69/10:yr./nos.) Order from: Director; Rocky Mountain Forest and Range Experiment Station; 240 West Prospect Street; Fort Collins, Colo. 80521.

1011. **Marketing Information Guide.** 1959-71. Monthly. LC Card No. 59-30923. (C 41.11:v. and nos.)

Contains annotations of selected current publications and reports with basic information and statistics on marketing and distribution. Discontinued with the December 1971 issue, but now privately published by TMIG, Inc., 1028 Connecticut Avenue, N.W., Suite 815; Washington, D.C. 20036.

1012. **Mental Retardation Abstracts.** 1964— . Quarterly. $3.00/yr. LC Card No. 66-60248. (HE 17.113:v. and nos.)

Intended to aid investigators and other workers in the field of mental retardation. In two sections: the first is by broad subjects with full bibliographic citations and abstracts; the second is by author with full bibliographical data. Author and subject indexes are also provided.

1013. **Monthly Bibliography of Medical Reviews.** 1968— . Monthly. $4.50/yr. (HE 20.3610:v. and nos.)

Designed to provide quick guidance to the latest reviews in the journal literature of biomedicine. This bibliography will also continue to be listed in the monthly *Index Medicus* (q.v.).

1014. **Monthly Catalog of United States Government Publications.** 1895— . Monthly. $7.00/yr. LC Card No. 4-18088. (GP 3.8:yr./nos.)

Lists, by agencies, the publications (printed and processed) issued during each month. It includes the publications sold by the Superintendent of Documents, those for official use, and those which are sent to Depository Libraries.

1015. **Monthly Checklist of State Publications.** 1910— . Monthly. $8.00/yr. LC Card No. 10-8924. (LC 30.9:v. and nos.)

Arranged alphabetically by states and issuing agencies. Lists publications received by the Library of Congress. Cumulative index is published annually.

1016. **National Library of Medicine Current Catalog.** 1966— . Monthly. $7.50/yr. LC Card No. 67-62762. (HE 20.3609:v. and nos.)

1017. **National Library of Medicine Current Catalog.** 1966— . Quarterly. $13.00/yr. LC Card No. 67-62762. (HE 20.3609:v. and nos.)

Cites monographic publications cataloged by the National Library of Medicine during each month. The final quarterly issue is an annual cumulation.

1018. **NBS Publications Newsletter.** 1963— . Irregular. (C 13.36/5:yr./nos.) Order from: National Bureau of Standards; Gaithersburg, Md. 20760.

Lists new publications and services of the National Bureau of Standards.

1019. **New Publications (List).** Monthly. (L 1.34/3:yr. no.) Order from: Office of Information, Publications and Reports; Labor Department; Washington, D.C. 20210.

Lists publications by subject with price, number of pages, and issuing agency given for each.

1020. **New Publications, Bureau of Mines.** Monthly. (I 28.5/2:yr./nos.) Order from Mines Bureau; 4800 Forbes Avenue; Pittsburgh, Pa. 15231.

Lists publications issued each month. See entries 649 and 650 in this volume for cumulative works.

1021. **New Publications in Wages and Industrial Relations.** 1954— . Irregular. (L 2.74/2:nos.) Order from: Labor Statistics Bureau; Washington, D.C. 20210.

1022. **New Publications of the Geological Survey.** 1910— . Monthly. LC Card No. GS 11-221. (I 19.14/4:nos.) Order from: Geological Survey, Washington, D.C. 20242.

This is the only annotated listing of Geological Survey publications. When cumulated annually, annotations are omitted. See entry number 622 for cumulated edition.

1023. **New Serial Titles.** 1960— . Monthly. $115.00/yr. LC Card No. 53-60021. (LC 1.23/3:date) Order from: Card Division; Library of Congress; Building 159, Navy Yard Annex; Washington, D.C. 20541.

Arranged by titles with place of publication, beginning date and date of cessation (if applicable). Cumulated quarterly and annually.

1024. **New Serial Titles: Classed Subject Arrangement.** 1955— . Monthly. $25.00/yr. LC Card No. 55-60037. (LC 1.23/5:date and nos.) Order from: Card Division; Library of Congress; Building 159, Navy Yard Annex; Washington, D.C. 20541.

Arranged by Dewey Decimal Classification number. Provides LC holdings information.

1025. **Nuclear Science Abstracts.** 1948— . Semimonthly. $42.00/yr. LC Card No. 50-4390. (Y 3.At 7:16/v. and nos.)

Abstracts literature relating to nuclear science and engineering, including materials of the AEC, other government agencies, universities, and industrial research establishments.

1026. **Nuclear Science Abstracts: Indexes.** 1948— . Quarterly. $34.50/yr. LC Card No. 50-4390. (Y 3.At 7:16-5/v. and nos.)

Subscription to quarterly indexes includes an annual report number index. See entry numbers 741 and 742 in this volume for cumulative volumes.

1027. **Occupational Outlook Quarterly.** 1957— . Quarterly. $1.50/yr. LC Card No. 67-5477. (L 2.70/4:v. and nos.)

Contains current information on employment trends and outlook, based primarily on the continuous research and statistical programs of the Bureau of Labor Statistics.

1028. **Outdoor Recreation Action.** 1966— . Quarterly. $2.00/yr. LC Card No. 67-60945. (I 66.17:nos.)

This series is the forum for reporting private, local, state, and federal action in the areas of outdoor recreation and natural beauty. Indexed by states, government agencies and private organizations.

1029. **Parkinson's Disease and Related Disorders, Citations from the Literature.** 1970— . Monthly. $2.50/yr. (HE 20.3511:v. and nos.)

This bibliography is intended to provide current, selected, systematically categorized citations from the literature in a sizable but limited area of interest. Arranged in two sections—subject and author.

1030. **Personnel Literature.** 1941— . Monthly. $6.00/yr. (CS 1.62:v. and nos.)
Cites selected books, pamphlets, and other publications received in the Library of the Civil Service Commission during the previous month. Periodical articles, unpublished dissertations, and microfilms are also listed.

1031. **Pesticides Documentation Bulletin.** 1965-69. Biweekly. LC Card No. Agr 65-150. (A 17.20:v. and nos.)
Discontinued with volume 5, no. 26, December 26, 1969. Indexed by keywords in titles, by title and by author. Semiannual cumulative indexes were also issued.

1032. **Preliminary Determination of Epicenters.** Monthly. $1.50/yr. (C 55.690:yr./nos.)
Lists earthquakes recorded throughout the world, during each monthly period, by date and time and with preliminary data on location, depth and magnitude. It is suited to earth science courses and for statistical studies of seismicity.

1033. **Problems of Communism.** 1952— . Bimonthly. $3.00/yr. LC Card No. 54-61675. (IA 1.8:v. and nos.)
Provides analyses and significant background information on various aspects of world communism today.

1034. **Psychopharmacology Abstracts.** 1961— . Monthly. $13.00/yr. LC Card No. 63-1143. (HE 20.2409/2:v. and nos.)
This service is designed to meet the needs of investigators in the field of psychopharmacology for rapid and comprehensive information about new developments and research results. Cumulative indexes are published separately.

1035. **Publication Announcements.** Irregular. (C 13.36/2:nos.) Order from: National Bureau of Standards; Gaithersburg, Md. 20760.

1036. **Publications of the Bureau of Sport Fisheries and Wildlife.** 1968— . Monthly. LC Card No. 68-62318. (I 49.18/6:yr./nos.) Order from: Bureau of Sport Fisheries and Wildlife; Washington, D.C. 20240.

1037. **Recent Publications of Southern Forest Experiment Station.** Irregular. (A 13.40/8-2:yr./nos.) Order from: Southern Forest Experiment Station; 701 Loyola Avenue; New Orleans, La. 70113.

1038. **Reliability Abstracts and Technical Reviews.** 1963-70. Monthly. LC Card No. 63-2548. (NAS 1.35:v. and nos.)
Discontinued with the annual index for 1970.

1039. **Research in Education.** 1966– . Monthly. $21.00/yr. LC Card No. 72-216727. (HE 5.77:nos.)

Provides up-to-date information about educational research sponsored by the Bureau of Research, Office of Education. The semiannual and annual indexes are not included as part of the subscription service but are sold separately.

1040. **Scientific and Technical Aerospace Reports.** 1963– . Semi-monthly. $54.00/yr. LC Card No. 64-39060. (NAS 1.9/4:v. and nos.)

This series announces, abstracts, and indexes reports issued by NASA, other government agencies, universities, and research organizations. Referred to as STAR. Semiannual indexes are published separately.

1041. **Selected Abstracts of Planning Publications.** 1968– . Quarterly. (HH 8.9:yr.-nos.) Order from: Department of Housing and Urban Development; Washington, D.C. 20410.

This series abstracts planning reports prepared under the Urban Planning Assistance Program. Arranged by subjects and within each subject by states. Not indexed.

1042. **Selected List of Recent Additions to Library.** Weekly. (L 1.19:3/nos.) Order from: Department of Labor; Washington, D.C. 20210.

1043. **Selected Publications and Audio-Visual Materials.** Quarterly. (S 1.30/2: yr./nos.) Order from: Department of State; Washington, D.C. 20520.

Each issue in this series, usually two to four pages, lists State Department documents published during the preceding three months. Most entries are annotated.

1044. **Selected References on Environmental Quality as It Relates to Health.** 1971– . Monthly. $4.00/yr. (HE 20.3616:v. and nos.)

Cites journal articles pertaining to the effects of environmental pollution on human health. Annual cumulations supersede monthly issues.

1045. **Selected United States Government Publications.** 1928– . Biweekly. Free. LC Card No. 28-26554. (GP 3.17:nos.)

These annotated guides to GPO-published documents list materials on a wide variety of subjects. Useful for anyone—housewife to scientist.

1046. **Selected Urban Storm Water Runoff Abstracts.** Quarterly. Prices vary. (EP 2.10:11024EJC-nos.)

1047. **Selected Water Resources Abstracts.** 1968– . Semimonthly. $22.00/yr. (I 1.94/2:v. and nos.) Order from: National Technical Information Service; Springfield, Va. 22151.

Contains abstracts of current and earlier pertinent monographs, journal articles, reports and other publications which cover the water-related aspects of the life, physical, and social sciences as well as related engineering and legal aspects of the characteristics, conservation, control, use or management of water. Annual indexes are published separately.

1048. **Solid Waste Management: A List of Available Literature.** Quarterly. (EP 3.9:L 71/yr.-nos.) Order from: Publications Distribution Unit; Solid Waste Management Office; Environmental Protection Agency; 5555 Ridge Avenue; Cincinnati, Ohio 45213.

1049. **Sport Fishery Abstracts.** 1957— . Quarterly. LC Card No. 59-38041. (I 49.40/2:v. and nos.) Order from: Bureau of Sport Fisheries and Wildlife; Fish and Wildlife Service; Washington, D.C. 20240.

Contains signed abstracts of works in many areas of sport fisheries research. Arranged by author with subject indexes. Cumulative indexes are also published.

1050. **Technical News Bulletin.** 1925— . Monthly. $3.00/yr. LC Card No. 25-26527. (C 13.13:v. and nos.)

Announces all new publications by members of the staff of the National Bureau of Standards including those appearing in other journals.

1051. **Toxicity Bibliography.** 1968— . Quarterly. $14.00/yr. (HE 20.3613: v. and nos.)

A highly specialized medical bibliography which includes the entire range of chemical and biological interactions, covering reports of toxicity studies, adverse drug reactions, and poisoning in animals and humans.

1052. **U.S. Government Research and Development Reports.** 1946— . Semimonthly. $30.00/yr. LC Card No. 46-2794. (C 51.9/3:v. and nos.) Order from: National Technical Information Service; Springfield, Va. 22151.

1053. **U.S. Government Research and Development Reports: Index.** 1946— . Semimonthly. $22.00/yr. LC Card No. 46-2794. (C 51.9:v. and nos.) Order from: National Technical Information Service; Springfield, Va. 22151.

1054. **U.S. Government Research and Development Reports: Quarterly Cumulative Index.** 1946— . Quarterly. $6.00/yr. LC Card No. 46-2794. (C 51.9/2:v. and nos.) Order from National Technical Information Service; Springfield, Va. 22151.

USGRDR is a detailed listing of unclassified and unrestricted technical reports generated by various federal agencies. All publications listed are available from NTIS. Now published under the title *Government Report Announcements*.

1055. **Wildlife Review: An Abstracting Service for Wildlife Management.** 1935— . Quarterly. LC Card No. 53-17432. (I 49.17:nos.) Order from: Bureau of Sport Fisheries and Wildlife; Fish and Wildlife Service; Washington, D.C. 20240.

Cumulative indexes entitled *Wildlife Abstracts* appear irregularly.

INDEX

ADP Glossary, 610
Abbreviations and Definitions of Terms Used in Civil Defense Training, 697
Abridged Index Medicus, 958
Abstracts of Literature on Distillation of Seawater and on the Use of Nuclear Energy for Desalting, 743
Abstracts of North American Geology, 959
Abstracts of the Standard Edition of the Complete Psychological Works of Sigmund Freud, 878
Academic deans, 247
Accessions List: Ceylon, 960; Eastern Africa, 961; India, 953-954, 962; Indonesia, Malaysia, Singapore, and Brunei, 963; Israel, 964; Middle East, 965; Nepal, 966; Pakistan, 955, 967;
Accident Bibliography, 725
Accredited Higher Institutions, 246n
Accredited Postsecondary Institutions and Programs, 246
Ackley, Richard M., 549
Activation Analysis: A Bibliography, 605
Adams, John Quincy. 925
Administration of Modern Archives: A Select Bibliographic Guide, 336
Adult Basic Education Program Statistics, 224
Adult Development and Aging Abstracts of the National Institute of Child Health and Human Development, Scientific Information Centers Branch, 968
Adult education, 224-226
Advanced Abstracts of Scientific and Technical Papers Submitted for Publication and Presentation, 969
Adverse drug reactions, 903
Aeronautical and space engineering, 685-696, 970, 1040
Aeronautical Engineering, Special Bibliography, 970
Aeronautics, 685
Aerospace Bibliography, 687
Aerospace Engineering: A Special Bibliography, 688
Aerospace Medicine and Biology: A Continuing Bibliography, 971
Africa, 286-296, 961
Aging, 434-439, 968

Aging Committee (Senate) publications lists, 439
Agricultural Economics Bureau, 281
Agricultural Sciences, 533-576
  Agriculture, 533-559
  Forestry, 560-567
  Home Economics, 568-570
  Wildlife Management, 571-576
Agricultural trade, 154, 167-168
Agriculture
  General Works, 521, 533-552
  Farm Products, 553-555
  Soil Management, 556-559
  Vocational Education, 267
Agriculture Department publications lists, 534, 536, 977
Agriculture Statistics, 544-545
Aids to Media Selection for Students and Teachers, 229
Air Force Scientific Research Bibliography, 686
Air pollution
  Abstracts, 972
  Bibliographies, 775-784
  Directories, 785-787
Air Pollution Abstracts, 972
Air Pollution Aspects of Emission Sources: Cement Manufacturing, 775; Electric Power Production, 776; Municipal Incineration, 777; Nitric Acid Manufacturing, 778; Sulfuric Acid Manufacturing, 779
Air Pollution Training Courses, 786
Air University Library Index to Military Periodicals, 973
Airlines, 170
Albania, 316
Algeria, 287
All Around You: An Environmental Study Guide, 772
All States Income Tax Guide, 196
Allard, Dean C., 354
Alphabetical Index of Industries and Occupations, 46
Altus, David M., 209, 232, 258, 260
American Doctoral Dissertations on the Arab World, 308
American Ephemeris and Nautical Almanac, 582

227

American Indian Calendar, 426-427
American Indian Education, A Selected Bibliography, 258
American Ships of the Line, 350
Americas, Gazetteer Supplement, 285
Analysis of Work Stoppages, 135
Andresen, John W., 591
Andrews, Henry N., 676
Annotated Bibliography of Attempts to Rear Larvae of Marine Fishes in the Laboratory, 596
Annotated Bibliography of Zooplankton Sampling Devices, 597
Annotated Bibliography on Children, 448
Annotated Bibliography on Hydrology and Sedimentation, 632
Annotated Bibliography on Maternal Nutrition, 822
Annotated Bibliography on the Fishing Industry and Biology of the Blue Crab, 598
Annotated Bibliography on Vital and Health Statistics, 479
Annotated Bibliography: The Relationship Between Vehicle Defects and Vehicle Crashes, 733
Annotated Reading List of Marine Corps History, 349
Antarctic Bibliography, 333-334
Antarctica, 333-334
Antitrust Laws, with Amendments, 363
Antitrust Subcommittee (House) publications lists, 31
Apparel and Accessories for Women, Misses, and Children, 60
Architecture, Building and Engineering, 923
Area Handbook for . . . Albania, 316; Algeria, 287; Brazil, 321; Burma, 288; Ceylon, 297; Colombia, 322; Congo (Kinshasa), 289; Costa Rica, 323; Cuba, 324; Cyprus, 317; El Salvador, 325; Ethiopia, 291; Ghana, 292; Guatemala, 326; Honduras, 327; India, 299; Indonesia, 300; Iran, 309; Iraq, 310; Israel, 311; Malaysia, 303; Mongolia, 304; Nicaragua, 328; Oceania, 331; Pakistan, 305; Saudi Arabia, 312; Somalia, 293; Syria, 313; Thailand, 306; the Indian Ocean Territories, 335; the People's Republic of the Congo (Congo Grazzaville), 290; the Peripheral States of the Arabian Peninsula, 307;

Area Handbook for . . . (cont'd) the Republic of South Africa, 294; the Republic of Tunisia, 295; the Republic of Turkey, 314; the Soviet Union, 318; the United Arab Republic (Egypt), 296; Uruguay, 329; Venezuela, 330
Arms control, 376, 974
Arms Control Achievements, 376
Arms Control and Disarmament: A Quarterly Bibliography with Abstracts and Annotations, 974
Art and Architecture, 923-926
Arthritis and Rheumatic Diseases Abstracts, 975
Artificial Kidney Bibliography, 976
Arts and Crafts, 403
Ashby, Charlotte, 282
Asia, 297-306, 382
Asper, Ardys, 818
Associations, 217, 407-408, 424-425, 432, 896-897
Astronautics and Aeronautics, 693-694
Astronomy, 578-585
Atkin, Charles K., 451
Atlas and Gazetteer of the Near Side of the Moon, 578
Atlas of Oral Cytology, 814
Atlas of United States Trees, 586
Atlases
  China, 274
  Forests, 560
  Indian Ocean, 658
  Medical, 814
  Moon, 578-579
  Trees, 586
  U.S., 275-280, 386
Atomic Energy Joint Committee, 762-763
Atomic spectra, 764-765
Atomic transition probabilities, 752-753
Audiovisual personnel, 393-394
Automatic Indexing: A State-of-the-Art Report, 616
Author and Permuted Title Index to Selected Statistical Journals, 489
Automated Multiphasic Health Testing, 841
Automation for Small Offices, 49
Available Publications of the USDA's Consumer and Marketing Service, 533
Aviation, 709-718
Aviation medicine, 853-857
Aviation Medicine, 971n

BLS Publications on Productivity and Technology, 102
Baker, Simon, 275-278
Balima, Mildred G., 938
Ballon, Eleanor F., 952
Banking and Currency Committee (House) publications lists, 149
Banking and Finance, 143-149
Bankruptcy, 143
Barhyte, Diana Y., 206
Basic Library Reference Sources, 16
Basic Readings in Social Security, 181
Basic Religious Books and Chaplains' Services, 934
Basler, Roy P., 340
Beckman, Theodore N., 80
Behavior, 451, 879
Behavior Modification in Child and School Mental Health, 879
Belgium, 420
Bell, Thelma I., 572
Benjamin, Gwen P., 63
Benton, Mildred, 948
Bern, Betty, 354
Bernier, Bernard A., 944
Berthold, Jeanne S., 206
Bibliographies on Fabric Flammability, 704-706
Bibliography, Collaborative Study on Cerebral Palsy, Mental Retardation, and Other Neurological and Sensory Disorders of Infancy and Childhood, 835-836
Bibliography of . . . Desalting Literature, 603; Federal Grants-in-Aid to State and Local Governments, 387; Insect-Resistant Packaging, 51; Investment and Operating Costs for Chemical and Petroleum Plants, 56; Lobsters, 594; Medical Reviews, 825; North American Geology, 617-619, 959n; Potato Diseases, 554; Research on the Utilization of Rice, 553; the History of Medicine, 826; Tritium Studies Related to Hydrology, 629
Bibliography on . . . Atomic Transition Probabilities, 752-753; Early Childhood, 446; Electronic Composition, 71; Marketing to Low-Income Consumers, 53n; Meteorology, Climatology, and Physical/Chemical Oceanography, 645; Mortgage Finance, 144; Motor Vehicle and Traffic Safety, 724; Smoking and Health, 823-824; Speech, Hearing, and Language in Relation to Mental Retardation, 892;

Bibliography on . . . (cont'd) the Comprehensive Health Service Program, 907; the Epidemiology of Mental Disorders, 883; the Geology and Resources of Vanadium to 1968, 620; the High Temperature Chemistry and Physics of Materials, 920
Biblio-Profile on Human Communication and Its Disorders, 837-838
Bimonthly List of Publications and Motion Pictures, 977
Biographic Register, 370-371
Biographical Directory of the American Congress, 388
Biography, 9, 320, 370-371, 388, 390-391
Biological Sciences, 521, 586-598, 971
Birth records, 485
Bivins, Harold A., 349
Black Americans, A Chartbook, 429
Black Literature, 430
Blair, B. E., 512
Blindness, 861-862
Blutstein, Norman L., 323-325, 327
Boating Statistics, 719-720
Books Related to Adult Basic Education and Teaching English to Speakers of Other Languages, 225
Books Related to English Language and Literature in Elementary and Secondary Schools, 230
Botany, 586-592
Botswana, Lesotho, and Swaziland: A Guide to Official Publications, 938
Bowker, David E., 579
Bowker, H. Thomas, 333
Brash, Charlene, 442-443
Brazil, 321
Breden, Leslie H., 529
Briggs, Mary K., 685
Broadcasting Stations of the World, 83
Browne, Theodore D., 510
Brunei, 285, 963
Bryson, Carolyn Q., 882
Built Environment for the Elderly and the Handicapped, 438
Bureau of the Census Catalog, 978
Burma, 288
Burnside, Virginia W., 593
Business and Industry, 37-80
Business Machine Market Information Sources, 52
Business Service Checklist, 12n, 979
Business Statistics, 36

Calibration and Test Services of the National Bureau of Standards, 522
Callahan, John J., 766
Campbell, Colleen A., 252
Camping in the National Park System, 410
Camping Opportunities for Disadvantaged Youth, 408
Canada, 383, 709
Cancer, 831-832, 980-981
Cancer Chemotherapy Abstracts, 980
Carberry, Frank J., 49
Carcinogenesis Abstracts, 981
Career Education in the Environment, 238
Careers in the U.S. Department of Commerce, 188
Careers in the United States Department of the Interior, 189-190
Carmody, James, 820
Carpenter, Carmen, 395
Carter, Yvonne, 229
Cartographic Records of the Bureau of Agricultural Economics, 281
Catalog: Department of Health, Education, and Welfare Publications, 1
Catalog of . . . Basic Education Systems, 256; Chemical Analysis of Rocks from the Intersection of the African Gulf, Gulf of Aden, and Red Sea Rift Systems, 624; Copyright Entries, Cumulative Series Motion Pictures, 1960-1969, 931; Federal Domestic Assistance, 4-6; Federally Financed Housing and Building Research and Technology, 490; HEW Assistance, 2; Illustrated Paleozoic Plants in the National Museum of Natural History, 677; Information on Water Data; 938-941; Nautical Charts, 659; Publications, 423, 663;Research Reagents, 608; the 22d National Exhibition of Prints Held at the Library of Congress, 924; Type Specimens of Invertebrate Fossils: Conodonta, 678
Catalogue of Forms, Form Letters, and Notices, 198
Cement manufacturing, 775
Census Bureau Methodological Research, 476-477
Census Bureau publications lists, 476-477, 978
Census Users' Guide, 480
Centre International de l'Enfance, 444
Cerebral palsy, 835-836
Ceylon, 297, 960

Characteristics of General Assistance in the United States, 7
Chase, E. B., 639, 793
Chase, John L., 247
Checklist, International Business Publications, 150-151
Chemical analysis of rocks, 624
Chemical plants, 56, 58-59
Chemistry, 599-608, 920
Chemotherapy, 980
Child labor, 362
Children and Youth, 440-450
Children's Books, 227-228
China, 274, 298
Chintz, 926
Chismore, W. Dale, 234
Chlorine and Air Pollution: An Annotated Bibliography, 780
Christie, Marjorie B., 537
Citizen and Business Participation in Urban Affairs, 491
Civil Aeronautics Board publications lists, 710
Civil Aircraft Register, 715-718
Civil and Public Safety Engineering
   Civil Defense, 697-700
   Fire Sciences, 701-706
   Law Enforcement, 707-708
   Transportation, 709-735
Civil defense, 697-700
Civil Defense Motion Picture Catalog, 698
Civil Defense Office publications lists, 698
Civil rights, 356, 423
Civil Rights Commission publications lists, 423
Civil Rights Directory, 356
Civil Service, 8-9
Civil War Naval Chronology, 351
Civilian Conservation Centers, 98
Clark, Willie E., 740
Clarke, James W., 617, 619
Classified Index of Industries and Occupations, 47
Climate of Cities: A Survey of Recent Literature, 646
Climatological Data: National Summary, 982
Climatology, 645-648, 701, 982
Clinical Programs for Mentally Retarded Children, 895
Clothing stores, 60
Cloud, William K., 681-682
Coast and Geodetic Survey publications lists, 660, 679-680

Cocknell, Edna, 755
Coding Supplement to Standard Nomenclature of Veterinary Diseases and Operations, 918
Coffman, Jerry L., 681
Collier, Frederick J., 678
Colombia, 321
Color Filmstrips and Slide Sets of the United States Department of Agriculture, 534
Commerce Department publications lists, 11-12, 979
Commercial Fisheries Abstracts, 983
Committee Publications and Policies Governing Their Distribution, 10
Communications and Electronics, 736
Communications-Electronics Terminology, 737
Communications, 81-88, 736-737
Communism, 368-369, 1033
Communist China: A Bibliographic Survey, 298
Communist Eastern Europe, An Analytical Survey of Literature, 315
Communist North Korea: A Bibliographic Survey, 302
Community Health Centers, 886
Community Health Service publications lists, 906
Community Health Services, 909-910, 913
Compilation of Statutes Relating to the Consumer and Marketing Service and Closely Related Activities, 543
Compilation of Statutes Relating to Soil Conservation, Acreage Diversion . . ., 542
Comprehensive Tax Guide to U.S. Civil Service Retirement Benefits, 199
Computer Applications in Psychotherapy, 880
Computer Program Abstracts, 984
Computer Program Abstracts, Cumulative Issue, 609
Concise History of the United States Marine Corps, 348
Congo, 289-290
Congressional Committee Hearings, 395
Congressional Directory, 390-391
Congressional District Atlas, 386
Congressional Pictorial Directory, 389
Connolly, John A., 792
Conservation, 558, 774
Conservation Tools for Educators, 774

Constitution, Jefferson's Manual, and Rules of the House of Representatives, 396
Construction Industry: Selected References, 61
Consulates, 372-373, 998
Consultation Research in Mental Health and Related Fields, 876
Consumer and Marketing Service publications lists, 533
Consumer Education Bibliography, 93
Consumer Information, 89-94
Consumer Prices in the United States, 89
Consumer Product Information: Index of Selected Federal Publications, 90-92
Continuing Education Programs and Services for Women, 226
Contours of Change, 551
Controlled Fusion and Plasma Research, 744
Conventions, 30
Cooper, Margaret, 604
Cooperative Studies in Psychiatry: An Annotated Bibliography Summarizing 15 Years of Cooperative Research in Psychiatry, 885
Coordination Directory for Planning Studies and Reports, 636
Coping and Adaptation: A Behavioral Sciences Bibliography, 881
Corrections: A Bibliography, 452
Costa Rica, 323
Courts (U.S.), 357-358
Courville, Donovan A., 595
Crabtree, D. Glen, 788
Crabs, 598
Crafts Techniques in Occupational Therapy, 403
Cresswell, Mary A., 344
Crime and Delinquency Abstracts, 985
Criminology, 452-457, 985
Cryogenic Data Center Current Awareness Service, 986
Cuba, 324, 935
Cuban Acquisitions and Bibliography, 935
Cumulated Abridged Index Medicus, 808-809, 1005n
Cumulative Index of Congressional Committee Hearings, 395
Cumulative Index to Foreign Market Surveys, 156
Cumulative Index to NASA Tech Briefs, 689
Cunningham, Sylvia, 608
Curran, Mary A., 206

Current Catalog (NLM), 826n, 828, 1016-1017
Current Index to Journals in Education, 209n, 232n, 258n, 260n
Current Literature on Venereal Diseases: Abstracts and Bibliography, 987
Current Membership of the Joint Committee on Atomic Energy, 762-763
Cyprus, 317

Daily Newspapers, General Periodicals and Official State (U.S.) Periodicals Received in the Department of Labor Library, 951
Dakan, Norman E., 430
Data Preparation Manual for the Conversion of Map Cataloging Records to Machine-Readable Form, 615
Data Processing
  Abstracts, 609, 984
  Dictionaries, 610-611
  Equipment, 612-614
  Handbooks and Guides, 615-616
David, Charlotte M., 944
Deafness and deaf education, 262, 837-838
Dean, Gloria D., 952
Death and dying, 877
Death records, 485
DeBoer, Lloyd M., 55
Definitions of Selected Ground-Water Terms, 634
Demography, 478-479, 481-483, 485-486, 488
Denny, Lyle M., 647
Dental Science Handbook, 875
Dentistry, 815, 874-875
Desalination, 58-59, 603, 743
Desalting Plants Inventory Report, 58-59
Dewey, Lucretia, 136
Diabetes Literature Index, 803-804, 988
Dictionary of ... American Naval Fighting Ships, 352; International Agricultural Trade, 154; Military and Associated Terms, 739
Digest of Educational Statistics, 222
Digest of Selected Pension Plans, 180
Dill, Henry W., 275-278
Diplomatic List, 989
Diplomatic Social Usage, 380
Directory, Aviation Medical Examiners, 854-857

Directory: Coordinators of Children's Services and of Young Adult Services in Public Library Systems Serving at Least 100,000 People, 946
Directory, Federal Job Information Centers, 24
Directory for Reaching Minority Groups, 425
Directory for Economic Development Districts, 99
Directory, Medicare Providers and Suppliers of Services, 182
Directory, Public and Nonpublic Elementary and Secondary Day Schools, 236
Directory of ... Aviation Medical Examiners, 853; Community Mental Health Centers, 886; Companies Filing Annual Reports with the Securities and Exchange Commission, 28-29; Consultants on Migrant Education, 259; Consumer Protection Programs, 990n; Federal and State Officials Engaged in Water Resources Development, 635; Federal R & D Installations, 524; Federal Recreation Entrance, Admission, and User Fee Areas, 409; Federally Supported Information Analysis Centers, 519; Field Contacts for Coordination of Use of Radio Frequencies, 82; Full Year Head Start Programs, 257; Graduate Deans at United States Universities, 247; Health Occupations Training Programs, 866; Information Resources in Agriculture and Biology, 521; Information Resources in the United States: Physical Sciences and Engineering, 520; International Mail, 86n; Job Corps Centers, Civilian Conservation Centers, Men's Centers, Residential Manpower Centers, Women's Centers, Residential Support Centers, 98; Library Resources for the Blind and Physically Handicapped, 861; Meat and Poultry Inspection Program Establishments, Circuits and Officials, 990; Narcotic Addiction Treatment Centers, 466; National and International Labor Unions in the United States, 136; National Wildlife Refuges, 574; Non-Federal Statistics for Local Areas, 484; On-Going Research in Smoking and Health, 863; Organizations Serving Minority Communities, 424;

Directory of . . . (cont'd)
  Personnel Responsible for Radiological Health Programs, 859; Post Offices, 84-85; Private Programs Assisting Minority Business, 95; Public Elementary and Secondary Schools, 235; Research, Development and Demonstration Projects, 506; Selected Community Health Services, 909-910; Shipping Containers for Radioactive Materials, 759; Spanish Speaking Organizations in the United States, 432; Special Education Personnel in State Education Agencies, 263; Standards Laboratories, 523; State and Areawide Comprehensive Health Planning Agencies Supported under Sec. 314, Public Health Service Act as of July 1, 1970, 911; State and Local Resources for the Mentally Retarded, 893; State, Territorial, and Regional Health Authorities, 912; Studies and Reports Related to Training and Education, 138; U.S. Government Audiovisual Personnel, 393-394
Disadvantaged, 256-261, 408
Diseases and handicaps, 830-839, 975-976, 980-981, 987-988, 994, 1000, 1029
Diseases of Forest and Shade Trees, 587
Dissertations (academic), 308
Diving, 665
Division of Nursing Selected Publications, 898
Dombrowski, John, 326
Donehoo, Irene A., 643-644
Doody, Alton F., 80
Dorn, Georgette M., 936
Dougherty, Verda M., 629
Doughty, Richard M., 588
Dowdy, Emily, 599-601
Doyel, W. W., 639
Drama, 932
Drought Bibliography, 647
Drug Abuse
  Bibliographies, 458-461
  Dictionaries, 462
  Directories, 463-470
  Filmographies, 471-473
Drug Abuse Information, Education, and Rehabilitation Programs Supported by State Health Agencies and Voluntary Organizations, 468
Drug Abuse Prevention Materials for Schools, 465

Drug Abuse Information Programs Supported by National Organizations, 469
Drug Abuse Education Programs Supported by State Education Agencies, 467
Drug Dependence and Abuse: A Selected Bibliography, 458
Drugs of Abuse, 463
Drugstores, 62
Dupuy, Trevor N., 304
Duda, John R., 56
Dybwad, Rosemary F., 897

EDA Directory of Approved Projects, 100, 991
ERIC Products, 1967-68: A Bibliography, 253
Early Childhood Psychosis: Infantile Autism, Childhood Schizophrenia and Related Disorders, 882
Earnings Distributions in the United States, 123
Earth Sciences
  Geology, 617-625
  Hydrology, 626-641
  Meteorology, 642-648
  Mineralogy, 649-657
  Oceanography, 658-675
  Paleontology, 676-678
  Seismology, 679-682
Earthquakes, 681-682, 1032
Ecological Effects of Pesticides on Nontarget Species, 791
Economic Development Programs, 95-100, 991
Economics and Business, 8-205
  General Works:
    Bibliographies, 8-23, 979, 1042
    Directories, 24-30
    Indexes, 31-33
    Statistics, 34-36
Edgerly, David E., 922
Education, 206-273
  General Works:
    Bibliographies, 1, 206-210
    Dictionaries, 211
    Directories, 212-221
    Statistics, 222-223
Education Directory, 212-217
  Education Associations, 217; Higher Education, 215-216; Public School Systems, 213-214; State Governments, 212

233

Education (Drug Abuse Prevention), 464-465, 467, 470-472
Education (Environmental), 772-774
Education (Health), 866
Education, Literature of the Profession, 208
Education Office publications lists, 210
Educational research, 253-254, 1039
Educational technology, 206-207
Educational Technology and the Teaching-Learning Process, 206
Edwards, Robert D., 893
Egypt, 296
El Salvador, 325
Electric utilities, 76-79
Electric power production, 401, 776
Electrical and electronic engineering, 736-737
Electromagnetic Metrology Current Awareness Service, 992
Electronic composition, 71
Elementary and Secondary Education, 227-239
    Bibliographies, 227-233
    Dictionaries, 234
    Directories, 213-214, 235-237
    Handbooks and Guides, 238-239
Eligible Institutions: Guaranteed Student Loan Program, 248
Emergency Health Services Selected Bibliography, 819
Employee Benefits and Services, 125
Employee-Management Relations in Public Service, 126
Employer's Tax Guide, 200
Employment and Earnings, States and Areas, 114-115
Employment and Earnings, United States, 116
Employment and labor, 101-142, 1030
Endocrinology Index, 993
Engineering, 683-765
    General Works, 509, 520, 683-684, 923
Engineering Design Handbook: Tables of Cumulative Binomial Probabilities, 797
Engineers' Overseas Handbook, 63
Environment and the Community, 492
Environmental Data Service: Services and Publications, 642
Environmental-Ecological Education: A Bibliography, 231
Environmental education, 231, 238, 772-774

Environmental monitoring, 771, 785
Environmental Pollution: A Selective Bibliography—Information for Business and Industry, 769
Environmental quality, 766, 1044
Environmental Science Services Administration publications lists, 642
Environmental Sciences, 766-795
    General Works:
        Bibliographies, 766-769, 1044
        Directories, 770-771
        Guides, 772-774
Ephemeris of the Sun, Polaris and Other Selected Stars with Companion Data and Tables, 580-581
Epilepsy Abstracts, 805-806, 994
Equal Opportunity in Employment, 107
Equilibrium Critical Phenomena in Fluids and Mixtures, 606
Equivalency and Testing, 840
Ervin, Sharon, 218
Essential United States Foreign Trade Routes, 174
Estate and gift tax, 202
Ethical Issues in Health Services, A Report and Annotated Bibliography, 820
Ethiopia, 291
Europe, 285, 315-319, 383
Europe and U.S.S.R. Gazetteer Supplement, 285
Evans, Frank B., 336
Everyman's Guide: An ERIC Search System, 218
Executive Development Programs, 140n
Executive Manpower Management, 127
Export/import data, 163-169

FAA Catalog, 711
FAA Inspection Authorization Directory, 712
FAA Statistical Handbook of Aviation, 713-714
Fabric flammability, 704-706
Fact Book of U.S. Agriculture, 539
Fair Labor Standards Act, 113, 360-362
Falkner, Frank, 444
Fallout shelters, 699-700
Family Food Budgeting for Good Meals and Good Nutrition, 568
Family planning, 474
Farley, Judith R., 941

Farm products, 541, 550, 553-555, 990
Farmer Cooperative Service publications list, 537
Farmer cooperatives, 549
Farmer's Tax Guide, 201
Fast Announcement Service, 995
Federal and State Indian Reservations, 428
Federal and State Student Aid Programs, 252
Federal Assistance in Outdoor Recreation, 404
Federal Aviation Administration publications lists, 711
Federal Buying Directory, 27
Federal Civil Service: History, Organization, and Activities, 8
Federal Health Programs Service publications lists, 801-802
Federal Income Tax Information for Armed Forces Personnel, 197
Federal libraries, 948
Federal Outdoor Recreation Programs and Recreation-Related Environmental Programs, 405
Federal Population Censuses, 1790-1890: Catalog of Microfilm Copies of the Schedules, 478
Federal Reserve Chart Book, 148n
Federal-State Market News Reports, 54
Federal Statistical Directory, 487
Federal Wage Hour Law, 360-361
Fertilizer Abstracts, 996
Festival U.S.A., 402
Fibrinolysis, Thrombolysis, and Blood Clotting Bibliography, 833-834
Fiction Men Read, 929
Field Directory (HEW), 3
Fifty United States Civil Service Commissioners, 9
Film Reference Guide for Medicine and Allied Sciences, 817
Films on Drug Abuse, 473
Finance and Banking, 143-149
Financial Management Research in Farming in the United States, 535
Fire in Northern Regions, 702
Fire Weather, 701
Fire sciences, 701-706, 1009
Firearms, 708, 738
Firearms Identification for Law Enforcement Officers, 708
Fireline Handbook, 703
Fischer, R. P., 620

Fish Kills Caused by Pollution, 794
Fisher, Janet, 799
Fisheries, 573, 575, 983, 1036, 1049
Fishery Statistics of the United States, 571-572
Flag Manual, 397
Floss, Ludmilla, 557
Fluoridation Census, 874
Follow Through Project Directory, 237
Food and Agricultural Export Directory, 167-168
Food exporting, 167-168
Food products, 541, 550, 602, 990
Food processing and retailing, 64-66
Foreign Affairs Research Papers Available, 997
Foreign Affairs Research, Special Papers Available: Near East and South Asia, 382
Foreign Affairs Research, Special Papers Available: Western Europe, Great Britain, and Canada, 383
Foreign Affiliate Financial Survey, 162
Foreign Business Practices, 164
Foreign Commerce and Navigation of the United States, 157
Foreign Consular Offices in the United States, 372-373
Foreign Curriculum Consultant Program, 221
Foreign policy, 374
Foreign Service List, 998
Foreign Statistical Publications, 999
Foreign trade routes, 174-179
Forest Atlas of the South, 560
Forest Service Films Available on Loan, 561-562
Forest Service Health and Safety Code, 566
Forest Service Organizational Directory, 564
Forest Service publications lists, 561-563, 1007-1008, 1010, 1037
Forestry
    Atlases, 560
    Bibliographies, 561-563
    Directories, 564-565
    Guides, 566-567
Forestry Schools in the United States, 565
Fossils, 676-678
14-MeV Neutron Generators in Activation Analysis: A Bibliography, 754
Freer, Alice B., 355
Freud, Sigmund, 878
From Spanish to Portuguese, 927

Galactosemia, 830
Gastroenterology Abstracts and Citations, 1000
Gazetteers, 285
Gelman, Anna C., 842
General Catalogue of Homoptera, 593
General Reference Works
  General Bibliographies, 935-937
  Government Publications, 938-945
  Library Science, 946-948
  Microforms, 949
  Periodicals and Serials, 950-957
Geographical Guide to Summaries of Plant Quarantine Import Requirements of Foreign Countries, 163
Geography
  Atlases, 274-280
  Bibliographies, 281-283
  Dictionaries, 284
  Gazetteers, 285
Geological Survey publications lists, 621-622, 1022
Geology
  Abstracts, 959, 1001
  Bibliographies, 617-623
  Catalogs, 624
  Geologic Names, 625
Geophysical Abstracts, 1001
Gephart, Ronald M., 341
Ghana, 292
Gillespie, Karen R., 60
Gilmore, John S., 510
Glenn, Bruce P., 796
Glossary of Mapping, Charting, and Geodetic Terms, 284
Glossary of Terms in Drug Culture, 462
Goetz, Delia, 230, 233
Gold, 604
Good Life for More People, 552
Gorham, Kathryn A., 889
Goring, Sylvia M., 714
Government Publications on Drug Abuse, 460
Government Reports Announcements, 1052-1054
Government-Supported Research: International Affairs, 384-385
Grain standards, 538
Grant, W. Vance, 222
Grasses, 589
Great Britain, 383
Greenfield, Sidney H., 704-706
Grey, Milton K., 67

Guatemala, 326
Guide and Resources for the Community Coordinated Child Care Program, 445
Guide for Colleges and Universities; Cost Principles and Procedures, 243
Guide Posts for Supervisors, 110n
Guide to . . . Cartographic Records in the National Archives, 282; Child Labor Provisions of the Fair Labor Standards Act, 362; Drug Abuse Education and Information Materials, 470; Federal Career Literature, 187; Federal Consumer Services, 94; Federal Estate and Gift Taxation, 202; Foreign Trade Statistics, 158-159; Nutrition Terminology for Indexing and Retrieval, 570; Programs, National Science Foundation, 525-526; Record Retention Requirements, 48; Research in Air Pollution, 787; Soviet Literature Accessions in the Atmospheric Sciences Library and the Geophysical Sciences Library, 643-644; Student Assistance, 244; the Medicinal Plants of Appalachia, 588; the Study of the United States of America, 340; Training Resources and Information Publications, 139; Using Interest Factors in Economic Analysis of Water Projects, 796
Guidelines for Drug Abuse Prevention Education, 464
Guidelines for Health Occupations Education Programs, 264
Guides for Supervisors, 110
Gurewitz, Pauline H., 921

HUD Library Periodicals List, 950
HUD Statistical Yearbook, 499-501
Hagermann, Madeline G., 212
Hall, Ann B., 598
Halstead, Bruce W., 595
Handbook for Job Restructuring, 111
Handbook of . . . Agricultural Charts, 546-547; Airline Statistics, 170; Electromagnetic Propagation in Conducting Media, 919; Labor Statistics, 117-118; Mathematical Functions: With Formulas, Graphs and Tables, 798; Selective Placement in Federal Civil Service Employment of the Physically Handicapped, the Mentally Restored, the Mentally Retarded, the Rehabilitated Offender, 109;

Handbook of . . . (cont'd)
  Statistical Procedures for Long-Range Projections of Public School Enrollment, 239; Toxicity of Pesticides to Wildlife, 788
Handbook on the Law of Search and Seizure, 359
Handicapped, 109, 262-263, 266, 411, 861-862, 869
Handy Reference Guide to the Fair Labor Standards Act, 113, 360
Harris, A. S., 592
Harris, Deane, 476-477
Harris, Yeuell Y., 211
Harrison, Virden L., 535
Hauptman, Herbert, 799
Haviland, Virginia, 227-228
Hayes, Jack, 551-552
Health—Almanacs, 810-811
Health and Hygiene, 818
Health and safety, 566, 870
Health Aspects of Pesticides: Abstract Bulletin, 1002
Health Careers for American Indians and Alaskan Natives, 867
Health, Education, and Welfare Department publications lists, 1, 890-891
Health Facilities Planning and Construction Service publications lists, 843
Health Manpower: A County and Metropolitan Data Book, 871
Health occupations, 269, 866-868
Health Resources Statistics, Health Manpower and Health Facilities, 872
Health services, 819-820, 907, 909-910
Health Services and Mental Health Administration publications lists, 844
Health—Statistics, 479, 871-873
Health testing, 840-842
Hearing and speech, 892
Heerwagen, Arnold J., 590
Helium: Bibliography, 599-601
Heller, Terry S., 510
Henderson, Harry W., 154
Henderson, John W., 288, 300, 303, 306, 331
Herbicide Manual for Noncropland Weeds, 556, 790
Heynen, William, 281
Higher Education
  Bibliographies, 240
  Directories, 96, 215-216, 241-252, 527, 565, 664, 786, 860

Higher Education (cont'd)
  Financial Assistance, 243-244, 248, 250-252, 900-901
Higher Education Administration: An Annotated Bibliography of Research Reports, 240
Higher Education Aid for Minority Business: A Directory of Assistance Available, 96
Highland, Henry A., 51
Highway Safety Bibliography, 727
Highway Safety Literature, Annual Cumulation, 725-729
Highway Safety Literature: Announcement of Recent Acquisitions, 1003
Highway Safety Literature: Annual Indexes, 730
Highway Statistics, 721-722
Highways and traffic safety, 721-735, 1003
Hijacking: A Selected List of References, 455
Hintgen, Joseph N., 882
Historical Chart Book, 147-148
History and Area Studies
  Africa, 286-296
  Asia, 297-306
  Europe, 315-319
  Latin America, 320-330
  Middle East, 307-314
  Oceania, 331-335
  U.S., 336-354
Hobby Shops, 67
Home Delivered Meals, A National Directory, 434
Home economics, 270, 568-570
Homemaking Handbook for Village Workers in Many Countries, 569
Honduras, 327
Hormuth, Rudolf P., 895
House Manual, 396
Household Survey Manual, 488
Housing and planning, 502-504, 1004, 1041
Housing and Planning References, 502
Housing and Planning References, New Series, 1004
Housing and Urban Development Department Library acquisitions lists, 951
Houston, D. F., 553
How to Find U.S. Statutes and U.S. Code Citations, 364
Hughes, J. Kentrick, 579
Human Factors Bibliography, 726
Hurlburt, Margaret, 899
Hydraulic Research in the U.S., 921

Hydrocarbons and Air Pollution: An Annotated Bibliography, 783
Hydrochloric Acid and Air Pollution: An Annotated Bibliography, 781
Hydroelectric power projects, 401
Hydrology
    Abstracts, 1047
    Bibliographies, 626-632, 1006
    Dictionaries, 633-634
    Directories, 635-636
    Handbooks, 559
    Indexes, 637-641
Hygiene, 818

Impact of Medicare: An Annotated Bibliography, 183
Import/export data, 163-169
Important Events in American Labor History, 133
In Service to the Mentally Retarded: Directory of National Voluntary Agencies, 896
Income tax, 196-197, 199-201, 203-205
Index-Catalogue of Medical and Veterinary Zoology, 917
Index Medicus, New Series, 808-809, 826n, 827, 958, 1005, 1013n
Index of . . . Antitrust Subcommittee Publications, 31; Current Regulations of the Maritime Administration, Maritime Subsidy Board, National Shipping Authority, 175-176; Deposits of Country Banks, 146; Generic Names of Fossil Plants, 676; Institutions of Higher Education by State and Congressional District, 249; Patents, 530-531; Surface-Water Records, 637; Trademarks, 32-33; U.S. Voluntary Engineering Standards, 683
Index to . . . Areal Investigations and Miscellaneous Water Data Activities, 638; Clinical Research in the Federal Health Programs Service, 801-802; Conferences Relating to Nuclear Science, 740; Ground Water Stations, 639; Publications of the Manpower Administration, 142; the Surface Water Section, 640; the Water Quality Section, 641
Indexed Bibliography of the Tennessee Valley Authority, 630-631

Indexes of Output Per Man-Hour, Selected Industries, 119-120
Indexing, 616
India, 299, 953-954, 962
Indian Ocean, 335, 658, 668-669
Indians (American), 258, 426-428, 867
Indonesia, 300, 963
Industry Profiles, 43-44
Insects, 593
Insurance, 180-185
Interest rates, 796
Interior Department—Careers, 189-190
International Affairs
    General Works, 370-375
    Military Affairs, 376-379
    Protocol, 380-381
    Research, 382-385, 997
International commerce, 150-179
International Commerce Bureau publications lists, 150-151
International Directory of Mental Retardation Resources, 897
International Mail, 86
Introductory Guide to Exporting, 165
Inventory and record control, 48-50
Inventory Management, 50
Inventory of . . . Air Pollution Monitoring Equipment Operated by State and Local Agencies, 785; Automatic Data Processing Equipment in the United States Government, 612-613; Computers in U.S. Higher Education, 245; Congressional Concern with Research and Development, 518; Federal Programs that Support Health Manpower Training, 858; Federal Tourism Programs, 406; Vocational Educational Statistics Available in Federal Agencies, 265
Inventory Report on Real Property Owned by the United States, 194-195
Iran, 309
Iraq, 310
Israel, 285, 311, 964

JANAF Thermochemical Tables, 607
Jackson, Dorothy G., 422
Jaffe, A. J., 239
Janezeck, Elizabeth G., 16
Japan, 418
Jefferson's Manual, 396n, 400n

Job Corps Centers, 98
Job Descriptions and Organizational Analysis for Hospitals and Related Health Services, 868
Job Information Centers, 24
Johnson, Constance R., 301
Johnson, Harold E., 738
Johnson, Mae L., 934
Johnson, Mattie W., 536
Johnsson, K. O., 743
Joiner, Brian L., 489
Joint Economic Committee publications lists, 10
Jones, Mildred V., 555
Jones, William B., 81
Jossi, Jack W., 597
Justice Department, 357-358

Kaplan, Irving, 291-294
Katell, Sidney, 56
Keefe, Eugene K., 316-318
Kelly, Robert C., 749
Kern, Karl, 66
Kidney Disease Services, Facilities, and Programs in the United States, 865
Kidney diseases, 976
King, Billy Joe, 599
Kittner, Dorothy R., 180
Klement, Alfred W., 745
Knuths, Thelma M., 225
Korea, 301-302, 419
Korea, 301
Kramer, Lucy M., 858
Krochmal, Arnold, 588
Kron, Veronica B., 629
Krusiewski, S. Victoria, 750
Kudrle, Albert E., 69
Kulin, Gershon, 921

LEAA Reference List of Publications, 453
LSD-25, A Factual Account: Layman's Guide to the Pharmacology, Physiology, Psychology and Sociology of LSD, 902
Labor Department Library acquisitions lists, 951
Labor Department publications lists, 13-14, 1019
Labor history, 133
Labor-Management relations, 124-134, 1021

Labor organizations, 135-137
Labor Standards Bureau publications lists, 101
Labor Statistics Bureau publications lists, 102-107, 1021
Landlord-Tenant Relationships, 493
Languages, 230, 927-928
Lanier, Sidney F., 756
Larsen, S. Y., 606
Larson, Signe M., 702
Latin America, 320-330, 935-936
Latin America, Spain, and Portugal, 936
Laugdon, Lois M., 264
Law, 355-367
  General Works:
    Bibliographies, 355
    Directories, 356
    Handbooks and Guides, 357-365
Law enforcement, 707-708
Law Enforcement Assistance Administration publications lists, 453
Lawrence, Deloris, 923
Laws
  Agriculture, 542-543
  Fish and Wildlife, 576
  Foreign Relations, 375
  Handicapped, 869
  Labor, 113, 360-363, 365
  Medicine, 869-870
  Occupational Health, 870
  Urbanology, 498
Layman's Guide to Basic Law Under the National Labor Relations Act, 365
Lazarow, Arnold, 803-804
Lead poisoning, 916
Leary, Majella A., 180
Lebanon, 285
LeClerg, E. L., 554
Legal Bibliography for Juvenile and Family Courts, 355
Legislation on Foreign Relations, 375
Legg, N. J., 805-806
Leithead, Horace L., 589
Le Rocco, August, 821
Lesotho, 938
Lewis, R. D., 594
Lexicon of Geologic Names, 625
Library Accessions, 1006
Library of Congress Catalogs in Book Form and Related Publications, 939
Library of Congress Publications in Print, 940-941
Library of Congress publications lists, 940-941

Library science, 946-948
Life Portraits of John Quincy Adams, 925
Lin-Fu, Jane S., 916
Link, Albert D., 258
List of . . . Available Publications, 1007-1008; Available Publications of the Department of Agriculture, 536 ; Bureau of Mines Publications and Articles, 649-650; Bureau of Reclamation Bibliographies, 626; Chemical Compounds Authorized for Use Under the USDA Poultry, Meat, Rabbit, and Egg Inspection Programs, 602; Equipment Approved for Use in Federally Inspected Meat and Poultry Plants, 64; Fishery Cooperatives in the United States, 573; Foreign Firms with Some Interest/Control in American Manufacturing and Petroleum Companies, 155; Journals Indexed in Index Medicus, 827; Library Accessions, 1009; National Fish Hatcheries, 575; Plants Operating Under USDA Poultry and Egg Grading and Egg Products Inspection Programs, 65; Publications, 537, 710, 1010; Publications and Committee Membership of the Select Committee on Small Business, 15; Publications by Subject, 563; Publications Issued by the Committee on Banking and Currency, 149; Record Groups in the National Archives and Federal Records Centers, 337; Seismological Publications, 679-680; U.S. Government Medical and Dental 8mm Films for Sale by the National Audiovisual Center, 815
Literature Relating to Neurological and Neurosurgical Nursing, 899
Literature, 230, 929-930
Little, Elbert L., 586
Little, Silas, 591
Lobsters, 594
Lohman, S. W., 634
Lonergan, Bobbie, 210, 217
Look of Our Land: An Airphoto Atlas of the Rural United States, 275-279
Lunar Orbiter Photographic Atlas of the Moon, 579
Lutz, G. J., 605, 754, 768
Luxembourg, 420
Lyles, Charles H., 571

Maintainability Engineering Handbook, 684
Major Conventions, Exhibitions, and Trade Shows, 30n
Major Statistical Series of the Department of Agriculture, 548
Malawi, 285
Malaysia, 285, 303, 963
Man, His Job, and the Environment: A Review and Annotated Bibliography, 108
Management, 39-41, 126-131, 134, 141
Management: Continuing Literature Survey with Indexes, 38-39
Management (Excluding Personnel), 37
Managing Human Behavior, 128
Managing Overseas Personnel, 129
Mannino, Fortune V., 876
Manpower Administration publications lists, 142
Manpower research and training, 138-142, 256
Manual on Uniform Traffic Control Devices for Streets and Highways, 723
Manufacturers' Sales Representative, 68
Manufacturing, 68, 155, 775, 778-779
Manuscripts, 937
Map cataloging, 615
Maps, 274, 280, 283
Margolin, Victor, 449
Maritime Administration publications list, 153
Maritime Administration regulations, 175-176
Marketing, 51-55, 1011
Marketing and the Low Income Consumer, 53
Marketing Information Guide, 1011
Marriage records, 486
Mass media, 81-83
Maternal and Child Health Service publications lists, 845-846
Maternal Nutrition and the Course of Pregnancy, 822n
Mathematics, 233, 796-799
Matheny, William D., 746-747
Mather, William G., 108
May, Robert C., 596
McAnallen, Harry W., 736
McCormick, Jack, 591
McCrum, Blanche P., 340
McCuistion, George K., 351
McDonald, Gordon, 289, 290

McEnally, Susan, 37
McEvilla, Joseph D., 62
McGee, Mary, 183
McGinnis, Doris H., 740
McKee, Harley J., 342
McLaughlin, Patrick D., 283
Medical and Health Related Sciences Thesaurus, 852
Medical and Pharmacal Coding Guide, 903n
Medical reviews, 825
Medical Sciences
 General Medicine, 800-873
 Dentistry, 874-875
 Mental Health and Psychiatry, 876-888, 1034
 Mental Retardation, 889-897, 1012
 Nursing, 898-901
 Pharmacology, 902-905
 Public Health, 906-913
 Toxicology, 914-916
 Veterinary Medicine, 917-918
Medical Subject Headings, 1005n
Medical history, 826
Medicare, 182-183
Medicinal plants, 588
Medicine (General)
 Abstracts and Indexes, 800-809, 958
 Almanacs and Yearbooks, 810-813
 Atlases, 814
 Audiovisual Guides, 815-817
 Bibliographies, 812-813, 818-851, 971
 Dictionaries, 852
 Directories, 812-813, 853-865
 Health Occupations, 866-868
 Laws, 869-870
 Statistics, 871-873
Meat processing, 64-65
Men's centers, 98
Mental Health and Psychiatry
 Abstracts, 1034
 Bibliographies, 876-885
 Directories, 886-888
Mental Health Directory, 887-888
Mental Health Film Guide, 884
Mental retardation, 109, 835-836, 889-897, 1012
Mental Retardation Abstracts, 1012
Mental Retardation Construction Program: Research Centers, University Affiliated Facilities, and Community Facilities, 894
Mental Retardation Publications of the Department of Health, Education, and Welfare, 890-891

Merchant Fleets of the World, 177
Merchant Vessels of the United States, 171-172
Mercury Contamination in the Natural Environment, 767
Meteorology
 General Works, 642-645
 Climatology, 646-648
Metts, C. E., 51
Metz, Stafford, 223
Mexican Americans, 122, 241-242, 432-433
Meyjes, F. E. P., 805-806
Michaels, S., 606
Microforms, 949
Middle East, 307-314, 965
Migrant Education, A Selected Bibliography, 260
Military affairs, 376-379
Military engineering, 738-739, 973
Milwaukee, Wisc., 124
Migrant education, 259-260
Miller, Helen A., 207
Mineral Facts and Problems, 651
Mineralogy, 649-657
Minerals Yearbook, 652-657
Mines Bureau publications lists, 649-650, 1020
Miniature Environments, An Environmental Education Guidebook, 773
Minority Business Opportunities: A Manual on Opportunities, 26
Minority Group Relations
 General Works, 423-425
 American Indians, 426-428
 Negroes, 429-431
 Spanish Americans, 432-433
Minority groups in business, 25-26, 95-97
Mohr, Paul A., 624
Mongello, Beatrice O., 213-214
Mongolia, 285, 304
Montague, Jacqueline, 214
Monthly Bibliography of Medical Reviews, 1005n, 1013
Monthly Catalog of United States Government Publications, 1014
Monthly Checklist of State Publications, 1015
Moon, 578-579
Moore, Coralie B., 889
More Words on Aging, 437
Morgan, William J., 353
Morocco, 285
Morrey, Lon W., 875

241

Mortgages, 144
Motels, 69
Motion pictures and drama, 931-932
Motor vehicle accidents, 725, 733
Motor vehicle and traffic safety, 724, 727, 729
Mugridge, Donald H., 340
Multiphasic Health Testing Systems, 842
Mulvihill, Donald F., 50
Municipal incineration, 777
Municipal Labor-Management Relations: Chronology of Compensation Developments in Milwaukee, 124
Murphy, Sidney E., 225
Murray, John P., 451
Music, 933
Myers, Beverly M., 793
Myers, Robert H., 73

NAPCA Abstract Bulletin, 972n
NBS Publications Newsletter, 1018
NHSB Corporate Author Authority List, 731
NHSB Thesaurus of Traffic and Motor Vehicle Safety Terms, 732
NIH Publications List, 847-851
Nalty, Bernard C., 347
Narcotic Addiction Treatment Centers, 466
National Adverse Drug Reaction Directory, 903
National Aeronautics and Space Administration publications lists, 689
National and International Environmental Monitoring Activities: A Directory, 771
National and Regional Export Expansion Councils Directory, 166
National Archives publications lists, 338
National Atlas of the United States, 280
National Bureau of Standards publications lists, 511, 513, 1018, 1035, 1050
National Bureau of Standards Films, 511
National Defense Graduate Fellowships, Graduate Programs, 250
National Directories for Use in Marketing, 55
National Directory of Latin Americanists, 320
National Directory of Qualified Fallout Shelter Analysts, 699-700
National Drug Code Directory, 904-905

National Handbook of Conservation Practices, 558
National Institutes of Health Almanac, 810-811
National Institutes of Health publications lists, 847-851
National Jail Census, 454
National Labor Relations Act, 365
National Library of Medicine Current Catalog, 828, 1016-1017
National Marine Fisheries Service, 667
National Medical Audiovisual Center Catalog, 816
National Museum publications lists, 945
National Park Guide for the Handicapped, 411
National Parks and Landmarks, 412
National Parks and Recreation Areas, 409-412
National Register of Microform Masters, 949
National Roster of Minority Professional Consulting Services, 25
National Science Foundation programs, 525-526
National Science Foundation publications lists, 514
National Transportation Safety Board publications lists, 734-735
National Union Catalog of Manuscript Collections, 937
National ZIP Code Directory, 87-88
Natural Environmental Radioactivity, 745
Natural gas companies, 74-75
Nautical Almanac, 583-584
Nautical charts, 659
Naval aviation, 695
Naval Documents of the American Revolution, 353
Naval Oceanographic Office publications lists, 663
Navigation, 157, 583-585
Nayman, Oguz B., 451
Near East, 382
Negro in the United States, 431
Negroes, 429-431
Nelsen, Robert J., 875
Nelson, Stewart B., 666
Nepal, 966
Netherlands, 420
Neurological and neurosurgical nursing, 899
New Communities: A Bibliography, 503

242

New Publications . . . (List), 1019;
   Bureau of Mines, 1020; in Wages
   and Industrial Relations, 1021; of
   the Geological Survey, 1022
New Serial Titles, A Union List of Serials,
   956, 1023
New Serial Titles: Classed Subject
   Arrangement, 1024
New Technology in Education, 207
Newspapers—Bibliography, 950-951, 957
Newspapers Currently Received and Permanently Retained in the Library of
   Congress, 957
Nicaragua, 328
1971 Catalog of Federal Domestic
   Assistance, 6
Nitric acid manufacturing, 778
Nitrogen Oxides: An Annotated Bibliography, 784
Noe, Betty G., 600-601
Non-GPO Imprints Received in the
   Library of Congress, 942-943
**North Atlantic Treaty Organization
   (NATO)**, 379
Norwegian Language Guide, 928
Nuclear Engineering
   Abstracts and Indexes, 740-743,
      1025-1026
   Bibliographies, 744-754
   Classification, 755-756
   Dictionaries, 757-758
   Directories, 759-763
   Tables, 764-765
Nuclear Reactors Build, Being Built or
   Planned in the United States, 760-761
Nuclear Science Abstracts, 1025; Annual
   Index, 742; Cumulative Report Number
   Index, 741; Indexes, 1026
Nuclear Weapons and NATO, 379
Nursery Business, 70
Nursing, 898-901
Nursing Division publications lists, 898
Nursing Homes, A County and Metropolitan Area Data Book, 873
Nutrition, 568, 570, 822
Nyrop, Richard F., 297, 305, 313

Oberholtzer, Betty, 513
O'Brien, Donough, 830
O'Brien, Julie M., 929
O'Brien, Muriel J., 554

Occupational Employment Statistics, 121
Occupational Health and Safety Legislation, 870
Occupational Outlook Handbook, 186
Occupational Outlook Quarterly, 1027
Occupations
   General, 46-47, 121, 186-190, 1027
   Agricultural, 267
   Environmental, 238
   Health, 264, 269, 866-868
   Home Economics, 270
   Office Work, 271
   Trade and Industrial, 273
Oceania, 331-335
Oceanographic Atlas of the International
   Indian Ocean Expedition, 658
Oceanographic ships, 666-667
Oceanographic Ships, Fore and Aft, 666
Oceanography, 658-675
   General Works:
      Atlases, Maps and Charts, 658-659
      Bibliographies, 645, 660-663
      Directories, 664
      Manuals, 665
Oceanography: A Bibliography of
   Selected Activation Analysis Literature, 662
O'Connell, Dorothy, 442-443
Office employment, 271
Official Congressional Directory, 390-391
Official Grain Standards of the United
   States, 538
Ohl, Jane P., 620
Oil Pollution of the Marine Environment:
   A Legal Bibliography, 795
100 Native Forage Grasses in 11 Southern
   States, 589
Operation Breakthrough: Mass Produced
   and Industrialized Housing, 504
Opportunities Abroad for Teachers, 219-220
Oral cytology, 814
Organization Manual, 398-399
Osbourn, Sandra, 766
O'Shaughnessy, Frank, 59
Osso, Nicholas A., 224
Outdoor Education: A Selected Bibliography, 209
Outdoor Recreation
   Assistance Programs, 404-408
   National Parks, 409-412
   Research, 413-414, 1028
   Statistics, 415

Outdoor Recreation Action, 1028
Outdoor Recreation Research, 413-414

Pacific Islands and Trust Territories: A Select Bibliography, 332
Packaging, 51
Pakistan, 305, 955, 967
Paleontology, 676-678
Palmer, Wayne C., 647
Pariseau, Earl J., 935
Parker, James S., 475
Parkinson's disease, 839, 864, 1029
Parkinson's Disease and Related Disorders, Citations from the Literature, 1029; Cumulative Bibliography, 839; International Directory of Scientists, 864
Partial Bibliography on Human Cancer Involving Viruses, 831
Partial Bibliography on Type-B and Type-C Viruses in Relation to Animal Neoplasia, 832
Partial Directory of American Poets, 930
Patents, 530-531
Patterson, Carol B., 740
Pearce, Lilla M., 207
Peins, Maryann, 892
Pennington, Robert M., 608
Pension plans, 180
People's Republic of China Atlas, 274
Periodical Literature on the American Revolution, 341
Perry, Sarah B., 106
Personnel Literature, 1030
Personnel Management, 134
Personnel Management Function—Organization, Staffing, and Evaluation, 130
Personnel Policies and Practices, 131
Pesticides, 788-791, 1002, 1031
Pesticides Documentation Bulletin, 1031
Peterson, James T., 646
Petroleum companies, 155
Petroleum plants and refineries, 56-57
Petroleum Refineries in the United States and Puerto Rico, 57
Pharmacology, 902-905, 1034
Phillips, J. Edmund, 111
Photochemical Oxidants and Air Pollution: An Annotated Bibliography, 782
Photography, 692
Physical Sciences (General), 520
Physics, 919-922

Pimentel, David, 791
Pinney, John J., 70
Planning for a Nationwide System of Library Statistics, 947
Planning for Hospital Discharge, 821
Planning, Organizing, and Evaluating Training Programs, 140
Plant quarantines, 163
Plant Tours for International Visitors, 42
Plants (Industrial), 42, 56-59, 64-65
Plastics standards, 529
Pocket Data Book USA, 481
Pocket Guide to . . . Foreign Policy Information Materials and Services of the Department of State, 374; Japan, 418; Korea, 419; the Low Countries, 420; Vietnam, 417
Poets, 930
Poison Control Centers Directory, 915
Poisonous and Venomous Marine Animals of the World, 595
Police Telecommunication Systems, 707
Political Science and International Relations
  Communism, 368-369
  International Affairs, 370-385
  U.S. Government, 386-400
Pollution Analysis: Bibliography of Activation Analysis, 768
Popular Names of U.S. Government Reports, 944
Popular Publications of the Geological Survey, 621
Population censuses, 478
Porter, Dorothy B., 431
Portraits of the American Stage, 932
Ports, 179
Portugal—Bibliography, 936
Portuguese language, 927
Position Classification and Pay in the Federal Government, 132
Postage Stamps of the United States, 416
Postal guides, 84-88
Potatoes, 554
Poultry, 64-65, 602, 990
Poverty, 53, 475
Poverty Studies in the Sixties, 475
Pre-Federal Maps in the National Archives, 283
Preliminary Determination of Epicenters, 1032
President's 1971 Environmental Program, 770

Presidents of the U.S., 388
Priester, William A., 918
Printing, 71
Prisons, 452, 454
Private Assistance in Outdoor Recreation, 407
Problems of Communism, 1033
Productivity, Motivation and Incentive, 128n
Professional Workers in State Agricultural Experiment Stations, 540
Project Follow Through, 237
Project Head Start, 257
Protocol, 380-381
Psychiatry and Mental Health
  Bibliographies, 876-885
  Directories, 886-888
Psychopharmacology Abstracts, 1034
Psychoses, 882
Psychotherapy, 880
Public Land Statistics, 191-192
Public lands, 191-195
Publication Announcements, 1035
Publications and Films, 450
Publications Catalog, 906
Publications Index, 800
Publications List, 439
Publications of . . . the Bureau of Labor Statistics, 103-106; the Bureau of Sport Fisheries and Wildlife, 1036; the Centre International de l'Enfance Coordinated Growth Studies, 444; the Committee on Science and Astronautics, 516-517; the Geological Survey, 622; the Health Facilities Planning and Construction Service, Hill-Burton Program, 843; the Health Services and Mental Health Administration, 844; the Maritime Administration, 153; the Maternal and Child Health Service, 845-846; the National Bureau of Standards, 513; the National Science Foundation, 514; the National Transportation Safety Board, 734-735; the Office of Education, 210; the Office of the Chief of Military History, 345-346; the U.S. Department of Labor: Subject Listing, 13-14; the United States National Museum, 945; the Women's Bureau Currently Available, 20-23
Pulsars, A Bibliography, 746-747
Putnam, John F., 234

Quest for Environmental Quality: Federal and State Action, 1969-70; An Annotated Bibliography, 766

Radio, 81-83
Radioactivity, 745, 750, 759
Radiological Health Bureau publications lists, 800
Radiological health programs, 859-860
Raleigh, Henry D., 748
Rapp, J. R., 639
Reactor Safety Literature Search, 748
Reagents, 608
Real estate, 191-195
Recent Publications of Southern Forest Experiment Station, 1037
Reclamation Bureau publications lists, 626
Recording Historic Buildings, 342
Recordkeeping, 48
Recreation and travel, 401-420, 1028
Recreation Opportunities at Hydroelectric Projects, 401
Reese, Howard C., 295
Refuse Collection and Disposal, 792n
Regional medical programs, 908
Register of the Department of Justice and the Courts of the United States, 357-358
Reinhart, Hilda W., 704-706
Related Areas Bibliography, 728
Reliability Abstracts and Technical Reviews, 1038
Religion, 934
Report Number Codes Used by the USAEC Division of Technical Information in Cataloging Reports, 755
Research and development, 518, 524
Research and Training Opportunities Abroad, 251
Research Grants, Index, 807
Research in Education, 209n, 232n, 254-255, 258n, 260n, 1039
Research 1970, 421
Research Relating to Children, 440-443
Research Vessels of the National Marine Fisheries Service, 667
Residential Manpower Centers, 98
Residential Support Centers, 98
Resources for Scientific Activities at Universities and Colleges, 527
Retirement benefits, 180, 199

Review of Selected Program Activities in the Education of the Deaf, 262
Revolutionary War (U.S.), 341, 353
Rheumatic diseases, 975
Rhodehamel, Edward C., 629
Rice, 553
Richelieu, Judith L., 941
Rima, Donald R., 793
Roberts, Thomas D., 314
Rothgeb, Carrie L., 878
Rural Education and Small Schools, 232
Ruth, Robert H., 592
Ryan, John M., 328
Rzonca, Chester S., 264

SCS National Engineering Handbook, 559
Sachs, Milton S., 58
Safeguards Dictionary, 757
Safeguards Glossary, 758
Safety Guide for Pesticides, 789
Sargent, Polly, 395
Saudi Arabia, 312
Sauer, Mary Louise, 134
Sawyer, E. Nell, 11-12
Schacter, Francine E., 484
Scheina, Robert L., 351
Schmidt, Fred H., 122
Schools Offering Nurse Traineeships for Full-Time Academic Study, 1971-72, Under the Professional Nurse Traineeship Program, 900
Schools Participating in Nursing Student Assistance Programs, 901
Science and Astronautics Committee (House) publications lists, 516-517
Science and Mathematics Books for Elementary and Secondary Schools, 233
Science and Society: A Bibliography, 508
Science and Technology
  General Works:
    Abstracts, 969, 1038
    Bibliographies, 508-518, 1018, 1035, 1050, 1052, 1054
    Directories, 519-527
    Guides, 528
    Indexes, 529-531
    Statistics, 532
Science Facilities Bibliography, 515
Scientific and Technical Aerospace Reports, 1040

Scientific and Technical Aerospace Reports: Indexes, 690-691
Scientific and Technical Personnel in Industry, 532
Scientific Directory and Annual Bibliography, 812-813
Scientists, 509, 532
Scientists and Engineers in the Federal Government, 509
Seafaring Guide and Directory of Labor-Management Affiliations, 137
Search and seizure, 359
Secondary and Elementary Education
  Bibliographies, 227-233
  Dictionaries, 234
  Directories, 213-214, 235-237
  Handbooks and Guides, 238-239
Sedimentation, 632
Seeney, Daniel J., 80
Segal, Dorothy B., 917
Seibert, Ivan N., 211
Seismology, 1032
Select List of Publications of the National Archives and Records Service, 338
Select List of Sound Recordings: Voices of World War II, 339
Selected Abstracts of Planning Publications, 1041
Selected and Annotated Bibliography of Pitch Pine, 591
Selected Annotated Bibliography of Civil, Industrial, and Scientific Uses for Nuclear Explosives, 749
Selected Annotated Bibliography of the Minor-Element Content of Marine Black Shales and Related Sedimentary Rocks, 623
Selected Annotated Bibliography on the Geochemistry of Gold, 604
Selected Bibliography of Natural Plant Communities in 11 Midwestern States, 590
Selected Bibliography of Regional Medical Programs, 908
Selected Bibliography on . . . Death and Dying, 877; Drugs of Abuse, 461; Lead Poisoning in Children, 916; Radioactive Occurrences in the United States, 750; the Use of Drugs by Young People, 459
Selected Drug Abuse Education Films, 471-472

Selected Economic Data for Less Developed Countries, 34-35
Selected List of Federal Laws and Treaties Relating to Sport Fish and Wildlife, 576
Selected List of Recent Additions to Library, 1042
Selected Outdoor Recreation Statistics, 415
Selected Publications and Audio-Visual Materials, 1043
Selected Publications of the Bureau of Labor Standards, 101
Selected Reading Suggestions for Parents of Mentally Retarded Children, 889
Selected References for Social Workers on Family Planning, 474
Selected References on Environmental Quality as It Relates to Health, 1044
Selected Statistics on Educational Personnel, 223
Selected Tables of Atomic Spectra, 764-765
Selected United States Government Publications, 1045
Selected Urban Storm Water Runoff Abstracts, 1046
Selected Water Resources Abstracts, 1047
Self Development Aids for Supervisors and Middle Managers, 141
Selim, George D., 308
Sells, S. B., 466
Senate Manual, 400
Senior Centers in the United States, 435
Serial Titles Cited in Nuclear Science Abstracts, 751
Serials—Publication Calendar, 952
Shale, 623
Sheridan, William H., 355
Shiflet, Thomas N., 589
Shinn, Rinn-Sup, 299
Ship Metallic Material Comparison and Use Guide, 72
Shipbuilding, 72
Ships
    Merchant, 171-172, 177-178
    Military, 350, 352
Shopping centers, 73
Shore, Milton F., 876
Sickness and Poverty, a Handbook for Community Workers, 913
Sietsema, John P., 213-214
Silverman, Leslie J., 223
Simon, Kenneth A., 222

Singapore, 285, 963
Sitka Spruce: A Bibliography with Abstracts, 592
Slattery, William J., 683
Small Arms Identification and Operation Guide: Eurasian Communist Countries, 738
Small Business Administration Publications: Classification of Management Publications, 40; For-Sale Booklets, 17-19; Free Management Assistance Publications, 41
Small Business Administration publications lists, 17-19, 40-41
Small Business Committee (House) publications lists, 15
Smart, James R., 933
Smith, Cameron C., 110
Smith, Harvey H., 296, 309-311
Smoking, 823-824, 829, 863
Social and Rehabilitation Service publications list, 421
Social Conditions
    Aging, 434-439
    Children and Youth, 440-450
Social Problems
    Behavior, 451
    Criminology, 452-457
    Drug Abuse, 458-473
    Family Planning, 474
    Poverty, 475
Social Sciences—General Works, 1-7
Social Security, 181, 184-185
Social Security Programs in the United States, 184
Social Security Programs Throughout the World, 185
Social studies, 218
Social Usage and Protocol, 381
Sociology, 421-475
    General Works, 421-422
    Minority Group Relations, 423-433
    Social Conditions, 434-450
    Social Problems, 451-475
Soft-Frozen Dessert Stands, 66
Soil management, 556-559, 996
Soldier and Brave: Historic Places Associated with Indian Affairs and the Indian Wars in the Trans-Mississippi West, 343
Solid Waste Management: A List of Available Literature, 1048
Solid Waste Management: Abstracts from the Literature, 792

Somalia, 293
Source Data Automation Equipment Guide, 614
Sources of Information on American Firms for International Buyers, 152
Sousa Band: A Discography, 933
South African Republic, 294
South China Sea, 285
Soviet Space Program, 1966-1970, 696
Space Photography, 1971 Index, 692
Spain, 936
Spanish language, 927
Spanish Speaking in the United States: A Guide to Materials, 433
Spanish Surnamed American College Graduates, 241-242
Spanish Surnamed American Employment in the Southwest, 122
Special Catalog of Federal Programs Assisting Minority Enterprise, 97
Special education, 256-263
Special libraries, 519-521
Speech and hearing, 892
Sport Fishery Abstracts, 1049
Sport Fisheries and Wildlife Bureau publications lists, 1036
Spotter's Guide for Identifying and Reporting Severe Local Storms, 648
Sprinkler Irrigation: A Bibliography, 557
Staffing the Higher Federal Civil Service, 127n
Stainback, Sandra E., 792
Stamp collecting, 416
Standard Nomenclature of Veterinary Diseases and Operations, 918
Standard Terminology for Curriculum and Instruction in Local and State School Systems, 234
Standards laboratories, 523
Stanfield, Rochelle L., 766
Stanley, Caroline, 230
State Department publications lists, 1043
State Education Agency: A Handbook of Standard Terminology and Guide for Recording Information, 211
State Laws Enacted in 1969 of Interest to the Department of Housing and Urban Development, 498
Statistical Abstract of the United States, 482-483
Statistical Analysis of the World's Merchant Fleets, 178
Statistical Appendix to the Annual Report of the Secretary of the Treasury, 145
Statistics and Demography
   Bibliographies, 476-479, 999
   Compendia, 480-483
   Directories, 484-487
   Handbooks, 488
   Indexes, 489
Statistics of Farmer Cooperatives, 549
Statistics of Interstate Natural Gas Pipeline Companies, 74-75
Statistics of Privately Owned Electric Utilities in the United States, 76-77
Statistics of Publicly Owned Electric Utilities in the United States, 78-79
Storm warnings, 648
Study of Resources and Major Subject Holdings Available in U.S. Federal Libraries Maintaining Extensive or Unique Collections of Research Materials, 948
Subject Headings Used by the USAEC, Division of Technical Information, 756
Sub-Saharan Africa: A Guide to Serials, 286
Subsurface Waste Disposal by Means of Wells, 793
Suburban Shopping Centers, 73
Sulfuric acid manufacturing, 779
Summary of Coast and Geodetic Survey Technical Publications and Charts, 660
Summary of Selected Legislation Relating to the Handicapped, 869
Supervisory Development Practices, 140n
Supervisory Responsibilities, Selection, and Evaluation, 127n
Surface Water Records, 637, 640
Survey of Current Business, 36n
Swaziland, 938
Sylvester, Rita D., 649-650
Syria, 313

Table of All Primitive Roots for Primes Less than 5000, 799
Tables of bankruptcy statistics, 143
Tables of Compound-Discount Interest Rate Multipliers for Evaluating Forestry Investments, 567
Tables of Computed Altitude and Azimuth, 585
Tagatz, Marlin E., 598
Talbot, Janet B., 626

Tariff Schedules of United States Annotated, 169
Tax Guide for Small Business, 203
Taxes, 196-205
Taylor, Kent, 880
Technical News Bulletin, 1050
Technology Transfer, A Selected Bibliography, 510
Television, 83, 451
Television and Social Behavior: An Annotated Bibliography, 451
Tennessee Valley Authority, 630-631
Territorial Areas Administered by the United States, 193
Thailand, 306
Theatrical arts, 932
Thermochemical Tables, 607
Thesaurus of Water Resources Terms, 633
Thomas, Myra H., 225, 231
Thrombolysis, 833-834
Thuronyi, Geza T., 334
Tide Tables, High and Low Water Predictions, 668-675
Tides, 668-675
Timberg, Eleanor E., 889
Time and Frequency: A Bibliography of NBS Literature, 512
Todhunter, E. Neige, 570
Tomlinson, Robert M., 264
Tools and Their Uses, 528
Tourtelot, Elizabeth B., 623
Toxic Substances, 914
Toxicity Bibliography, 1051
Toxicology, 914-916, 1051
Trade Goods: A Study of Indian Chintz in the Collection of the Cooper-Hewitt Museum of Decorative Arts and Design, 926
Trade shows, 30
Trademarks, 32-33
Traffic control devices, 723
Transport Statistics in the United States, 173
Transportation Engineering
    Aviation, 709-718
    Boating, 719-720
    Highways and Traffic Safety, 721-735, 1003
Transportation and foreign trade, 157; 170-179
Travel guides, 417-420
Treaties in Force, 366-367
Trees, 586-587, 591-592

Tritium, 629
Tucker, Richard K., 788
Tully, Philip C., 599-601
Tunisia, 295
Turkey, 314
Turner, Anthony, 454
Turnley, Edwin R., 940

USDA Standards for Food and Farm Products, 541
Underdeveloped areas, 34-35
Uniform Crime Reports, 456-457
U.S.S.R., 285, 318-319, 643-645, 661, 696
USSR: Strategic Survey, A Bibliography, 319
United Arab Republic, 296
United States
    Archives, 336-339
    Army, 345-346, 392
    Atlases, 275-280, 386
    Civil War, 351
    Congress, 386, 388-391
    Courts, 357-358
    Government, 386-400
    Marine Corps, 347, 349
    Revolutionary War, 341, 353
    States, 387, 484, 1015
United States Air Force History: An Annotated Bibliography, 344
United States Army Installations and Major Activities, 392
United States Civil Aircraft Register, 715-718
U.S. Code, 364n
United States Conventions and Trade Shows, 30
United States Department of Commerce Publications: Catalog and Index, 11-12
United States Earthquakes, 681-682
United States Foreign Trade Annual, 161
U.S. Foreign Trade Statistics: Classifications and Cross-Classifications, 160
United States Government Organization Manual, 398-399
United States Government Publications: A Partial List of Non-GPO Imprints, 943n
U.S. Government Research and Development Reports, 1052-1054
U.S. Industrial Outlook, 45
United States Marine Corps Ranks and Grades, 347

United States Naval Aviation, 695
U.S. Naval History Sources in the Washington Area, 354
U.S. Navy Diving Manual, 665
U.S. Statutes, 364n
United States Tax Guide for Aliens, 204
University Curricula in the Marine Sciences, 664
University Curriculums and Fellowships in Radiological Health, 860
Update of 1970 Catalog, 5
Upward Bound, Ideas and Techniques, 261
Urban Mass Transportation: A Bibliography, 505
Urban Renewal Directory, 495-497
Urban Transportation Bibliography, 507
Urban Vocabulary, 494
Urbanology, 490-507, 646
    General Works, 490-501
    Housing and Planning, 502-504, 1004
    Urban Transportation, 505-507
Uruguay, 329
Utility companies, 74-79

Vanadium, 620
Vegh, Emanuel, 799
Vehicle Safety Bibliography, 729
Venereal disease, 987
Venezuela, 330
Vernick, Joel J., 877
Veterans' Reemployment Rights Handbook, 112
Veterinary medicine, 917-918
Vietnam, 285, 417
Vital statistics, 479
Vocabulary for Information Processing, 611
Vocational education, 264-273
Vocational Education for Handicapped Persons, 266
Vocational Instructional Materials Available from Federal Agencies, 267-273
Volunteers Who Produce Books, Braille, Large Type, Tape, 862
von Ende, Eunice, 208, 233
von Hake, Carl A., 682
Voress, Hugh E., 508

Wages and earnings, 114-116, 123, 132, 1021
Wake, Sandra B., 442-443
Walkowicz, J. L., 611
Walpole, Norman C., 312
Walters, Russell S., 588
Warren, John C., 68
Warner, Elizabeth R., 704-706
Waste disposal, 792-793, 1048
Water pollution, 794-795, 1046
Water quality records, 641
Water Resources Research Catalog, 627-628
Watson, Deena, 466
Watt, Arthur D., 677
Watt, Lois B., 227-228, 230-231, 233
Watts, Mary E., 474
Weights and Measures Labeling Handbook, 922
Weil, Thomas, 321-322, 329-330
Wells, Jean A., 226
West, Robert G., 749
What's New on Smoking in Print and on Film, 829
When to Buy What: A Buying Calendar for Annual Publications, 952
Where to Write for Birth and Death Records, 485
Where to Write for Marriage Records, 486
White, Helen W., 755
Whitston, Milton O., 744
Wholesaling, 80
Wildlife Abstracts, 1055n
Wildlife and pesticides, 788
Wildlife management, 571-576, 1055
Wildlife refuges, 574
Wildlife Review: An Abstracting Service for Wildlife Management, 1055
Willis, Dawn E., 505
Women's Bureau publications lists, 20-23
Women's Centers, 98
Wood, Jennings, 943n
Wool Statistics and Related Data, 555
Words on Aging, 436
Work stoppages, 135
Working Reference of Livestock Regulatory Establishments, 990n
World Data Center A: Oceanography; Catalogue of Accessioned Soviet Publications, 661
World Index of Plastics Standards, 529
World Maps of Atmospheric Radio Noise in Universal Time by Numerical Mapping, 81

World Military Expenditures, 377-378
World of Children: Films from the 1970 White House Conference on Children, 449
World Port Index, 179
World Strength of the Communist Party Organizations, 368-369
World Survey of Civil Aviation: Canada, 709
Wyrtki, Klaus, 658

Yarlett, Lewis L., 589
Yearbook of Agriculture, 551-552
Your Federal Income Tax, 204
Youth Development and Delinquency Prevention Administration publications lists, 450
Youth Resources Manual for Coordinators, 447

Zacharisen, Donald H., 81
ZIP codes, 87-88
Zoology, 593-598
Zooplankton, 597
Zusman, Jack, 883